The Gospel of

MATTHEW

Also by James Montgomery Boice

Witness and Revelation in the Gospel of John
Philippians: An Expositional Commentary
The Sermon on the Mount
How to Live the Christian Life (originally, *How to Live It Up*)
Ordinary Men Called by God (originally, *How God Can Use Nobodies*)
The Last and Future World
The Gospel of John: An Expositional Commentary (5 volumes)
"Galatians" in the *Expositor's Bible Commentary*
Can You Run Away from God?
Our Sovereign God, editor
Our Savior God: Studies on Man, Christ and the Atonement, editor
Does Inerrancy Matter?
The Foundation of Biblical Authority, editor
Making God's Word Plain, editor
The Epistles of John
Genesis: An Expositional Commentary (3 volumes)
The Parables of Jesus
The Christ of Christmas
The Minor Prophets: An Expositional Commentary (2 volumes)
Standing on the Rock
The Christ of the Open Tomb
Foundations of the Christian Faith (4 volumes in one)
Christ's Call to Discipleship
Transforming Our World: A Call to Action, editor
Ephesians: An Expositional Commentary
Daniel: An Expositional Commentary
Joshua: We Will Serve the Lord
Nehemiah: Learning to Lead
The King Has Come
Romans (4 volumes)
Mind Renewal in a Mindless Age
The Glory of God's Grace (originally, *Amazing Grace*)
Psalms (3 volumes)
Sure I Believe, So What!
Hearing God When You Hurt
Foundations of God's City (originally, *Two Cities, Two Loves: Christian Responsibility in a Crumbling Culture*)
Here We Stand: A Call from Confessing Evangelicals, editor with Benjamin E. Sasse
Living by the Book: The Joy of Loving and Trusting God's Word
Acts: An Expositional Commentary
The Heart of the Cross, with Philip G. Ryken
What Makes a Church Evangelical?

The Gospel of MATTHEW

Volume 2
The Triumph of the King
Matthew 18–28

JAMES
MONTGOMERY
BOICE

 Baker Books

A Division of Baker Book House Co
Grand Rapids, Michigan 49516

© 2001 by Linda Boice

Published by Baker Books
a division of Baker Book House Company
P.O. Box 6287, Grand Rapids, MI 49516-6287

Second printing, June 2002

Printed in the United States of America

Library of Congress Cataloging-in-Publication Data

Boice, James Montgomery, 1938–2000
    The Gospel of Matthew / James Montgomery Boice.
      p.   cm.
    Includes bibliographical references (v. 2, p.) and indexes.
    Contents: v. 2. The Triumph of the King (Matthew 18–28).
    ISBN 0-8010-1202-3 (cloth)
    1. Bible. N.T. Matthew—Commentaries. I. Title.
BS2575.53.B65   2001
226.2'077—dc21   00-064147

For current information about all releases from Baker Book House, visit our web site:
http://www.bakerbooks.com

To him whose
"dominion is an everlasting dominion
that will not pass away,
and his kingdom . . . one that will never be destroyed."
Daniel 7:14

Contents

Preface

What an extraordinary book Matthew is! It is the first of the Gospels, the longest, the most Jewish, the most evangelistic, and, in many ways, the most compelling. Nowhere does the Gospel name its author, but it has been ascribed to Matthew from the earliest days of church history, and for the first three or four centuries, it was the most highly regarded and most often quoted Gospel of the four. To some people, now as well as then, Matthew is the most important book ever written.

It is about Jesus of Nazareth, of course. That is what each of the Gospels is about. But each writer has his own way of handling the material regarding Jesus' life and has his own unique emphasis. In Matthew's case, the emphasis is on Jesus being the Messiah or King of Israel. Jesus is introduced this way at the beginning: "Jesus Christ [Messiah] the son of David" (Matt. 1:1), and the theme is evident throughout.

I have tried to capture Matthew's emphasis by the titles given to the various sections of the Gospel. The first six were covered in volume 1 of this two-volume work: (1) "The Coming of the King" (chapters 1–4); (2) "The Sermon on the Mount" (chapters 5–7); (3) "The Power of the Kingdom" (chapters 8–10); (4) "Is Jesus Really God's King?" (chapters 11–12); (5) "The Parables of the Kingdom" (chapter 13); (6) "The Withdrawal of the King" (chapters 14–17). This volume picks up where the first left off, exploring: (7) "The Citizens of the Kingdom" (chapters 18–20); (8) "The King's Final Break with Judaism" (chapters 21–23); (9) "The Sermon on the Mount of Olives" (chapters 24–25); and (10) "The King's Death and Resurrection" (chapters 26–28).

At this point in the narrative Jesus has withdrawn from the vicinity of Jerusalem, the headquarters of the leaders of the people who are his enemies, and he is concentrating his time on training the disciples, whom he is soon to leave behind. They were precisely like us, thinking in worldly categories and jockeying with each other to see who might be greatest in the kingdom of heaven. Peter has confessed Jesus to be the Christ, which they

371

had all presumably come to understand. But neither Peter nor any of the others had the faintest idea what it meant to take up Christ's cross and follow him. They needed to learn that to be great one has to become a servant first, then learn to treat others with mercy and love, which is how God in Christ has treated us.

Many will be especially interested in my study of Christ's teaching on the endtimes in the Sermon on the Mount of Olives (Matthew 24–25). The disciples wanted to know when the end would come and what the signs of the end would be. Jesus replied by telling them of many signs but insisting that they would not be signs of his second coming in judgment since the second coming would be sudden, without warning. The bottom line of this teaching is that his followers must therefore always be watching and ready.

As the first of the Gospels, Matthew is a bridge book linking the Old Testament with its fervent anticipation of the Messiah to the realization of the Messiah's kingly rule over the new people of God, which is the church. Now the King has come. He has triumphed over death by his resurrection and rules today by his Spirit in the church. He is coming again. Until then his disciples are to carry the gospel of salvation from sin by his death to all people. The Great Commission is the Gospel's climax (Matt. 28:18–20). Matthew does not let us forget that his message about this Jewish King and Savior is not only for Jews but for everyone. He insists that Jesus is "the Savior of the world" (John 4:42).

Is the Book of Matthew relevant today? It certainly is. In a largely secular age, as ours is, we need to know that Jesus is truly God's King. In a day of nominal Christianity, we need to hear Christ's call to "follow me." In a day of lax and lazy discipleship, we need to hear once again the command of Jesus to take the message of his death and resurrection to the world.

It has been thirty years since I first began to preach from the Gospels, starting with the Gospel of John in 1971, the third year of my ministry at Tenth Presbyterian Church in Philadelphia. Like most preachers I have returned to the Gospels again and again over the years, since they are the very heart of the Bible and tell of the life, death, and resurrection of Jesus Christ, who is the heart of Christianity. I have preached on the Sermon on the Mount, the parables, Jesus' teaching about discipleship, the cross, the resurrection, and other passages. But it is only in these studies that I have returned once again to explore an entire Gospel in detail.

May God bless this work by calling many to faith in Christ and deepening the discipleship of others, and to God be *all* the glory.

James Montgomery Boice
Philadelphia, Pennsylvania

PART SEVEN

The Citizens of the Kingdom

40

Who Is Greatest in the Kingdom?

Matthew 18:1–9

At that time the disciples came to Jesus and asked, "Who is the greatest in the kingdom of heaven?"

He called a little child and had him stand among them. And he said: "I tell you the truth, unless you change and become like little children, you will never enter the kingdom of heaven. Therefore, whoever humbles himself like this child is the greatest in the kingdom of heaven.

"And whoever welcomes a little child like this in my name welcomes me. But if anyone causes one of these little ones who believe in me to sin, it would be better for him to have a large millstone hung around his neck and to be drowned in the depths of the sea.

"Woe to the world because of the things that cause people to sin! Such things must come, but woe to the man through whom they come! If your hand or your foot causes you to sin, cut it off and throw it away. It is better for you to enter life maimed or crippled than to have two hands or two feet and be thrown into eternal fire. And if your eye causes you to sin, gouge it out and throw it away. It is better for you to enter life with one eye than to have two eyes and be thrown into the fire of hell."

What was it that Shakespeare wrote?

Be not afraid of greatness: some men are born great, some achieve greatness, and some have greatness thrust upon them.

Twelfth Night, act 2, scene 5

Pity the disciples! They were with true greatness in the person of the Lord Jesus Christ. He was great as only God is great. They were not. They had not been born great. They had not achieved greatness. They had not had greatness thrust upon them. Yet they wanted so much to be great.

375

They were thinking of an earthly kingdom that would be established by Jesus, whom they now believed to be the Messiah, and they were wondering which of them would be the greatest when Christ's kingdom came. Luke says they were arguing about it and that Jesus knew what they were thinking (Luke 9:46–47). Mark adds that they had been on their way to Capernaum, and when they got to Capernaum, Jesus asked what they had been arguing about. They were silent, probably because they were embarrassed by their worldly thoughts (Mark 9:33–34). Matthew says they then asked Jesus directly, "Who is the greatest in the kingdom of heaven?" (Matt. 18:1).

This question becomes the catalyst for a new direction in Jesus' private teaching of these men, which takes place in Matthew 18–20. This new direction has to do with what the citizens of the kingdom should be like, the fourth of six collections of Jesus' teachings in the Gospel. Earlier collections included the Sermon on the Mount (Matthew 5–7), the commissioning of the disciples (Matthew 10), and the seven parables of the kingdom (Matthew 13). The others are in Matthew 23 and Matthew 24–25. Matthew 18 is a collection of teachings gathered from talks given over the course of Jesus' ministry, as more than likely were the earlier collections.

The Disciples' Question

In some ways, the disciples' question was amazing. For one thing, Jesus had already taught about the type of people who would be citizens of his kingdom: "the poor in spirit," "the meek," "the merciful," and so on (Matt. 5:3, 5, 7). Even more amazing is the fact that almost immediately before this Jesus had explained that he would be betrayed and killed (Matt. 17:23). Matthew says they "were filled with grief," but their grief didn't last long. They were convinced Jesus was the Messiah, and the Messiah was going to establish a glorious earthly kingdom. Therefore they began to anticipate who would be greatest in that kingdom and to jockey for position.

The kind of kingdom they were thinking about becomes clear in Acts 1, where they ask Jesus, even after the resurrection, "Lord, are you at this time going to restore the kingdom to Israel?" (v. 6). John Stott notes, "The verb *restore* shows that they were expecting a political and territorial kingdom; the noun *Israel* that they were expecting a national kingdom; and the adverbial clause *at this time* that they were expecting its immediate establishment."[1] They were wrong on all counts. The kingdom was going to be a spiritual kingdom of those who were saved from sin through faith in Jesus. It was for all people, not just the people of Israel, and it was to develop over time as God, through the preaching of the gospel and the power of the Holy Spirit, brought individuals to faith.

But those were concepts the disciples would need to learn later. In this chapter Jesus is concerned about teaching what the citizens of the kingdom must be like, since at this point the minds of the disciples are still miles away from genuine Christianity.

Entering the Kingdom

What will the citizens of the kingdom be like? "They will be something like children," Jesus explains, as he calls a little child to him and sets the child in the center of the group.

Children have some characteristics that the people of God are *not* to copy. Children do not know very much; they lack the ability to focus on one thing for long periods of time; and they are foolish and easily deceived. We are not to be childlike in those ways. Children have positive characteristics too, such as open-mindedness and trust, though Jesus was not thinking of those here either. Jesus was thinking about humility, which he makes clear in verse 4: "Therefore, whoever humbles himself like this child is the greatest in the kingdom of heaven." He stresses humility because humility is the exact opposite of the disciples' greedy pride.

D. A. Carson says, "The child is a model, in this context, not of innocence, faith, or purity, but of humility and unconcern for social status. Jesus assumed that people are not naturally like that; they must *change* to become like little children."[2]

The use of a child as an illustration is striking and is typical of the teaching devices Jesus used so often and so well. But it is the words that are important, more than the illustration, and the words are more than striking. They are shocking, for two reasons.

1. *Jesus changed the nature of the question.* The disciples had been asking about greatness in the kingdom they believed Jesus would establish. They assumed that greatness was all they had to worry about. They assumed they would be in the kingdom. But instead of answering them only on that level, Jesus explains that unless they possessed a nature that was entirely different from what they were betraying by their question, they would not even enter the kingdom. Forget about who was going to be most important, Jesus said. What they needed to worry about was being there at all!

This response is similar to the way Jesus answered people who asked him why God allowed some apparently innocent people to be killed by Herod's soldiers or others to be killed when the tower of Siloam fell on them. Jesus said they were asking the wrong question. They should not ask why others had suffered but why they themselves had not, since they were sinners. The question should have been, "Why am I not in hell at this moment?" (Luke 13:1–5).

Obviously, we have much to learn if we are to learn the ways of God.

2. *Jesus insisted on the disciples' conversion.* D. A. Carson made this point in the words I quoted earlier. To enter the kingdom people must possess the humility of children, but to do so they need to be radically changed. People are not humble by nature. We are self-seeking, selfish, and driven by pride. What do we need if we are to become humble, trusting what God has done for our salvation and not what we can accomplish for ourselves? The answer is clear: We need to "turn" or "be converted," which is God's work. We need

to pray the prayer of Jeremiah 31:18: "Turn me, and I shall be turned, for you are the LORD my God" (my translation). We "must be born again" (John 3:7).

How do we know if we are converted? The evangelical bishop John Ryle said, "The surest mark of [any] true conversion is humility."[3] It is when we humble ourselves and trust Jesus alone to save us that we can be sure we are converted.

The Danger of Harming Others

In the first three verses of this section, Jesus uses children as examples of humility, which he demands of those who would be saved. In the next two verses, however, he seems to think of children not in terms of their humility but as those who are weak or helpless. He is not thinking of children literally, however. He is thinking of believers who, because they have become like children in their humility, have come to "believe in me" (v. 6). Jesus is concerned about and warns about harming such believing persons spiritually.

Let me make that point again. When Jesus speaks of "one of these little ones who believe in me" (v. 6), he is not speaking of children literally, though he does not exclude them. He is speaking of normal believers, and he warns against placing harmful obstacles in a true believer's way.

This should be a frightening matter for a person who thinks it is somehow fun to get a Christian to sin. Such a person will provoke a Christian to anger or excessive loose talk, sometimes even to overt sinful behavior. When he succeeds in this, he is pleased and feels vindicated: "If I have been able to get this Christian to sin, what I do must be all right, or at least, he is no better than I am." A person can feel good about that. But Jesus says that instead of feeling good, such a person should be terrified. In fact, it would have been far better for him that a large millstone had been hung around his neck and he had been thrown into the sea to drown than that he should have lived long enough to harm a new or weak believer. If you have ever mocked a Christian, tempted a Christian, or discouraged a Christian from serving Christ, you should tremble before these categorical statements by the Lord.

Yet religious people can do this same harm too. We need to remember Paul's denunciation in Romans 2:17–24. He had been arguing that everyone, not just obviously depraved people, needs the gospel, and at this point he turns to those who consider themselves religious. In Paul's day the most religious of all people were Jews, and they made eight important claims: (1) God has given us his law, and (2) he has entered into a special relationship with us. (3) Because we have been given his law, we know his will, and thus (4) we approve only the most excellent of moral standards. Therefore, (5) we are guides for the blind, (6) light for those who are in the dark, (7) instructors for the foolish, and (8) teachers of spiritual infants (vv. 17–20). Strikingly, each of these claims was absolutely true, and Paul admits it.

But knowledge of the ways of God is not enough! God judges according to truth and not according to appearances, according to what men and women actually do and not according to their mere professions.

Paul then brings forth three examples of the Jew's "superior" way: the eighth of the Ten Commandments (against stealing), the seventh of the Ten Commandments (against adultery), and a statement joining the first and second of the Ten Commandments (concerning the right worship of God). The Jews of Paul's day considered these good examples of the superior religious way of life they followed, as opposed to the godlessness of the heathen. But what Paul tells the Jews is that God is not satisfied with knowledge of the right way only. He is concerned with deeds, exactly what Paul has told the moral pagan (Rom. 2:6–16), and by that standard a Jew is condemned exactly as a pagan is condemned. A Jew judges another, but he is judged out of his own mouth because he himself has done what he condemns.

When Paul comes to the end of this paragraph, he quotes the Old Testament to show that "God's name is blasphemed among the Gentiles because of you" (v. 24; see Isa. 52:5 and Ezek. 36:22). This is always the case when religious persons violate the upright standards they proclaim. They become a stumbling block to others. Jesus warns about this in Matthew 18, and it is as true for us today as it was in the first Christian century. "Be warned," Jesus says. If you are living like this, it would be better for you that a large millstone had been hung around your neck and you had been drowned in the sea than that you had lived to harm one of Jesus' little ones.

That is what happens when people try to become great, of course. They put themselves ahead of others, particularly the small and the weak. They trample on them to get to the top. "What Jesus is saying in verses 1–6 is . . . that, instead of striving to become greatest in the kingdom of heaven (v. 1) [and] in the process of attempting this hurting others instead of guarding them (v. 6), the disciples should rather learn to forget about themselves and to focus their loving attention upon Christ's little ones, upon the lambs of the flock and upon all those who in their humble trustfulness . . . resemble those lambs."[4]

Determinism and Free Will

It is difficult to know whether verse 7 belongs with what comes immediately before or with what comes after because it applies to both passages. It is a standout verse that deals with the matters of sin, determinism, human responsibility, and free will.

It is not difficult to understand why Jesus said this or why Matthew added it to his collection of Jesus' teachings at this point. Sinful people want to excuse their behavior by saying that they just can't help what they are doing. In our day this usually takes a materialistic form. I do bad things because of my genetic makeup, or because of the bad neighborhood in which I grew up, or because I wasn't properly loved and cared for by my parents. In religious circles it sometimes takes a theological form. I sin because God has ordained it; it isn't my fault. In Paul's day some people used this argument to approve of increased sinning. God has willed to bring good from it, so "let us do evil that good may result" (Rom. 3:8).

Interestingly enough, Jesus does not deny the determinism, though that is not the best word to describe the Bible's teaching in this area. He acknowledges that this *is* an evil world and that "the things that cause people to sin . . . *must come*" (v. 7, emphasis added). We can even rightly say that God has determined that it should be so, at least passively, since God is not the originating cause of sin. Yet at the same time Jesus is equally insistent that the person who sins or causes others to sin is responsible.

It is impossible in this fallen evil world to avoid enticements to sin, but woe to the one through whom the enticements come. That is the point. The judgment of such a person will be just, and the judgment will be most severe if the enticement causes one of Jesus' own followers to stumble. Remember that when you look into your heart and examine your actions. Woe to such a person, Jesus says. *Woe* is the word the Bible uses to lament the terrible end of a person who is judged by God in "eternal fire" or "the fire of hell" for his or her sins (vv. 8–9).

The Need for Self-Discipline

This is not only a warning about harming another believer, however. We can also harm ourselves, and it is to this point that Jesus turns in verses 8 and 9: "If your hand or your foot causes you to sin, cut it off and throw it away. It is better for you to enter life maimed or crippled than to have two hands or two feet and be thrown into eternal fire. And if your eye causes you to sin, gouge it out and throw it away. It is better for you to enter life with one eye than to have two eyes and be thrown into the fire of hell."

These verses are an almost exact repetition of Matthew 5:29–30, from the Sermon on the Mount. Jesus was talking about adultery in the Sermon on the Mount, and he was teaching that adultery or any other sin should be taken seriously. Sin is so serious that any inclination toward it must be dealt with radically. What should be done? Many people know that because of these verses the early church father Origen had himself castrated in order to avoid sexual temptation. But this is not exactly what Jesus means, since here, in Matthew 18:8–9, Jesus explains his reference to hands and feet (v. 9 adds "eyes") by speaking of "things that cause people to sin" (v. 7). He means, get rid of whatever is tempting you to sin: suggestive movies, especially the kind you can rent at video stores and bring home to watch privately; the daily talk shows that wallow in depravity almost endlessly; books that urge you to get ahead by stepping on others; or talk that promotes racial bias. Get rid of the poison. Protect your mind from the defilement.

Of course, in the final analysis the answer to any problem is not merely to run away, especially since it is so difficult to avoid temptations in our culture. The real answer is a love for God and the transformed mind and heart that flow from it.

Did They Get It?

"Who is the greatest in the kingdom of heaven?" Jesus answered the question, and we have been trying to understand Jesus' answer. But here I want to follow up by asking, Did the disciples get it? Were they actually turned and changed to become like little children?

We know they didn't get it right away, because they are still fighting for the top position two chapters later. On that occasion the mother of James and John came to Jesus asking that one of her sons be chosen to sit at his right hand and the other son be chosen to sit at his left hand when he came into his kingdom (Matt. 20:21). They had probably put her up to it. So when the other disciples heard what she had asked Jesus, "they were indignant with the two brothers" (v. 24). They wanted those positions themselves.

What did Jesus do? He got them together and went through it all again. "You know that the rulers of the Gentiles lord it over them, and their high officials exercise authority over them. Not so with you. Instead, whoever wants to become great among you must be your servant, and whoever wants to be first must be your slave—just as the Son of Man did not come to be served, but to serve, and to give his life as a ransom for many" (vv. 25–28).

As long as Jesus was with them, they didn't get it. But when he died, they did, for they understood at last that he had given himself for them and had bought their salvation at the cost of his own life. And they really were changed.

It is beautiful to see. The disciples were all guilty of this self-advancing spirit, according to the Gospel. But among the many who were guilty, James and John stand out as the most guilty because of their compliance with the efforts of their mother to get them the first places. Yet think what happened to them! At one time Jesus called them "Sons of Thunder," no doubt because of their arrogant, boisterous attitudes (Mark 3:17). On another occasion they wanted to call down fire from heaven to destroy a village of the Samaritans that did not receive them (Luke 9:54). They were changed when they finally got their minds off themselves and onto Jesus.

We are not told much about James, but he must have changed. We do not hear of him struggling for prominence after the crucifixion and resurrection of the Lord, and he eventually died for Jesus, being executed by King Herod (Acts 12:1–2). John lived to be a venerable old man, known at last as the "apostle of love." He spoke humbly when he said, "This is how we know what love is: Jesus Christ laid down his life for us. And we ought to lay down our lives for our brothers" (1 John 3:16). If Jesus can turn a "son of thunder" into an "apostle of love," he can conquer your pride and teach you humility so that you can become like one of Jesus' "little children." He needs to, if you are to belong to his kingdom.

41

The Parable of the Lost Sheep

Matthew 18:10-14

"See that you do not look down on one of these little ones. For I tell you that their angels in heaven always see the face of my Father in heaven.

"What do you think? If a man owns a hundred sheep, and one of them wanders away, will he not leave the ninety-nine on the hills and go to look for the one that wandered off? And if he finds it, I tell you the truth, he is happier about that one sheep than about the ninety-nine that did not wander off. In the same way your Father in heaven is not willing that any of these little ones should be lost."

Many images in the Bible convey the protecting care of God for his people, but probably no image is more greatly loved than that of the shepherd and his sheep. What Christian can consider God as a shepherd without thinking of the Twenty-third Psalm: "The LORD is my Shepherd, I shall not want" (v. 1 KJV)? Or the tenth chapter of John, where Jesus applies the image to himself: "I am the good shepherd. The good shepherd lays down his life for the sheep" (v. 11)?

Yet it is not only in these well-known passages that the image occurs. A psalmist wrote, "We are his people, the sheep of his pasture" (Ps. 100:3). Isaiah said about God,

> He tends his flock like a shepherd:
> He gathers the lambs in his arms
> and carries them close to his heart;
> he gently leads those that have young.
>
> Isaiah 40:11

The image also occurs several times in Matthew. The first was in chapter 2, which cites this prophecy from Micah:

> But you, Bethlehem, in the land of Judah,
>   are by no means least among the rulers of Judah;
> for out of you will come a ruler
>   who will be the shepherd of my people Israel.
>
> Matthew 2:6, quoting Micah 5:2

In chapter 9 Matthew wrote of Jesus' compassion for the crowds "because they were harassed and helpless, like sheep without a shepherd" (Matt. 9:36; see Mark 6:34). In chapter 26 he reports Jesus as saying, "This very night you will all fall away on account of me, for it is written:

> 'I will strike the shepherd,
>   and the sheep of the flock will be scattered.'"
>
> Matthew 26:31, quoting Zechariah 13:7

As far as the rest of the New Testament is concerned, Hebrews describes Jesus as "that great Shepherd" (Heb. 13:20), and Peter calls him the "Chief Shepherd" to whom the undershepherds are accountable (1 Peter 5:4).

The Eighth Parable

The notable thing about Jesus' use of this image in Matthew 18 is that here it is a parable. Parables were an important teaching device for Jesus. Seven of them were introduced in chapter 13, and although this is the first Jesus used since that chapter, we will encounter eight more in Matthew 18:23–35; 20:1–16; 21:28–32, 33–46; 22:1–14; 25:1–13, 14–30, and 31–46.

A parable is a story drawn from real life that makes a single or at most a few spiritual points. It differs from a fable, which is not drawn from real life. In Aesop's fables, for example, animals or inanimate objects talk. Again, a parable differs from an allegory in which nearly everything stands for something else. The best-known example of an allegory is *Pilgrim's Progress* by John Bunyan.

This parable is found again in Luke 15:3–7, but the setting and points are different in the two Gospels. In Luke, Jesus answers the teachers of the law who are criticizing him for associating with known "sinners." Jesus uses the parable to explain that he is associating with sinners in order to save them, just as a shepherd exerts himself for a lost sheep and rejoices when he finds it. He calls the lost but found sheep a "sinner who repents" (v. 7). In Matthew, Jesus is teaching his disciples, and the point he makes is that they must be like shepherds in their care for other believers, particularly the weakest ones.

This parable fits into the context of Matthew 18. At the beginning of the chapter the disciples ask Jesus, "Who is the greatest in the kingdom of heaven?" (v. 1). Jesus answers: (1) the one who is humble, like a little child

(vv. 2–9); (2) the one who cares for the weak or lost believer (vv. 10–14); and (3) the one who forgives other people (vv. 15–20).

Howard Vos traces the progression in this way:

> Disciples who wish to be great are told that first they must accept and show kindness to other believers (vv. 5–9), facilitating their Christian walk and doing everything possible to avoid being a stumbling block to them. Second, they are not to despise or show contempt for other believers but are to offer help to those who may be in danger of going astray or who may have gone astray (vv. 10–14). Third, they are taught what to do if one Christian sins against another (vv. 15–17).[1]

This is a pattern of behavior entirely opposite of the pattern the world associates with personal greatness or success.

Ministering Angels

The first verse of this section makes clear that Jesus is talking about new or weak believers, still using the image of little children. It serves as an introduction to what he is going to say about the lost sheep. "See that you do not look down on one of these little ones," he says. "For I tell you that their angels in heaven always see the face of my Father in heaven" (v. 10).

People have turned to this Bible verse above all others for the idea of guardian angels, though there is not much in the Bible elsewhere to support that idea. In Daniel the archangel Michael appears as a protector of the Jewish people (see Dan. 12:1). Hebrews 1:14 refers to "ministering spirits sent to serve those who will inherit salvation." The first three chapters of Revelation refer to the angels of the seven churches, though it is not certain whether these are meant to be spirit beings. The "angels" may be the pastors of these churches. None of these verses proves clearly that each individual believer has a specific angel assigned to him or her.

What does Jesus' reference to the angels of these little ones mean then? B. B. Warfield had an interesting idea. He thought it refers to the spirits of the little ones after death and that this is a reminder of their eternal security or destiny. The problem with this interpretation is that the verse speaks of "angels," and we certainly do not become angels when we die.

John Broadus probably has it right when he connects this to Christians as a class. "However humble in the estimation of worldly men, believers have angels as their attendants, sent forth to serve God for their benefit (Heb. 1:14), and these angels of theirs enjoy in heaven the highest dignity and consideration, like persons admitted to the very presence of a monarch and allowed, not once but continually, to behold his face."[2] The point is that the angels have access to the presence of the Father at all times on behalf of "these little ones."[3]

The Shepherd and His Sheep

Yet it is not the angels who are important in this passage. They may be interceding on behalf of weak or wandering Christians, an encouraging thing to know. But what is really important here is that God is compared to the shepherd who seeks and finds the lost sheep. Why should we focus on angels when God is our Savior?

The parable tells us many important things about God.

1. *God cares for us individually.* When I see a hundred sheep in a meadow, I cannot begin to imagine how a shepherd can distinguish one sheep from another and miss one if it is caught by a predator or wanders off. All sheep look alike to me. But I am told that shepherds know their sheep. They know them individually, and, what is more, their sheep know them and respond to their voices. Jesus was building on this fact when he told the people of his day, "I am the good shepherd; I know my sheep and my sheep know me— just as the Father knows me and I know the Father—and I lay down my life for the sheep" (John 10:14–15).

We know that God knows his people individually and cares for them individually because when he calls them to faith he calls them "by name" (John 10:3). We see this clearly in the earthly ministry of Jesus. Think of Matthew himself. We are told that Jesus "saw a man named Matthew sitting at the tax collector's booth. 'Follow me,' he told him, and Matthew got up and followed him" (Matt. 9:9). Here was a lost sheep who had been given to Jesus by the Father. Jesus called him by name, and when he did, Matthew recognized his Master's voice and followed him.

Zacchaeus was another lost sheep. He was a little man who could not see Jesus as he passed by because of the large crowd of people. So he climbed a tree to get a better view. "When Jesus reached the spot, he looked up and said to him, 'Zacchaeus, come down immediately. I must stay at your house today.' So he came down at once and welcomed him gladly" (Luke 19:5–6).

An even more powerful example occurred in Bethany. The brother of Mary and Martha was sick. Word was sent to Jesus, but Lazarus died before Jesus arrived. But Jesus stood before the tomb and cried loudly, "Lazarus, come out!" (John 11:43). And he did! Lazarus was another of Jesus' lost sheep, and he responded by returning from the dead.

Or how about Mary. Mary was weeping in the garden where Jesus had been buried following his crucifixion. He spoke to her, but she supposed him to be the gardener. Then he spoke her name: "Mary." Immediately she knew him. Her doubts and sorrow fled, faith rose up, and Mary cried, "Rabboni!" which means Teacher (John 20:16).

It is always that way. If you are a believer, it is because God called you individually, and when you heard him call you by name, you turned from trusting yourself and trusted him instead. That is the kind of relationship God has with his people. It is an individual relationship. He knows you, even you. If he called you by name when you first believed on Jesus, you can be sure that he will exercise that same individual care in keeping you and seeking you if you wander away. You may be one in a hundred, but you are the one he will go to find and bring home.

2. *God understands our weaknesses.* I have never taken care of sheep or even had anything to do with them, except for seeing them in fields from time to time. But I am told that sheep are stupid creatures, probably the most stupid animals on earth. One way they show their stupidity is by so easily wandering away. They can have a good shepherd who has brought them to the best grazing lands, near an abundant supply of water, but they will still wander off to where the fields are barren and the water undrinkable. Again, by contrast, they are creatures of habit. They will stay in the same spot, grazing on the same land, until every blade of grass and every root is eaten, the fields ruined and themselves impoverished. This has actually ruined land in many sheep-raising areas of the world.

The wonderful thing is that God does not berate us for being stupid. The Bible says, "He knows how we are formed, he remembers that we are dust" (Ps. 103:14).

3. *God seeks us when we stray.* Doesn't God have anything better to do than to hunt for lost sheep? He does other important things too, of course. He runs the universe. He directs the flow of history. He sets up kings and brings kings down. But there is a sense in which all these other actions are only a backdrop for the drama of salvation, which means that seeking and saving lost sheep are the most important things God does.

Jesus is described as "the Lamb that was slain from the creation of the world" (Rev. 13:8). This means God created the world as a stage upon which the drama of salvation would be acted out. Moreover, when Jesus came, he described his mission by saying, "The Son of Man came to seek and to save what was lost" (Luke 19:10). Indeed, when the drama is over and the curtain has come down on the final act, the angelic audience and those who have been saved will praise the author and chief actor, crying,

> "Worthy is the Lamb, who was slain,
> to receive power and wealth and wisdom and strength
> and honor and glory and praise!" . . .
>
> "To him who sits on the throne and to the Lamb
> be praise and honor and glory and power,
>   for ever and ever!"

Revelation 5:12–13

We should remember one more thing: God does not wait for us to come to him, because we would not. "There is no one who . . . seeks God" (Rom. 3:11). "But God demonstrates his own love for us in this: While we were still sinners, Christ died for us" (Rom. 5:8).

4. *God rejoices when we repent and return to him.* The Greeks believed God cannot have emotions because, if he did and if we are the cause of his emotions—whether grief, anger, sorrow, love, or dismay—then to that extent we would have power over God and control him. That may be reasonable as philosophy,

but it is not the Bible's teaching. The Bible says that God grieves over sin and rejoices when a sinner is reclaimed. Jesus makes this explicit in the parable, saying of the great shepherd, "He is happier about that one sheep [that is found] than about the ninety-nine that did not wander off" (Matt. 18:13).

In the fifteenth chapter of Luke three stories tell about something that was lost. The first is the parable of the lost sheep, the parallel to the story we are studying (vv. 1–7). The second is a story about a lost coin (vv. 8–10). The last, which is the best known, is the story of the prodigal son (vv. 11–32). He too was lost, having squandered his inheritance on wild living. But at last he came to his senses and went back to his father to confess his sin and seek a place as his servant. We think of this as a story chiefly about the son; we even call it the parable of the prodigal son. But it is actually about the father, who represents God. The father was longing for his son, waiting for his return, and when he saw his son coming, the father ran to him, threw his arms around him, and kissed him. Then he said to his servants, "Quick! Bring the best robe and put it on him. Put a ring on his finger and sandals on his feet. Bring the fattened calf and kill it. Let's have a feast and celebrate. For this son of mine was dead and is alive again; he was lost and is found" (vv. 22–24).

Never think that if you go back to God, you will find him reproachful, angry, distant, or vindictive. Everything God has done is for your salvation, and no one in all the universe will be happier at your repentance than God.

5. *God's pursuit of the lost is effective.* We might suppose, if all we are thinking about is the parable of the prodigal, that the son might not have returned and that the love of the father might have been frustrated. But that is not what Jesus was getting at. In the first two parables in Luke 15 the shepherd finds the lost sheep and the woman finds the lost coin. Jesus is emphasizing God's joy over recovering whatever had been lost. This is what he means in Matthew too, for in Matthew 18 Jesus says, "Your Father in heaven is not willing that any of these little ones should be lost" (v. 14). And, of course, they are not. The Father seeks for them until he finds them and brings them home.

Remember that in Matthew Jesus is teaching the disciples how they are to care for weak believers, the "little ones" who are in view throughout the chapter. He is not teaching that all people will be saved, the doctrine known as universalism. He is teaching about the perseverance of the saints, the belief that not even one of those who has been given to Jesus by God will perish.

This is what Jesus teaches in John 10, the chapter we think of most often when we think of Jesus as our shepherd. In this chapter, after he has spoken of how he will call his sheep and how they will hear his voice and follow him, Jesus says, "I give them eternal life, and they shall never perish; no one can snatch them out of my hand. My Father, who has given them to me, is greater than all; no one can snatch them out of my Father's hand. I and the Father are one" (vv. 28–30). I call this clinching the nails, just as a carpenter drives nails through two pieces of wood and then bends the points of the nails over sideways into the wood. It is a way to secure the joint.

"I give unto them eternal life"—that is the nail. "They shall never perish"—that is the clinch by which the doctrine is made fast.

"No one can snatch them out of my hand"—that is the second nail. "My Father, who has given them to me, is greater than all; no one can snatch them out of my Father's hand"—that is the second clinch.

It is difficult to imagine how anyone could be made more secure than that. And if you think of being held by two hands—one hand Jesus' and the other the Father's—you can remember that God the Father and God the Son still have two hands free to defend you.

The Elder Brother

I want to go back to the story of the prodigal son, because one part of it is a picture of what we often wrongly do. It is a contrast to what Jesus was urging when he said in the chapter we are studying, "See that you do not look down on one of these little ones" (v. 10).

We are told that when the prodigal son came back, his older brother was not home. He was in the fields. But when he came in, heard the rejoicing, asked what it was about, and was told that the younger son had come back, he refused to go in. The father came out for him, but the son argued, "All these years I've been slaving for you and never disobeyed your orders. Yet you never gave me even a young goat so I could celebrate with my friends. But when this son of yours who has squandered your property with prostitutes comes home, you kill the fattened calf for him" (Luke 15:29–30).

Many find it easy to sympathize with the older son, but the only reason we do is because we often see ourselves in his shoes. We suppose that we are not like the prodigal. We have been faithful, hardworking, obedient. But we have not. Or if we have, it is only because God has already sought and found us. And it is probably true that we have also often wandered away and been brought back.

What were the disciples thinking about when Jesus told them about the lost sheep? They had been arguing about which of them should be greatest in the kingdom of heaven. With that in the immediate background, presumably they were thinking of themselves as among the ninety-nine who were still on the hillside and were wondering which of the ninety-nine would be the "top sheep." As long as they were thinking of such things, they would never be concerned for the one who was lost, and they would never do anything to help find him or her.

Who will be greatest? We should be beginning to understand the answer to that question by now. The greatest believer is the one who is most like the Shepherd, who gave himself for us. Like little children? Yes. But like the Shepherd too. We are never more like God than when we exert ourselves to help others, and if God rejoices over the one we help to bring home, he is probably rejoicing over what we are doing too.

42

The Parable of
the Unmerciful Servant

Matthew 18:15–35

"Therefore, the kingdom of heaven is like a king who wanted to settle accounts with his servants. As he began the settlement, a man who owed him ten thousand talents was brought to him. Since he was not able to pay, the master ordered that he and his wife and his children and all that he had be sold to repay the debt.

"The servant fell on his knees before him. 'Be patient with me,' he begged, 'and I will pay back everything.' The servant's master took pity on him, canceled the debt and let him go.

"But when that servant went out, he found one of his fellow servants who owed him a hundred denarii. He grabbed him and began to choke him. 'Pay back what you owe me!' he demanded.

"His fellow servant fell to his knees and begged him, 'Be patient with me, and I will pay you back.'

"But he refused. Instead, he went off and had the man thrown into prison until he could pay the debt. When the other servants saw what had happened, they were greatly distressed and went and told their master everything that had happened.

"Then the master called the servant in. 'You wicked servant,' he said, 'I canceled all that debt of yours because you begged me to. Shouldn't you have had mercy on your fellow servant just as I had on you?' In anger his master turned him over to the jailers to be tortured, until he should pay back all he owed.

"This is how my heavenly Father will treat each of you unless you forgive your brother from your heart."

The way we develop character and master godly conduct is one step at a time, and the disciples were learning it—

391

not very fast perhaps but surely. They had asked about being great in Christ's kingdom and had been taught that greatness begins with humility, like that of a child. They had been taught to avoid sin and were warned about causing another person to sin, especially a new or weak believer. But what if the other person sins against you? The answer to that question was Jesus' next important lesson.

The remarkable thing about Jesus' teaching here is that although he had been stressing humility and would teach forgiveness, he did not say that sin should just be overlooked. Offenses must be dealt with. His explanation of how they must be dealt with is the classic text for how Christians are to handle discipline problems in the church.

Dealing with Sin in the Church

The procedure for dealing with sin is both sensible and clear, as Jesus states it. It involves three steps.

1. *Go and talk to the person who has sinned against you,* attempting to show him his fault. He ought to listen and correct the fault. If he does, that is the end of the matter: "You have won your brother over" (v. 15).

2. *If talking about it does not achieve a correction and reconciliation, go again, this time taking one or two others with you,* "so that 'every matter may be established by the testimony of two or three witnesses'" (v. 16). This is a clear reference to the primary legal statute of the Old Testament, Deuteronomy 19:15.

3. *Bring the matter before the church.* If the offending brother still does not respond, he is to be treated "as you would a pagan or a tax collector" (v. 17).

It is obvious from the way Jesus develops these points that a number of important principles are involved. First, upright conduct matters; sin must be dealt with. Second, discipline is to be kept as private as possible, involving as few people as possible. If it can be worked out between two individuals, that is best. Third, the purpose of these steps is the restoration of the offender. We sometimes say that the purpose of discipline is restorative, not retributive. That is correct. Further, the final step is a function of the church, which means that it should be an official action. The word *church* occurs here for only the second time in Matthew's Gospel.[1]

In verse 18 Jesus gives the church the authority to bind and loose, the same authority he had given to Peter earlier.[2] This means verse 18 has bearing on how his earlier words to Peter should be understood. It indicates that the authority he gave to Peter was not an authority given to Peter as an individual or in virtue of a special office he was to hold. Rather, he gave it to the church as a whole in its official functions.

The final verses of this section seem to say that God will do anything that two or more Christians agree should be done. But that is not true. Actually, these verses belong with what was said in the previous verse about the binding and loosing function of the church, and they teach that God recognizes and validates that authority. What is most remarkable, however, is verse 20, because this verse puts Jesus in the role of God. Only God can be in more than one place at the same time, and that is what Jesus says of himself. He will be wherever two or three believers gather in his name.

Such a statement should be an encouragement to Christians, for however small the group or however insignificant we may think we are, we can know that the very God of the universe, even Jesus, is present with us. What can be more encouraging or more comforting than that?

Misusing the Steps

The most important principle in this passage is that discipline is intended for the restoration of the sinner and not for his or her condemnation, still less for the self-justification of the offended party. This is why the steps set out in verses 15–20 are followed by the parable of the unmerciful servant in verses 21–35. Before we look at the parable, let me share how the elders of Tenth Presbyterian Church discovered the misuse of the steps in verses 15–20, since the parable is an answer to the misuse of this procedure.

Several years ago the elders began to notice that some individuals who were having marriage problems attempted to use these verses to justify divorce so they could be declared free to get remarried. Their argument went like this. In 1 Corinthians 7:15 Paul says that if a believing person is married to an unbeliever and if the unbeliever insists on terminating the marriage, the believer is free to let the unbelieving spouse go: "A believing man or woman is not bound in such circumstances." That is perfectly understandable, of course. It is the apostle's way of saying that it takes two to live together and that if a non-Christian, who is not even attempting to live by biblical standards, wants to leave the marriage, in the final analysis there is no means of stopping him or her. Divorce is inevitable.

However, that concession was joined to Christ's teaching about reconciliation (or failure to achieve reconciliation) in Matthew 18. Jesus said that if a brother refuses to respond to proper attempts by the church to affect a reconciliation, the church is to "treat him as [one] would a pagan or a tax collector" (v. 17), that is, as an unbeliever. So the argument went that if in a Christian marriage one party refuses to be reconciled to the willing spouse after the church has been involved in the reconciliation attempt, the obstinate party may then be regarded as a non-Christian and be allowed to depart according to the principle of 1 Corinthians 7:15. The Christian may then be allowed to remarry with God's blessing—in spite of God saying that he hates divorce (Mal. 2:16) or Jesus' clear teaching that divorce followed by remarriage is adultery (Matt. 5:32).

The elders found they were being manipulated by the spouse who wanted a divorce. They were asked to approach the stubborn spouse to effect a change of mind. If they were unsuccessful, they were expected to declare that the rebellious spouse was either an unbeliever or (supposing it to be the same thing) was acting like one and allow the person making the complaint to get a divorce and remarry. They were maneuvered into facilitating divorces rather than restraining them.

Peter's Question

That particular problem is not in view in Matthew 18, of course. But it was because of this kind of foreseen abuse that the chapter continues with the parable of the unmerciful servant. The parable is about forgiveness, and it teaches that we must forgive without limits since that is how we have been forgiven by God.

The bridge to the parable is Peter's question: "Lord, how many times shall I forgive my brother when he sins against me? Up to seven times?" (v. 21). The rabbis had been teaching that one should forgive an offense three times, but not beyond that.[3] So Peter was probably thinking that he was going a long way toward mastering the spirit of Jesus when he suggested that one might actually forgive seven times.

We tend to look down on Peter for misreading Christ's mind, supposing that we would do better. But Peter was at least asking the right question. He realized that it was right to forgive and that he had an obligation to do so. He was trying. But do we even try? To put it another way, do we forgive even seven times, not to mention the seventy-seven times suggested by Jesus? Can you think of anyone who, in the last week or month or year, you have consciously forgiven for the same offense as many as seven times? You may have, but you probably have not. So at least grant Peter something. He had been in Jesus' school for only three years and had a great deal yet to learn, but he had learned this much at least. Some of us have barely matriculated in that school and are therefore far from graduating with even the rudiments of Christ's teaching.

When Jesus told Peter, "I tell you, not seven times, but seventy-seven times" (v. 22),[4] he did not mean that we do not need to forgive the seventy-eighth time, of course. It was a way of saying that we should never stop forgiving. Then Jesus told this story.

Forgiven but Unforgiving

A certain king wanted to settle accounts with his servants, so he called in one who had an enormous debt: ten thousand talents. It is difficult to estimate how much money that was, and it may only mean the largest conceivable debt, "ten thousand" being one of the largest common numbers and a "talent" being the largest denomination of currency. However, if we do estimate it, we get some interesting results.

A talent was seventy-five pounds, so ten thousand talents would be 750,000 pounds. We do not know whether these were talents of gold or silver, but since Jesus is trying to exaggerate the contrast between this debt and the relatively small debt of the other servant, we may suppose that he was thinking of the more valuable of the two talents. In troy weight there are twelve ounces to a pound. So we are now dealing with 750,000 times 12, or 9 million ounces of gold. Assuming that gold is selling at roughly $350 an ounce, we come to a figure of $3,150,000,000. That is beyond our comprehension, which is precisely Christ's point. It was an astronomical debt.

Since the servant was unable to pay, the king was going to have him, his wife, and his children sold into slavery and his goods sold on the market to reclaim as much of the debt as possible. Hearing this, the man fell on his knees and begged, "Be patient with me, and I will pay back everything" (v. 26). He could not, of course, but the king had pity on him and canceled the obligation.

This man then found a fellow servant who owed him money: one hundred denarii. A denarii was a day's wage for a common laborer, so that was approximately a third of a year's wages. Assuming (in our terms) that a low wage might be twelve or fifteen thousand dollars per year, the debt was only four or five thousand dollars. That was a significant debt, but it was a pittance compared to the enormous debt incurred by the first servant. When the man with the smaller debt begged for time to repay his obligation, which he could presumably have done, the first servant hardened his heart and had the other man thrown into prison.

Others heard what had happened and told the king. He called the first man in, demanding, "You wicked servant, I canceled all that debt of yours because you begged me to. Shouldn't you have had mercy on your fellow servant just as I had on you?" (vv. 32–33). Then, according to Jesus, the king turned him over to the jailers until he should pay back all he owed. The point is obvious: Christians must be limitless in forgiving others since God has been infinitely forgiving with them.

A Troubling Statement

We might wish that Jesus had stopped there, but he had this additional disturbing word: "This is how my heavenly father will treat each of you unless you forgive your brother from your heart" (v. 35). The statement is troubling because it seems to imply a "works" salvation, that is, if you forgive others (a work), you will be forgiven. But even if it does not teach that, it seems to imply that grace continues by means of works. We may be saved by grace, but if we fail to act rightly, God may cancel his forgiveness and have us thrown into hell anyway. Such an interpretation is unacceptable for several reasons. Therefore, some have tried to work out ways of getting around it.

Evasion number 1: Jesus did not mean what he said. Some regard the parable as simple hyperbole, an exaggerated statement given for its emotional or rhetorical effect. According to these writers, Jesus did not mean to say that God would send us to hell if we do not forgive our debtors, but only that forgiveness is an extremely important matter and that we really ought to forgive. We *should* forgive others just as God has forgiven us, but if we do not, we are not to suppose that we are not saved or that we will lose our salvation.

That approach is a bit childish, because it is what children do. When a mother is about to go out and instructs her children what is to be done in her absence, she says, "I have to go to the store for a few minutes. I want you to use the time while I'm gone to straighten up your rooms. Make your beds. Hang up your clothes. Put the toys back in the toy box. Don't waste time watching television. Do you understand that?"

"Yes," the children answer.

"And you're going to do it? You're not going to put it off so I find your rooms still a mess when I come back?"

"Oh, no," the children say. "We'll do it."

The mother goes out. When she comes back the rooms are exactly the way they were and the children are watching television. What do they say when she asks why they haven't cleaned up their rooms? "Did you want us to clean up our rooms today? We must have misunderstood you. We thought you wanted us to do it tomorrow."

Evasion number 2: Apply the words to someone else. According to this view, Jesus meant what he said, but his words do not apply to people living in this age. Jesus' teaching was for Jews living under the law, and therefore it does not apply to us. We are justified by faith apart from works. God's forgiveness does not depend in any way on our forgiveness of others and is, in fact, not even linked to it. Such an approach is like speeding down a highway and then, when you see a police car coming with its siren sounding and light flashing, you hope it is going after someone else. That won't work. It is not to other people but to *us* that Jesus is speaking.

Evasion number 3: Reject the rest of the New Testament. The first two of these evasions are found in evangelicalism, but the third is not. The third evasion is that of liberalism, which instead of trying to get around Jesus' teaching actually delights in it by sacrificing the New Testament. The liberal says, "Here we are getting to the heart of that beautiful and simple gospel that Jesus actually taught. He is not teaching the later Pauline doctrine of justification by faith in a so-called work of atonement. This is merely that beautiful teaching of doing to others as we would want them to do to us. Since God forgives us, we should want to forgive everyone."

Jesus is not repudiating Paul, of course. In fact, we can tell from even the most casual reading of the verse that if we do not forgive others, God is going to send us to hell. That is not the gospel of liberalism! Another way of understanding these words is needed.

Forgiven *and* Forgiving

What we need to recognize is that Jesus is not giving the whole of the gospel message in one story. What he says is true enough, that there is an unbreakable connection between God's forgiveness of us and our forgiveness of other people. Such a word is intended to snap us out of our lethargy and confront us with the life-changing power of the gospel. But it does not mean we are saved by forgiving others or that salvation, once acquired, can be lost. Jesus is only saying that, whatever else is involved (and a great deal more *is* involved), forgiveness must be part of what it means to be a Christian.

Here is the explanation. Although we are justified by faith apart from works, being justified is not the only thing that happens to us in salvation. In fact, it is not even the first thing. Justification is by faith, so faith at least comes before it. And since, as Jesus said to Nicodemus, we cannot "see" or "enter" the kingdom of God unless we are born again, regeneration or the new birth must come before entering or believing (John 3:3, 5). No one believes on Christ and is justified who has not already been given a new nature. This new nature is the nature of Jesus himself or, as we could also say, it is God's own forgiving nature. Thus, although the new nature does not manifest itself entirely at once, if we are justified, that nature will increasingly and inevitably express itself in our forgiveness of others, just as God for Christ's sake has forgiven us. We will be able to pray, as Jesus instructed us to pray, "Forgive us our debts, as we also have forgiven our debtors" (Matt. 6:12).

The Lutherans say, "We are justified by faith alone, but not by a faith which is alone." Faith comes first, but our new nature will express itself after that in what we do. The conclusion is, if we do not forgive others, we are not forgiven. We are not justified people. We are not God's children.

The parable of the forgiven but unforgiving debtor makes three points.

1. *A judgment is coming.* Jesus did not pass over that teaching. He spoke of forgiveness, but he also spoke of what happened to the wretched man in his story. He was cast into prison until he should pay back all he owed. That judgment hangs over everyone who has not experienced God's forgiveness through faith in Christ.

2. *There is forgiveness.* God *does* forgive. God sent Jesus to make forgiveness possible.

3. *The only sure proof that a person has received God's forgiveness through true faith in Jesus is a transformed heart and changed life.* How do we get that down into the practical areas of our lives so that we actually begin to treat others as we have been treated? By standing before the holy God and seeing ourselves as the sinners we are—vile and yet forgiven through the death of God's Son. We must know that we have been saved solely because of the undeserved mercy of God. That awareness should humble us so that we simply have no other option but to forgive others and to do it from the heart.[5]

43

Jesus' Teaching on Divorce

Matthew 19:1-12

When Jesus had finished saying these things, he left Galilee and went into the region of Judea to the other side of the Jordan. Large crowds followed him, and he healed them there.

Some Pharisees came to him to test him. They asked, "Is it lawful for a man to divorce his wife for any and every reason?"

"Haven't you read," he replied, "that at the beginning the Creator 'made them male and female,' and said, 'For this reason a man will leave his father and mother and be united to his wife, and the two will become one flesh'? So they are no longer two, but one. Therefore what God has joined together, let man not separate."

"Why then," they asked, "did Moses command that a man give his wife a certificate of divorce and send her away?"

Jesus replied, "Moses permitted you to divorce your wives because your hearts were hard. But it was not this way from the beginning. I tell you that anyone who divorces his wife, except for marital unfaithfulness, and marries another woman commits adultery."

Whom, therefore, God hath joined together, let no man put asunder." These are the words that end the most common form of marriage service used in Christian churches. But men *are* "putting asunder," as are women. The statistics tell us that nearly one in two marriages taking place in the United States today will end in divorce, and the statistics are not much better for Christian marriages. We see the evidence of decay all around us. What are we to make of these statistics, especially when we turn to the Bible and find that God requires chastity before marriage, fidelity afterward, and lifelong unions of wives and husbands without easy divorce as an escape?

When we compare our practices with God's standards, we might very well exclaim, as the disciples do in Matthew 19, "If this is the situation between a husband and wife, it is better not to marry" (v. 10).

But it is *good* to marry! The problem is not with the institution of marriage, since marriage is God's idea. It was God who brought the first bride to the first groom in Eden, after all. Everything God does is good. The problem is sin, or to put it another way, the problem is with our own hard hearts, which Jesus refers to explicitly in verse 8. Jesus says, referring to the Old Testament law about divorce (Deut. 24:1–4), "Moses permitted you to divorce your wives because your hearts were hard. But it was not this way from the beginning."

I am sure this is why, in Matthew's Gospel, the long discussion of divorce in chapter 19 (vv. 1–12) immediately follows the equally long discussion in chapter 18 (vv. 21–35) of the need of Christ's followers to forgive other people, knowing that they themselves have been forgiven much more by God. Marriage is the most intimate of all relationships, and in marriage the most piercing pain can be experienced. It follows that it is the relationship above all others that must be upheld by that "seventy-seven times" forgiveness about which Jesus speaks.

The Pharisees' Question

This important discussion of divorce and marriage was occasioned by a question the Pharisees asked Jesus. The question had been debated seriously among the rabbis, but Matthew says here that it was asked "to test him" (v. 3). "Is it lawful for a man to divorce his wife for any and every reason?" they asked. Presumably they wanted to force Jesus to one side of the issue or the other, thereby automatically alienating him from at least half the Jewish leaders. But perhaps, knowing that Jesus was conservative in his views and was likely to oppose divorce, or at least easy divorces, they also wanted to brand him with a view they knew would be unpopular.

The discussion among the rabbis was over the meaning of Deuteronomy 24:1–4, the only Old Testament passage that explicitly discusses divorce. It uses the words "something indecent" to describe what a man might find in his wife as a ground for his action. What does that refer to? And regardless of what it refers to, does the passage grant a husband the right to a divorce?[1] The adherents of the Qumran sect judged all divorces to be wrong. The well-known Rabbi Shammai permitted divorce but only because of gross indecency, though he did not spell out clearly what that was. The equally well-known Rabbi Hillel permitted divorce for all kinds of offenses, even preparing bad meals. Hillel was the liberal spokesman on this matter; Shammai was the conservative.[2]

Jesus' Teaching about Marriage

Jesus does not answer the Pharisees' question directly at first. Later he does (in verse 9). But here, instead of debating the matter on their level—

they were asking about the minimal grounds for divorce—Jesus raises the discussion to the level of God's original intention in marriage, directing his questioners to the first and second chapters of the Bible, where a description of the institution of the marriage relationship is found.

The first text Jesus cites is Genesis 1:27. "Haven't you read," he replies, "that at the beginning the Creator 'made them male and female'?" (v. 4). The implication is that God instituted marriage by the creation of humans in two genders, male and female, and that the woman was created for the man just as, in a corresponding way, the man was given to the woman.

The second text is Genesis 2:24. This is part of a longer passage that reads:

> The LORD God said, "It is not good for the man to be alone. I will make a helper suitable for him." . . . So the LORD God caused the man to fall into a deep sleep, and while he was sleeping, he took one of the man's ribs and closed up the place with flesh. Then the LORD God made a woman from the rib he had taken out of the man, and he brought her to the man.
> The man said,
>
> > "This is now bone of my bones
> > and flesh of my flesh;
> > she shall be called 'woman,'
> > for she was taken out of man."
>
> For this reason a man will leave his father and mother and be united to his wife, and they will become one flesh.
>
> Genesis 2:18, 21–24

According to these words, marriage was instituted by God for man's well-being, and the union that makes a man and a woman one flesh is to be permanent throughout both their lives—"'til death us do part," as one form of the marriage service states it. Therefore, Jesus stood against the common lax divorce practices of his day and for Scripture when he taught that marriage was a permanent institution.

Is Divorce Permitted?

As I read Matthew's account, I suspect that the Pharisees anticipated an answer such as this because they were ready at once with a follow-up question. "Why then," they asked, "did Moses command that a man give his wife a certificate of divorce and send her away?" (v. 7). They were talking about Deuteronomy 24:1–4, of course, and they were suggesting that Jesus must be wrong in his interpretation of Genesis 1 and 2, since later in the law, in Deuteronomy, Moses "commanded" divorce.

They were not reading their proof text correctly. They were reading it as follows: "If a man marries a wife and she displeases him (for some reason), he shall write her a bill of divorce and send her away." But that is not what

Moses said. Moses did not command divorce; he only recognized that it was happening and tried to regulate it. As Jesus says, he permitted divorce because of the hardness of the people's hearts. What the text actually says is something like this: "If a man marries a wife and she does not find favor in his eyes . . . *and* he writes her a bill of divorce and sends her away . . . *and* she marries another man . . . *and* her second husband also writes her a bill of divorce and sends her away, then the first husband must not marry her again." The text says nothing about a divorce being allowed, only about the sin of remarriage after the woman has been joined to another man.

What Is Fornication?

So far so good. But here is where the chief difficulty comes. It is clear that Jesus calls remarriage after divorce adultery, forbidding it. But then he added what is usually referred to as the exception clause. "I tell you that anyone who divorces his wife, *except for marital unfaithfulness,* and marries another woman commits adultery" (v. 9, emphasis added). Most people today understand "marital unfaithfulness" to mean adultery and conclude that this is the one valid ground for divorce, since adultery will already have broken the marriage relationship. This is the majority view even among the most conservative commentators, at least in our day. But I want to argue that this interpretation is wrong, that this is not what Jesus was referring to when he said "except for marital unfaithfulness."

Actually, the words "marital unfaithfulness" in the New International Version prejudge the issue because they mean "adultery." But "adultery" is not the actual meaning of the word they translate. The Greek word for adultery is *moicheia.* It is the equivalent in Greek of the Latin words *ad alterius torum,* which mean "to another's bed." We have condensed the three Latin words into our single word *adultery.* This is what *moicheia* means, but it is not the word in this passage. The word that occurs here is *porneia,* which most older versions of the Bible rightly translate as "fornication." It is broader than *moicheia. Porneia* refers to different kinds of sexual sin. It is based on the verb *pernemi* ("to sell"), referring to prostitution, first of all, but then also to other kinds of sexual conduct outside of marriage. The Latin term *fornix* has the same meaning, referring to the arch of a temple, which was where the temple courtesans collected. From this we get the word *fornication.*

If Jesus were referring to adultery as the one legitimate ground for divorce, the text would have used the word *moicheia.* That it doesn't suggests we should look elsewhere for Jesus' meaning. I would suggest that if the exception clause does not refer to adultery, the only thing it can reasonably refer to is impurity in the woman discovered on the first night of the marriage, in which case there would have been deceit in the marriage contract. Jesus would then be saying (in full accord with the accepted views of the day) that although a man may divorce a woman immediately after marriage if he finds her not to be a virgin (in which case he was allowed by the law to remarry and was not to be called an adulterer), he is not permitted to divorce her for any other reason. If he does, he places her into a position in which she may be forced to remarry, thereby becoming an adulteress, and he would become an adulterer if he remarried.

What Was Moses Teaching?

This is also the true meaning of the passage from Deuteronomy. The word translated "something indecent" (NIV) or "some uncleanness" (KJV) in verse 1 is actually the word for "nakedness" or "nudity." It was associated with being unclothed for the purpose of sexual relations and thus was often associated with sexual sin or impurity, which is the case here. It cannot refer to adultery because adultery was punishable by death, and in that case there would be no need for a divorce. If the word does not refer to adultery, which is sexual sin after marriage, the only thing it can refer to is sexual sin before marriage, which is what we mean by fornication. In other words, Jesus was reinforcing the Old Testament's teaching by his interpretation of Moses' specific "divorce" regulation.

Someone may object that fornicators were also put to death in Israel, but although that was true for some types of unchastity before marriage, it was not true for all. If a girl had been sexually abused or simply unchaste before an engagement, she was not punished by death and was free to marry, though the impurity had to be made known to the prospective groom beforehand.

There is one other interesting point to be considered. Mark also discusses this issue (Mark 10:1–12), but the exception clause that has been the cause of so much controversy does not appear in his Gospel. Matthew is the only Gospel that contains it. Why is that? Some liberal commentators (and even some conservative ones) argue that Mark's version of this saying is the original one and that Matthew added the exception because of divorce problems in the church of his day. That is hardly satisfactory.

Isn't it more reasonable to explain the addition, which Jesus certainly spoke, by noting that Matthew is also the only Gospel to record the reaction of Joseph when he learned of Mary's pregnancy. Matthew wrote, "Because Joseph her husband was a righteous man and did not want to expose her to public disgrace, he had in mind to divorce her quietly" (Matt. 1:19). Joseph and Mary were not married, though they were formally engaged, which was nearly as binding, and Joseph wanted to annul the engagement, which was regarded as a divorce, when he learned that Mary was expecting a child. If someone read that, followed by Jesus' statement in the nineteenth chapter that any divorce was wrong, the reader might conclude that Joseph was willing to break the law by what he planned to do. Matthew included the explanation to explain what had happened in the case of Jesus' parents.[3]

The Disciples' Question and Jesus' Answer

Chastity before marriage, fidelity after marriage, and a lifelong commitment of one married partner to the other with no thought of divorce! What a terribly high standard that is! No wonder the disciples reacted with the cynical comment I referred to at the beginning of this study: "If this is the situation between a husband and wife, it is better not to marry" (v. 10). We hear something very much like that today, especially from young people who often say, "I have never known a happily married couple; therefore, I am not going to get married."

The obvious answer to such cynicism is to model happy marriages, which Christians can do in spite of the sin that mars even Christian marriages and the need for repeated forgiveness that any close relationship entails. But strikingly, this is not the answer Jesus gives. Instead of reassuring the disciples that it is possible to have a happy marriage and instructing them on how they might achieve it, Jesus responds by saying that it is in fact better for some not to marry, if this is what they are called to do by God. Jesus refers to those who are unable to marry because of a physical lack or deformity and to others who are called to renounce marriage "because of the kingdom of heaven" (v. 12).

This is what Paul says in 1 Corinthians 7, where he advises remaining single "because of the present crisis" (v. 26). He was thinking of difficult missionary work and was acknowledging that it might be better done by single people than by those who are encumbered by a family. Yet he adds that there is nothing wrong with marriage (v. 28). Jesus spoke to the disciples as he did because he was giving them the same high calling.

Christian Marriages Today

That is the essence of Christ's teaching. It is consistent with the Bible's teaching as a whole, and there is no legitimate way of getting around it. But where do we come in? We can acknowledge the Bible's high standard and still struggle with how to do what is required. Or we can struggle over what to do when we fail to live up to Jesus' teaching. Many people are hurt by situations involving estrangement, divorce, or remarriage. I want to close by saying a few things about the application of these standards.

First, these are standards for Christians, not for the world. This means that believers must not try to impose them on other people. We believe that following Christian standards would make men and women happier than they are apart from them, and we can point with justified alarm to the weakening of the family and the decay of lasting relationships in today's society. But the majority of people are not Christians, and it would be both wrong and irrational to expect them to lead Christian lives.

C. S. Lewis offered a good suggestion when he argued that "there ought to be two distinct kinds of marriage: one governed by the state with rules enforced on all citizens, the other governed by the church with rules enforced by her own members. The distinction ought to be quite sharp, so that a man knows which couples are married in a Christian sense and which are not."[4]

Second, because many persons become Christians after they have been married and divorced, sometimes more than once, we must never forget that their previous conduct, along with their past, is wiped clean by their conversion to Christ and that they therefore have the right to marry for the first time as Christians. The church at Corinth must have been made up largely of persons in this category, for Paul wrote that many of them were fornicators, adulterers, and idolaters before their conversion (1 Cor. 6:9–11). Still, he calls them "new creatures" in Christ. When a new creature in Christ meets another new creature in Christ and God leads them to each other, do they not have a right to marry and establish a Christian home regardless of their previous marital history?

Third, there are cases in which one of the spouses is a Christian and the other is not. What is the Christian to do under these circumstances? Paul faced this situation not only in Corinth but in other cities, and his advice was this: First, the Christian should remain with the unbelieving spouse if at all possible, for, he says, how do you know that you will not be the means by which God will save your husband or wife (1 Cor. 7:16)? It is possible, however, that the unsaved spouse will not stay with the Christian. If that is the case, Paul says to let the unbeliever go. How can the Christian stop the unbeliever from doing so?

Fourth, we live in an imperfect, sinful world, and there will always be situations in which a Christian will have to choose the lesser of two evils. In some circumstances, this could be divorce. For instance, a woman may be married to a brute of a husband, a man who spends his money on drinking or gambling and then deserts his wife while she must raise and educate the children. Under the laws of the United States, it is entirely possible that the man might return just when the children are ready to go to college and claim the money the wife has saved and waste it. In a situation such as this, I believe it would be right for the wife to initiate the divorce, even if she is a Christian, since her chief responsibility at this point would be to the children and their future.

Finally, it is true that Christians who marry out of God's will and get divorced often remarry (frequently to Christians) and that God seems in grace often to sanctify and bless the second marriage. Does this mean that God modifies his standards? No. But it does mean that divorce and remarriage, as bad as they are, are not unforgivable and that God is always willing to begin again with us wherever we are or whatever we have done. Churches should never be closed to such people, and Christians above all should be understanding of others and show mercy.

There is hardly a matter in today's church that is treated with more laxity than the issue of divorce and remarriage. But identifying with and seeking to help people who have failed in their marriages does not mean lowering the standards. We must maintain the standards, but we must also be compassionate and understanding of those who have not followed them. We will never be of much help to anyone if we are not.[5]

44

Little Children and a Young Man

Matthew 19:13–30

Now a man came up to Jesus and asked, "Teacher, what good thing must I do to get eternal life?"

"Why do you ask me about what is good?" Jesus replied. "There is only One who is good. If you want to enter life, obey the commandments."

"Which ones?" the man inquired.

Jesus replied, "'Do not murder, do not commit adultery, do not steal, do not give false testimony, honor your father and mother,' and 'love your neighbor as yourself.'"

"All these I have kept," the young man said. "What do I still lack?"

Jesus answered, "If you want to be perfect, go, sell your possessions and give to the poor, and you will have treasure in heaven. Then come, follow me."

When the young man heard this, he went away sad, because he had great wealth.

Whenever you study the Bible, if you study it thoughtfully, you will find things that are wonderfully reasonable and balanced. For example, nothing is more reasonable than the balanced arrangement of material in Matthew 18 and 19. These chapters are about the character of those who belong to Christ's kingdom, and they are tied together by a series of relationships: (1) to other believers (Who shall be greatest?); (2) to those who sin against us (How often must I forgive?); (3) to a husband or wife (May I divorce?); (4) to children (Should they be included?); and (5) to money (Who, then, can be saved?).

On the other hand, we sometimes find material that is startling and even jarring. In Matthew 19:13–30 Jesus corrects his disciples for wanting to drive away people who were bringing little children to Jesus. Jesus says, "Let the little children come to me, and do not hinder them, for the kingdom of heaven belongs to such as these" (v. 14). Yet in the very next paragraph Jesus seems to drive away an earnest young man who wanted to become his disciple. The man is allowed to go because he is unwilling to part with his possessions. But even more puzzling, the chapter ends with Jesus promising the disciples houses, brothers, sisters, fathers, mothers, children, and fields in this life (v. 29). These contrasts are confusing, and it takes some careful thought to understand them.

Jesus and the Children

The one thing that is the same in the latter half of the chapter is that people are coming to Jesus: first the parents with their children and second the rich young man. We do not need to spend a great deal of time on Jesus' welcome of the children, for the meaning is on the surface. Jesus welcomed children, and it is proof of his gracious nature and visible goodness that children seem to have been drawn to him.

Jesus also used the incident to teach about the nature of those who are the citizens of his kingdom, almost exactly as he had done in the teaching recorded at the start of chapter 18. When the disciples were arguing about who should be greatest in the kingdom, Jesus put a little child in front of them, saying, "I tell you the truth, unless you change and become like little children, you will never enter the kingdom of heaven. Therefore, whoever humbles himself like this child is the greatest in the kingdom of heaven" (Matt. 18:3–4). Jesus is teaching the same thing in chapter 19 when he refers to the children who were brought to him: "The kingdom of heaven belongs to such as these" (v. 14).

The important words are "such as." Jesus is not teaching about the salvation of infants, though, as some theologians believe, God may graciously save those who die in infancy by Christ's work. Here Jesus is teaching that those who would be saved from sin must become like children in their humility and simple trust in Christ. Arguing about being greatest in the kingdom of heaven is the surest way not to enter it.

The Young Man's Question

Which brings us to the rich young man (vv. 16–22). Matthew, Mark, and Luke each tell us about him. All three say he was rich. Matthew adds that he was young (v. 20). Luke says he was a ruler, presumably in one of the local synagogues (Luke 18:18). He is the first (maybe the only) example of a person who comes to Jesus and is not saved.

What is striking is that Jesus does not seem to try to win him over in spite of the fact that he was apparently very earnest. In *Today's Gospel: Authentic or Synthetic?* Walter Chantry notes how radically different Jesus' approach was from what most evangelicals would do in like situations. The man was clean-cut and earnest. He wanted to be saved. He even asked a good question: "Teacher, what good thing must I do to get eternal life?" (v. 16). In that kind of encounter most of today's evangelicals would give the inquirer a three- or four-step presentation of the gospel, ask him to make a personal commitment to Jesus Christ, and send him away with the assurance of salvation. Jesus did nothing of the sort.

First, Jesus challenged the young man in regard to his notions about God: "Why do you ask me about what is good? There is only One who is good" (v. 17). He reminded him of God's written law: "'Do not murder, do not commit adultery, do not steal, do not give false testimony, honor your father and mother'" and "'love your neighbor as yourself'" (vv. 18–19). At the end he called for repentance and faith in himself: "Go, sell your possessions and give to the poor, and you will have treasure in heaven. Then come, follow me" (v. 21). That was the end of the interview. The young man was rich, and because he was unwilling to pay the cost of his possessions, he went away sorrowfully. Is that any way to win people to Christ?

Jesus thought so. Chantry points out that Jesus "demanded this turning from everything to himself as a condition of discipleship for everyone," concluding that because it fails to articulate this cost, much of today's church "isn't preaching Jesus' gospel!"[1]

What had Jesus done? He had confronted the man with the holiness of God and with the law's demands. In listing the commandments, Jesus referred to the sixth, seventh, eighth, ninth, and fifth commandments of Exodus 20, in that order, skipping over the tenth and coming directly to Leviticus 19:18 ("love your neighbor as yourself") as a summary. It was a probing response, and when the young man replied in sincere self-righteousness, "All these I have kept. What do I still lack?" Jesus returned to the last of the Ten Commandments, the one he had skipped, knowing it was the man's specific problem, and told him to sell his possessions. He was guilty of coveting his possessions, and because he was unwilling to sell them and give to the poor, he obviously did not love his neighbor as himself.

Does this mean that anyone who wants to follow Jesus must become poor? Not necessarily, for there are rich believers in the Bible. But it does mean two things. First, we have to recognize our sinfulness and know that we are condemned by God's law rather than justified by it. Second, we have to repudiate anything that would keep us from following Jesus. For some that is money. For others it may be something else.

John Broadus writes correctly:

> The test of this is different for different people. Some find it harder to renounce hopes of worldly honor and fame for Christ's sake, than to renounce wealth; and for others the hard trial is to abandon certain gratifications of the various appetites or of taste. Abraham left his native country at God's command, but became rich and famous. Moses gave up the distinction and refined pleasures

of court life, and tried patiently to rule a debased and intractable people. Elisha left his property at the call of God through Elijah. Paul abandoned his ambitious hope of being a great rabbi. All should be willing even to die for Christ (16:24ff), though not many are actually required to do so.[2]

The specifics may be different, but the demand is the same for all people. To be saved we must deny ourselves, take up our crosses daily, and follow Jesus (Matt. 16:24).

Jesus' Conclusion

Matthew tells us that the young man went away sad, but I think Jesus must have been sad too, for he commented on what had happened by saying to the disciples, "I tell you the truth, it is hard for a rich man to enter the kingdom of heaven. Again I tell you, it is easier for a camel to go through the eye of a needle than for a rich man to enter the kingdom of God" (vv. 23–24). It is difficult for any sinner to enter heaven, of course; in fact, it is impossible without a radical change of heart and faith in Christ. But we are not talking about other sins here. We are talking about the love of money, and we cannot forget that this is a chief, if not *the* chief, characteristic of our intensely commercial age.

The people of Christ's day regarded wealth as proof of God's blessing. They were not right, of course. But they were closer to being right than we are, because we think wealth is a proof of how successful we have been at blessing ourselves. They at least recognized that money, as well as every other good gift, is from God (James 1:17). But what Jesus is saying here is that, far from being a true blessing, wealth is actually a hindrance to gaining the greatest blessing of all, which is salvation. In fact, a great deal of money makes receiving salvation almost impossible.

The disciples seem to have understood this. After all, speaking about money was speaking on their level, and they were probably aware of how much they too coveted it. So they asked the obvious question: "If people who love money can't be saved, 'who then can be saved?'" (v. 25). Jesus' answer was direct: "No one, not the rich young man, nor you, nor anyone else, since everyone loves something or someone else more than God." Speaking only from a human point of view, the situation is hopeless. But fortunately this is not all that can be said, since "with God all things are possible" (v. 26).

Do you see where this is going? If you can't earn heaven by wealth or good works, which the young man hoped he could do, and if every desire of our hearts, even for good things, is actually a fatal desire because it keeps us from trusting Christ completely, the only way anyone will ever be saved is if God operates entirely apart from us and for his own good pleasure. In other words, *our only hope is God's grace!* Salvation is by grace alone through faith alone. Since this is the case, it is not surprising that in the next chapter Jesus goes on to teach about God's grace in the parable of the owner of the vineyard.

A Follow-up Question

A moment ago I said that Jesus was probably sad when he saw the young man leave. Let me add here that I think Peter probably noticed it since, as I read the story, he tried to cheer the Lord up. The young man had gone away, but Jesus still had his disciples, Peter thought. So he said, "*We* have left everything to follow you!" (v. 27). That was nice. In a sense they really had. Peter had left his fishing business, as had Andrew, James, and John. Matthew had left his tax collecting business. But the spirit of coveting was still in Peter, and probably in the others too, for Peter couldn't keep from adding, "What then will there be for us?" showing by his question that he still had much of the spirit of the rich young man and not much of the humble trusting spirit of the children Jesus had used as an illustration of what was needed for salvation.

Jesus' answer was that no one who follows him will ever be cheated out of anything. Instead, there will be rewards not only in the age to come ("at the renewal of all things"), but in the present age too. Nothing is comparable to God's blessings.

Commentators disagree as to what Jesus meant when he promised that the disciples would "sit on twelve thrones, judging the twelve tribes of Israel" (v. 28). Some see it as a literal rule by the disciples over Israel under Christ's overall messianic rule during a future earthly millennium. Others think it means the saved will participate in the judgment of Christ at the last day. Still others believe it refers to some kind of rule by Christians in this present age. I think the words "at the renewal of all things" and Christ's "glorious throne" decide the matter in terms of a future millennial age, however that may be conceived.

But that is not the most significant thing. What is profoundly striking is Christ's promise of blessing in the present age. All along Jesus has been telling his listeners that in order to be disciples they must deny themselves and be willing to give up their possessions. He did it in the case of the rich young ruler in this very chapter. Now Jesus says that if his disciples do that, they will receive a hundred times as much as what was given up, and not only in some future life, but now.

Mark's version is explicit. He adds, "in this present age," though he also adds, "and with them, persecutions" (Mark 10:30).

In Matthew, Jesus' exact words are, "I tell you the truth, at the renewal of all things, when the Son of Man sits on his glorious throne, you who have followed me will also sit on twelve thrones, judging the twelve tribes of Israel. And everyone who has left houses or brothers or sisters or father or mother or children or fields for my sake will receive a hundred times as much and will inherit eternal life" (vv. 28–29). He ends with the paradoxical statement, "But many who are first will be last, and many who are last will be first" (v. 30), meaning, I suppose, that those who have most here will not necessarily have the most in heaven.

An Astonishing Statement

This statement becomes more and more astonishing as we study it. It is surprising that it speaks of rewards, first of all, since nothing in the mere notion of discipleship requires them. At best we are unprofitable servants. However, in addition to speaking of rewards (perhaps spiritual rewards would suffice), the text speaks specifically of homes, brothers, sisters, mothers, fathers, children, and even fields.

"Fields" is the most interesting term. The other terms can be spiritualized to an extent. When Jesus mentions "homes" he is, I believe, speaking of literal, earthly homes, involving family members and houses and furniture and pots and pans and such things. But it might be possible to think instead of a "heavenly home" and thus remove this element from earthly life. The same might be done with brothers, sisters, mothers, fathers, and children, which might refer merely to the "family of God" in heaven. Such an interpretation cannot be applied to "fields." Fields mean earth. Thus, the mention of fields carries us back to the context, in which earthly possessions are discussed, and warns us about taking the other elements of this promise only in a spiritual sense.

And what about *a hundred times* as much? Even Job received only double his possessions after God restored his prosperity.

We must exercise some caution at this point, of course. For one thing, nothing in Christ's teachings encourages us to think in crass materialistic terms, as if Jesus were merely giving a formula for sure wealth. The words are ludicrous if taken in that way. If this is a formula for wealth, then we should first, earn all we can (taking years to do it if necessary); second, give up those earnings for Jesus; and finally, wait for Jesus to multiply our charitable gifts by one hundred. That would discourage discipleship rather than promote it.

Again, this promise does not necessarily apply to every individual. It is clear that some believers (though not all) are called to poverty. No matter how much they have and give up, they will always have only the most modest means, because that is what God has called them to have. I suppose that most of the disciples were in this category.

Still, the text is a true promise, and it does have to do with earthly relationships and material possessions. At the least, it means that the true follower of Christ will not lack for any good thing ("My cup overflows," Ps. 23:5) and that, under normal circumstances, a Christian will be blessed abundantly with earthly goods. Personally, I am convinced that Jesus gives us every good that he can possibly give us without rendering us unfit for his work or destroying our souls. The reason many of us do not have more is that the Lord knows we would misuse it.

Encouragement to Serve

In spite of these obvious qualifications, Christ's promise of homes, family, and fields is an encouragement for those willing to serve him. It tells us that God is good and that he is no man's debtor. Sometimes the idea that

"God is no man's debtor" has been used wrongly to try to control God, as it were. People have suggested that if we do such-and-such, then God is obliged to do such-and-such for us. That is manipulative, and the text does not support this view. However, properly received, it does encourage us to serve God in Christ's service, knowing that we will be blessed for it. There are several important grounds for this encouragement.

1. *Great blessings.* One thing that keeps many from following Jesus—the rich young ruler is an example—is the feeling that the cost of following him is too high. We would have to give up too much.

Matthew 19:28–29 teaches that the blessings found in Christ's service are greater than the blessings we could have apart from it. The rich young man was unwilling to give up his possessions, for he loved them more than he loved Jesus. Unfortunately, he could not be saved without loving God with all his heart and soul and mind and strength. However, if he had followed Christ, turning his back on his wealth, this text teaches that Jesus would have blessed him a hundred times over, possibly with a home, a large family, and fields. He could not be certain of the form Christ's blessing would take. He might have been called to a life of itinerant ministry, as Paul was. But whatever the form of his service, the blessings he would have received would have been many times greater than he could have given up.

2. *Secure blessings.* It is not only the greatness of the blessings that encourage us in Jesus' service; their security encourages us too. The young man turned away from Christ because he was unwilling to part with his possessions, but ironically, he turned from possessions that were certain to possessions that were at best uncertain. His possessions may have been lost before the year was out. His gold may have been stolen. He may have forfeited his lands. As was the case with the prodigal son, his friends may have grown cold and abandoned him.

This point can be made the other way. God may allow the ungodly to amass great wealth to their destruction. As for Christians, if you belong to Christ and put riches (or anything else) before service to Christ, God may take away your wealth until you repent and turn to him. However, if you are a follower of Christ and place him first in everything, you can be sure that whatever possessions God wants you to have will be safe.

3. *Blessings that are blessed.* The third reason the promise of Matthew 19:28–29 encourages us to serve Jesus is that the blessings promised by Jesus are themselves blessed by God. His favor rests on them, and his divine power makes them effective in assisting other people. It is not just that we are blessed. Others are blessed by them through us. To be blessed in this way is to be twice blessed, because the one receiving the gift is blessed along with the giver.

These promises are great. They are an encouragement to trust God and serve Christ. But we must always remember that they are for Christians only. Not only that, they are for Christians who have turned from all lesser loyalties to serve Christ. To these alone God promises homes, parents, children, friends, and fields—with persecutions—and in the age to come, eternal life.

45

The Parable of the Workers in the Vineyard

Matthew 20:1–16

"For the kingdom of heaven is like a landowner who went out early in the morning to hire men to work in his vineyard. He agreed to pay them a denarius for the day and sent them into his vineyard.

"About the third hour he went out and saw others standing in the marketplace doing nothing. He told them, 'You also go and work in my vineyard, and I will pay you whatever is right.' So they went.

"He went out again about the sixth hour and the ninth hour and did the same thing. About the eleventh hour he went out and found still others standing around. He asked them, 'Why have you been standing here all day long doing nothing?'

"'Because no one has hired us,' they answered.

"He said to them, 'You also go and work in my vineyard.'

"When evening came, the owner of the vineyard said to his foreman, 'Call the workers and pay them their wages, beginning with the last ones hired and going on to the first.'

"The workers who were hired about the eleventh hour came and each received a denarius. So when those came who were hired first, they expected to receive more. But each one of them also received a denarius. When they received it, they began to grumble against the landowner. 'These men who were hired last worked only one hour,' they said, 'and you have made them equal to us who have borne the burden of the work and the heat of the day.'

"But he answered one of them, 'Friend, I am not being unfair to you. Didn't you agree to work for a denarius? Take your pay and go. I want to give the man who was hired last the same as I gave you. Don't I have the right to do what I want with my own money? Or are you envious because I am generous?'

"So the last will be first, and the first will be last."

W hen Peter reacted to the unbelief of the rich young ruler by reminding Jesus that he and the other disciples had left everything to follow Jesus but were still wondering, "What then will there be for us?" Jesus answered by promising Peter rewards. "You who have followed me will . . . sit on twelve thrones, judging the twelve tribes of Israel. And everyone who has left houses or brothers or sisters or father or mother or children or fields for my sake will receive a hundred times as much and will inherit eternal life" (Matt. 19:28–29). When I commented on those words in the last study, I said that God will be no man's debtor.

But *debtor* isn't quite the word to describe what is going on in this passage. Debt implies obligation, that God owes us something. It was what Peter meant when he asked, "What then will there be for us?" Actually, God owes us nothing, and whatever we receive from him we receive only because he is gracious. To make sure the disciples understood this concept, Jesus told the parable of the workers in the vineyard. This parable occurs only in Matthew, where it serves to illustrate the principle of Matthew 19:30 ("many who are first will be last, and many who are last will be first"). This idea is repeated at the story's close.

A Straightforward Story

The parable itself is quite simple. A landowner needed men to work in his vineyard, so he went out early in the morning and hired all the workers he could find. He agreed to pay them a denarius, a normal day's wage, for their work. About nine o'clock he went out again and found other workers. He hired them too, but this time there was no set wage. He merely said, "I will pay you whatever is right" (v. 4). The new workers agreed with that arrangement and soon joined the others. The owner did the same thing at noon, at three in the afternoon, and at five o'clock, just one hour before quitting time.

At the end of the day he paid the workers, beginning with those he had hired last. He gave each one in that group a denarius, and so on with those hired at three o'clock, noon, and at nine in the morning. At last he came to those he had hired first. By that time they were rubbing their hands together happily, supposing that if those who had worked less than they had worked were being paid a denarius, they would receive more. But the owner paid them a denarius too, and they complained. The owner replied, "Friend, I am not being unfair to you. Didn't you agree to work for a denarius? Take your pay and go. I want to give the man who was hired last the same as I gave you. Don't I have the right to do what I want with my own money? Or are you envious because I am generous?" (vv. 13–15).

The parable is followed by a statement that is close to the one that ended the previous chapter: "So the last will be first, and the first will be last" (v. 16). It is a version of one of Jesus' favorite themes, appearing also in Matthew 18:4; 23:12; Luke 14:11; 18:14. Matthew 23:12 is a bit different but similar.

It reads, "Whoever exalts himself will be humbled, and whoever humbles himself will be exalted."

A Difficult Parable

The story itself is clear enough, but that does not mean it is without difficulties. The first difficulty is that it presents us with an admittedly strange situation. We have a businessman who pays people who work only one hour the same wage he pays those who work all day. We may say, as he does, that the pay for the full day's work is fair. That may be true, but what businessman operates that way? It seems irrational. It produces labor problems. More than that, it is bad business. A person who operated in this manner would soon be bankrupt.

But there is a further difficulty: The payment to the workers seems unjust. We may be reluctant to say it, knowing that the owner of the vineyard is God and that God is always just, regardless of what we may think. But still the procedure *seems* unjust. Why should those who were hired later be paid the same as those who were hired at the start of the day? Why shouldn't those who worked longer be paid more?

Many have attempted to interpret the parable so as to eliminate these difficulties, but the interpretations do not work. Some have suggested that those who began early in the day did not work well. They took extended coffee breaks and talked on the job. They knocked off for two and a half hours at lunch. Those who worked a shorter day worked harder. They accomplished as much in their one, four, or seven hours as the early risers did in their twelve hours. It was a simple case of equal pay for equal work. Unfortunately, nothing in the story indicates that we should interpret it this way, and much goes against it. If nothing else, the concluding words stress the generosity of the owner and not his accurate evaluation of the quality or quantity of the work that had been done (v. 15).

Others have suggested that the coins were different. In one case it was a gold denarius, in another silver, in another bronze, and so on. Still others have supposed that the parable teaches there are no rewards in heaven and that ultimately it will not matter how much or how little we do for Jesus. The problem with that view is that other texts teach there *will* be rewards and our work *does* matter.

Saved by Grace Alone

So how are we to understand this parable? At the very least it is a story intended to teach about the grace of God in salvation. Peter wanted to know what he and the others would get for their discipleship, which they considered a major contribution on their part. But when Jesus answered as he did, he was teaching that although the disciples would receive rewards for their service, anything they received from God—whether rewards for service or eternal life itself—was a gift flowing from the grace of God only. *Sola gratia!* God owes us nothing, not even a chance to hear and respond to the gospel.

Most people think he does, of course, which is why even church-going people think so little of grace in our day. "Amazing Grace" by John Newton used to be one of the most popular hymns. But today, as J. I. Packer says in *Knowing God,* "amazing grace" has become "boring grace" for many people. It is boring because we do not think of ourselves as sinners—at least not very great sinners—and because we think God owes us something anyway. We are kind, generous, forgiving. Why shouldn't God be?

What Jesus has to tell us is that God is not like human beings and does not operate in line with our ideas. Everything in God's kingdom is based on grace, which is why "the last will be first, and the first will be last."

Nothing in the immediate context of Matthew requires us to see anything more in the parable than that. But I cannot help but notice that it is one of a certain class of parables that deal in part with the problems the Jews had when Gentiles began to believe the gospel and embrace Christianity. The problem is reflected in the person of the older brother in Jesus' parable of the prodigal son (Luke 15:11–32). It is seen in the parable about the banquet to which many were invited but refused to come (Matt. 22:1–14) and in the parable of the Pharisee and the tax collector (Luke 18:9–14).[1]

In the earliest days of Old Testament history, from the calling of Abraham about two thousand years before Christ, God began to deal with the Jews in a special way. It is almost as though he turned his back on the Gentile nations, at least for a time, as he began to create, redeem, and eventually teach and disciple those to whom the Lord Jesus would eventually come. The Jews were proud of that heritage, as we ourselves would be.

But instead of remembering that what they had received was due entirely to God's grace (grace they had often resisted), the Jews began to suppose that the benefits of their position were really due largely to themselves. They thought they had earned their position by centuries of faithful labor for God. They were not complaining; they were glad for the arrangement. But when Jesus came, all the benefits they supposed they had earned by centuries of hard labor were now offered freely to the Gentiles, who had done nothing to deserve them. Gentiles were like the prodigal, who had squandered the father's wealth, or the tax collector, who was wicked to the Jewish way of thinking. Moreover, in time so many Gentiles were converted that it seemed as if the cherished Jewish traditions would be discarded.

As I have suggested, a number of parables deal with this problem, though in a variety of ways. The account of the older brother and the parable of the workers in the vineyard are similar. In each the faithful, hard-working people (the son in the one case and the workers who were hired at the start of the day in the other) resent the father's or owner's generosity to those they believe deserved less. The son stood outside and refused to go in (Luke

15:28). The workers grumbled against the landowner (Matt. 20:11). The root problem was *envy* of the ones who had been treated kindly.

In the parable of the banquet, the diagnosis is somewhat different. In the end the outcasts enter to enjoy the master's banquet, but the ones who were first invited are not there because *they refused the master's invitation.*

In the story of the Pharisee and tax collector, the root problem of the self-righteous Pharisee is *pride.* He was thankful that he was "not like other men— robbers, evildoers, adulterers—or even like this tax collector. I fast twice a week and give a tithe of all I get" (Luke 18:11–12). He was proud both of what he was not and of what he was.

These are different ways of analyzing the same problem, a problem that was evident in Jewish reactions to Gentile blessings. But it is not a uniquely Jewish problem. It is a problem for any who think that because they have served God faithfully for however many years they deserve something from him. We do not. I say it again: We never deserve God's favors. If we think we do, we are in danger of losing them entirely.

I remember a story told by Reuben Torrey, growing out of some meet- ings he held in Melbourne, Australia. He was teaching about prayer, stress- ing the power of true prayer, and one day just before a noon meeting a note was placed in his hand. It read:

> Dear Mr. Torrey,
> I am in great perplexity. I have been praying for a long time for something that I am confident is according to God's will, but I do not get it. I have been a member of the Presbyterian church for thirty years, and have tried to be a consistent one all that time. I have been the superintendent of the Sunday school for twenty-five years and an elder in the church for twenty years; and yet God does not answer my prayer. Can you explain why?

Torrey replied that he could explain it quite easily. He said, "This man thinks that because he has been a consistent church member for thirty years, a faithful Sunday school superintendent for twenty-five years, and an elder in the church for twenty years that God is under obligation to answer his prayer. He is really praying in his own name, and God will not hear our prayers when we approach him in that way. We must, if we would have God answer our prayers, give up any thought that we have any claims upon God. There is not one of us who deserves anything from God." At the close of the meeting a man came to Torrey, identified himself as the one who had writ- ten the note, and said that Torrey had described his case exactly.[2]

That story has to do primarily with prayer, but the principle applies in other areas too. It applies to anything we may do for God and anything we may expect from him. Jesus says we have to stop thinking of our service in terms of debt or obligation. Instead, we have to serve in the spirit of a son who serves because he loves his father, rather than in the spirit of a hireling who serves only for his wages.

People More than Things

Another lesson in the parable is that God cares for people more than things. Why is it that the owner of the vineyard gave those who had labored only one hour the same amount as those who had labored all day? Was it not because he knew they needed the denarius?

When we read the story carefully, we notice that not a word of criticism is spoken against those who were not hired in the morning. When the master came and asked them, "Why have you been standing here all day long doing nothing?" they replied, "Because no one has hired us" (vv. 6–7). It seems they had been willing to work, were eager to work, and undoubtedly needed the work, but they had not been hired. The owner hired them not for what he could get out of them in just a few hours, but because they needed the work, and he paid them the full denarius for the same reason. The owner was not thinking of his profit. He was thinking of people, and he was using his ample means to help them.

How different this is from the older son in the parable of Luke 15! He was angered because his father rejoiced in the return of his younger brother. He should have been rejoicing too, but instead he was thinking only of how his brother had wasted his inheritance (Luke 15:29–30). The older brother would have been happy if the property had come home and the son had been lost! As it was, the reverse was true, and he was displeased. God is exactly the opposite. He does not love us for what we do for him.

So who are we like? Do we serve because we love God rather than because of what we can get him to do for us? Are we like God in our estimate of others, evaluating them in terms of their worth as beings made in the image of God and for fellowship with God rather than just as tools for production? Or are we like the unhappy workers or the disconsolate older brother?

And speaking of the older brother, I cannot help remembering that his story appears in a chapter of Luke that contains three parables of something that was lost: a lost sheep, a lost coin, and a lost son. In each case the object remained valuable in the mind of the owner in spite of its lost condition. We can imagine an owner of sheep who might write off the loss of one sheep lightly. "After all," he might say, "what's one sheep when I still have ninety-nine? The loss is only 1 percent. A businessman has to expect a certain percentage of loss if he wants to run a business." The woman might have said, "I'm just not going to bother about one lost coin. It is one of ten, and I still have nine. I'll be happy with them." The father might have decided, "Well, my younger son is gone. It's sad, but such things happen. I'll focus my attention on the son I still have." That is not what the owners or the father did. The father longed after his prodigal son, and in the first two parables, the owners diligently searched until the lost object was recovered.

What is the explanation for their behavior? The object had value to its owner even though it was lost, and the owner was determined to recover it again. In all these parables, including the parable of the workers in the vineyard, God values what is lost and seeks it. In the story of the workers it is God himself who goes out to hire them, early in the day, throughout the day, and until the very end.

Shouldn't we who have been found by God have that same love for others who are lost? And shouldn't we tell them that if they are lost they are valuable to God even in their lost condition? If you are lost, you may be utterly worthless in your own sight, seeing only the ruin you have made, but you should know that you are valuable to God because (unlike yourself) he is able to see what you were created to be and what he can yet make of you.

Start Early and Work Hard

There is one last point. I am not sure Jesus had anything like this in mind when he told this provocative parable, but it is suggested by that most important verse that both introduces the story and ends it: "But many who are first will be last, and many who are last will be first" (Matt. 19:30). The important word here is *many,* for the teaching is not that every person who begins early with God and works for him throughout a lifetime will inevitably be last or that everyone who begins late will inevitably be first. That will be true for *many* people, but it will not be true for all.

Many who begin early will lose their reward or not even come to faith in Christ because they approach God in a false or mercenary spirit, on the basis of their merit and not on the basis of God's grace. Many who enter last will be first because, although they begin late, they nevertheless recognize that their status is due to God's grace alone and praise God for it. But neither of those cases is true for everyone.

It is not necessary either to start early and finish last or start last and finish first. In fact, neither is best. The truly desirable thing is to start early and work with all the might you have, not for reward but out of genuine love for our Master, Jesus Christ, and when you have finished still to say, "I am nevertheless an unprofitable servant." It is such people whom God delights to honor.

Daniel was such a person. He was carried off to Babylon with three of his friends at a very early age, probably when he was about fifteen or sixteen. He was immersed in the splendors of the great Babylonian court and was trained for high position and responsibility. He could have been swept away by the temptations. But Daniel decided at that early age not to "defile himself" with the royal enticements (Dan. 1:8). He determined to serve God, and he was still there decades later as an old man serving God and hearing God say, "Go your way till the end. You will rest, and then at the end of the days you will rise to receive your allotted inheritance" (Dan. 12:13).

Daniel served God for seventy years (from 606 to 536 B.C.).

Moses served God for eighty years.

Abraham served God for a hundred years.

Enoch served God for three hundred years.

This is the challenge I put before you, especially if you are young. Do not wait to serve God. Do not wait until the ninth or eleventh hour of your all-too-brief life. Start now. Serve now. Keep at your service year after year. And when you come to the end you will not say, "What am I owed for my service?" You will say, "What a joy it has been to serve my gracious and loving Lord!"[3]

46

On the Way to Jerusalem

Matthew 20:17–34

Now as Jesus was going up to Jerusalem, he took the twelve disciples aside and said to them, "We are going up to Jerusalem, and the Son of Man will be betrayed to the chief priests and the teachers of the law. They will condemn him to death and will turn him over to the Gentiles to be mocked and flogged and crucified. On the third day he will be raised to life!"

Time is running out. For seven chapters and for sixteen of my studies, ever since the parables of the kingdom in Matthew 13, we have witnessed Jesus' withdrawal from the leaders and even from the crowds so that he could teach his disciples about the nature of his kingdom and what they would have to be like if they were to be a part of it. Now the withdrawal stage is ending, and Jesus is on his way to Jerusalem to die by crucifixion.

This new change of direction is announced clearly for the first time in verse 17: "Now as Jesus was going up to Jerusalem . . ." By the start of the following chapter he is there. Chapter 21 begins, "As they approached Jerusalem and came to Bethphage on the Mount of Olives . . ." (Matt. 21:1). Sadly, the disciples still do not understand what Jesus is about to do or what it will mean for their discipleship.

Three linked events are in this final part of the middle section of the Gospel: (1) Jesus' third prediction of his passion (vv. 17–19), (2) further evidence of the disciples' struggle to be first in Christ's kingdom (vv. 20–28), and (3) the healing of two blind men (vv. 29–34).

The Third Prediction

Verses 17–19 contain the third prediction of Jesus' death and resurrection, and there are at least two reasons why this is repeated.[1] The obvious reason is that the disciples had not understood what Jesus had told them. They had gotten the idea that he was going to die, which is why they were "filled with grief" (Matt. 17:23), but they had only the vaguest notion of what this meant. They certainly did not understand why he would die or that he would be raised from the dead afterward.

When we compare these predictions, we also sense that Jesus added to his teaching bit by bit. In chapter 16 he spoke of his treatment by the elders, chief priests, and teachers of the law, that he must be killed and on the third day be raised to life (v. 21). In chapter 17 he added the fact of his betrayal (v. 22). In chapter 20 he revealed that the leaders of the people would turn him over to the Gentiles, who would mock and flog him, and that his death would be by crucifixion. This was the heart and substance of what Jesus had come to do, so it was both natural and necessary for Jesus to repeat it again and again for the disciples' benefit. Not long after this, these truths would be the very center of their preaching.

There is another reason why Jesus repeated these predictions: So the disciples might learn that self-denial, humility, and service were to be the pattern not merely of his life and ministry but of their own. This has been clear from the very first time Jesus spoke of his death. Peter had confessed Jesus as "the Christ, the Son of the living God" (Matt. 16:16), the first thing anyone needs to know about Jesus. Jesus had gone on to the second truth we need to know, namely, that he had come to die and then be raised to life. Immediately after this he used the example of his death to teach what the life of his disciples must be like: "If anyone would come after me, he must deny himself and take up his cross and follow me" (v. 24).

The disciples did not understand this. They did not want anything to do with bearing crosses. They wanted to be great in Christ's kingdom. When Matthew records Jesus' third prediction of his death in chapter 20, therefore, the words are also an introduction to the story of the disciples' continuing struggles to be great in verses 20–28. And they lead to this conclusion: "Whoever wants to become great among you must be your servant, and whoever wants to be first must be your slave—just as the Son of Man did not come to be served, but to serve, and to give his life as a ransom for many" (vv. 26–28).

Verses 26–28 are an application for the disciples of the principle laid down in verses 18 and 19 and show why the prediction of Jesus' death appears for a third time in this chapter.

Lord of Pots and Pans

"Not to be served but to serve." What a difficult lesson to learn. Yet how necessary. Do you know about Brother Lawrence, the Carmelite monk who lived in the seventeenth century? His birth name was Nicholas Herman. He was born in Lorraine, served as a soldier in the French army, and was converted through seeing a tree in winter, stripped of its leaves, and reflecting on the fact that within a short time its leaves would be renewed through the love and power of God. He became a monk in 1666.

In the Carmelite monastery where he was assigned, Lawrence, as he was then called, worked in the kitchen, where he had charge of the utensils. At first he hated the work, but he set himself to walk in God's presence so that he could worship God and serve others in these humble circumstances. In time he came to worship God more in the kitchen than in the cathedral, and he could pray, "Lord of all pots and pans and things, . . . make me a saint by getting meals and washing up the dishes." His meditations on the Christian life became *The Practice of the Presence of God,* which is a Christian classic. Brother Lawrence chose humility and by it achieved greatness.

How little we know of serving others, even after many years of Christian living! Yet how essential to discipleship! Humility reminds us of the need to die to ourselves, take up our crosses, follow Jesus, and serve others. It is one of the most difficult things we have to learn.

A Difficult School

Learning to serve others rather than themselves was a difficult lesson for the disciples. At the start of chapter 18, the disciples were arguing about who should be greatest in Christ's kingdom. To them, as for us, a kingdom meant pomp and power, not a cross. They assumed Jesus was going to take over the throne of his father David, and they were vying to see who would stand closest to that throne, exercise the greatest influence, and receive the greatest honor.

Jesus answered them by an illustration. He drew a little child into the middle of the group, saying, "I tell you the truth, unless you change and become like little children, you will never enter the kingdom of heaven. Therefore, whoever humbles himself like this child is the greatest in the kingdom of heaven" (Matt. 18:3–4).

We think the disciples would have gotten the point, particularly since it had been reinforced for them visually. But in the very next chapter we find the disciples actually turning children aside (Matt. 19:13). They told the mothers that Jesus was too important, too busy, but they were really thinking that *they* were too important and busy. Jesus rebuked the disciples. He said, "Let the little children come to me, and do not hinder them, for the kingdom of God belongs to such as these" (v. 14).

A third incident is the one we have come to now, before the triumphal entry. On this occasion the mother of James and John comes to Jesus asking if her sons may sit on the right and left sides of Jesus when he ushers in his kingdom. The other disciples hear about it and become angry with James and John, which shows that although James and John are the chief offenders on this occasion, the others are thinking in exactly the same way. They are angry because they resent James and John for getting the jump on them.

Jesus takes time to instruct the two brothers. He asks if they are able to "drink the cup" he is going to drink. This was a figure of speech referring to his suffering. He is saying that greatness in his kingdom has to do with suffering. It means denying themselves, taking up their crosses, and following him closely day by day. James and John do not understand this, of course, so they reply in naive self-confidence, "We can."

Jesus tells them they will indeed drink from his cup. James became one of the first Christian martyrs (see Acts 12:2), and John suffered for the faith by being imprisoned on the island of Patmos. "But," says Jesus, "to sit at my right or left is not for me to grant. These places belong to those for whom they have been prepared by my Father" (v. 23).

Then Jesus calls the entire group together and reinforces what he has already been saying: "You know that the rulers of the Gentiles lord it over them, and their high officials exercise authority over them. Not so with you. Instead, whoever wants to become great among you must be your servant, and whoever wants to be first must be your slave—just as the Son of Man did not come to be served, but to serve, and to give his life as a ransom for many" (Matt. 20:25–28). These verses are linked with the prediction of his own suffering in verses 18 and 19.

Sadly, this is not the end of the matter. We might think that the disciples would have dropped their feud at this point and that the fight for the chief place among them would have been forgotten. But this was not so. Apparently the conflict intensified and continued even into the upper room, for if Luke is giving us an accurate chronology of this evening, we learn that even after the institution of the Lord's Supper "a dispute arose among them as to which of them was considered to be greatest" (Luke 22:24). At this point Luke includes nearly the same words we find in Matthew 20 about the kings of the Gentiles lording it over them and about the need for the followers of Christ to be servants. It was at this point perhaps that the Lord laid his clothes aside, took a bowl of water and a towel, and washed the disciples' feet as a dramatic illustration of his teaching.

We should learn from this story that the desire to be foremost is also great in us and that we can be maneuvering for prominence even as we come to the communion service. We can be so caught up in thoughts of our own importance that we do not even hear Christ speaking. We need to become like little children so we can learn from Jesus, learning among other things what humility is and how it must function.

The Price of Redemption

Before looking at the last of the three incidents in the concluding part of chapter 20, we need to consider one of the most remarkable verses in Matthew, perhaps even in the entire Word of God. It is verse 28 of this chapter: "just as the Son of Man did not come to be served, but to serve, and to give his life as a ransom for many." The important word is *ransom*, the only occurrence of this precise form of the word in the New Testament.

To understand *ransom* we need to know that it is one of a number of related words that describes Christ's work of redemption. Other words for redemption are not related: *agorazo*, which means to buy in the marketplace, and *exagorazo*, which means to buy out of the marketplace so the object or person purchased might be set free. It is often used in reference to redeeming or setting free a slave. But these are not the terms I mean.

Ransom belongs to a word group based on the root verb *luo*, which means "to loose." These words have an interesting development. The root word originally meant nothing more than "to loose" or "to loosen," as in taking off clothes or unbuckling one's armor. When used of persons, it signified the loosening of bonds so that, for example, a prisoner might be released. It was usually necessary to pay a ransom to free a prisoner, however. So in time a second word developed from *luo* to signify this "ransom price." It was *lutron*, the word that occurs in Matthew 20:28. From *lutron* another verb developed: *lutroo*, which like *luo* meant "to loose" or "to set free" but unlike *luo* always meant to free by paying the redemption price. From these last two words the proper Greek term for redemption came about: *lutrosis* (and the cognate word *apolutrosis*). In the New Testament these words refer to the way Jesus freed us from sin's slavery by his death, which is what Jesus is talking about in Matthew 18.

We can go back even further, for *lutron* has parallels in the Hebrew of the Old Testament. The first parallel is the word *kopher*, which also means "a ransom price" but is richer than the Greek idea because it refers to the redemption of a person who, apart from the payment of that redemption price, would be executed.

Let me explain. Suppose a person owned an ox that had gored somebody to death. Under some circumstances (we would describe it as manslaughter rather than homicide) the owner of the ox would be fined. But suppose negligence had been involved. Suppose the ox was known to be dangerous and the owner had neglected to secure the animal properly. In this case the owner of the ox could be killed. He would have to forfeit his life for the one whose life had been taken. Little would be gained by one more death, of course, so the Old Testament provided a way by which, if the guilty owner could come to an agreement with the relatives of the dead man, it would be possible for him to pay a ransom price, an indemnity, instead of dying. This ransom price was called the *kopher*.

Jesus spoke Aramaic (a dialect of Hebrew) rather than Greek, of course, so this idea would have been in his and the disciples' minds when he spoke of his life becoming a ransom for others. This enriches our understanding of what the Lord did in dying for us, for it is not only in some vague way that his death freed us from sin's power. He delivered us from sin's power, but he also delivered us from *death,* which is the punishment God had established for transgressions ("The soul who sins . . . will die," Ezek. 18:4). He did this by dying in our place.

The final words I bring into this study are *gaal,* meaning "to redeem," and the related noun *goel,* which means "kinsman-redeemer." This latter term requires some separate explanation.

According to Jewish law, property should remain within a family if possible. If a Jewish person lost his or her share of the land through debt or by some other means, a near relative (if there was one) was supposed to buy the property back again. This person, because of his or her close relationship to the one who had lost the property, was a "kinsman," and if he was willing and able to purchase the property and restore it to the family, he became a "kinsman-redeemer." In some cases in which there was no male heir to inherit the property after the owner's death, the duty of the kinsman extended to marrying the widow in order to raise up heirs.

A kinsman-redeemer had to fulfill three qualifications:

1. He had to be a close relative (a stranger would not do).
2. He had to be willing to take on this responsibility (nobody could be compelled to do this work).
3. He had to be able to pay the ransom price; that is, he had to have sufficient means at his disposal.

These three conditions were fulfilled in the case of Jesus Christ, but they are best illustrated in the story of Ruth and her redeemer Boaz. In the days of the judges there was a famine in Israel, and a man from Bethlehem, whose name was Elimelech, left Judah with his wife, Naomi, and two sons to live in Moab. Not long after this, Elimelech died, and shortly after that the sons married two local girls from Moab. One was Orpah; the other was Ruth. Ten years later the sons also died, and Naomi and her daughters-in-law were left quite poor. When Naomi heard that the famine in Judah had passed and that food was available there, she decided to go back to her own land and live again in Bethlehem. Orpah, the first daughter-in-law, returned to her family, but Ruth insisted on staying with Naomi. Her appeal to Naomi is one of the most beautiful passages in the Bible:

> "Don't urge me to leave you or to turn back from you. Where you go I will go, and where you stay I will stay. Your people will be my people and your God my God. Where you die I will die, and there I will be buried. May the LORD deal with me, be it ever so severely, if anything but death separates you and me."
>
> Ruth 1:16–17

In Bethlehem, Naomi and Ruth were still poor, in spite of the fact that Naomi seems to have owned a piece of land (Ruth 4:3), and the only way they could survive was by Ruth going into the fields at harvest time to glean behind the reapers (following after the workmen and picking up any small bits of grain they missed or discarded).

Ruth went to a field belonging to an affluent man named Boaz, who, as it turned out, was a close relative of Naomi, a kinsman of her deceased husband, Elimelech. Boaz was kind to Ruth, in spite of the fact that she was a foreigner. He encouraged her to remain in his fields and instructed the workmen to protect her and be generous to her, allowing a good supply of the grain to fall behind.

Naomi seems to have recognized what was happening. She realized that God was arranging circumstances so that Boaz could perform the duties of a kinsman-redeemer for her, in regard to her inheritance, and for Ruth, in regard to raising up an heir. She advised Ruth as to how to make her claim known to Boaz. When she did, Boaz was delighted, for it meant that Ruth was interested in him also and had not, as he said, "run after the younger men, whether rich or poor" (Ruth 3:10). Unfortunately, there was another kinsman who was closer to Naomi and Ruth. Boaz promised to raise the matter with this kinsman and to perform the office of kinsman-redeemer if the other person was unable or unwilling.

As it turned out, the other relative was interested in the land but was unable to fulfill the obligation to Ruth, so Boaz willingly bought the land and married Ruth. They had a son named Obed, who became the father of Jesse, who was the father of King David.

In redeeming us, Jesus did exactly what this beautiful story illustrates: (1) he became our kinsman by the incarnation, being born in the town of Bethlehem, (2) he was willing to be our Redeemer, because of his love for us, and (3) he was able to redeem us because he alone could provide an adequate redemption price by dying. We rightly sing:

> There was no other good enough
> To pay the price of sin;
> He only could unlock the gate
> Of heaven, and let us in.

The redemption of Ruth may not have cost Boaz a great deal, at the most only money, but our redemption cost Jesus Christ his life.

Seeing Clearly

Do you understand how this applies to the life you are called to live as Jesus' follower? More specifically, do you *see* it? Let me suggest that this is where the final incident in this chapter comes in, the one involving the blind men who called to Jesus as he was passing by on his way from the area near Jericho to Jerusalem.

The healing of the two men is included at this point as an illustration of the disciples' spiritually blind condition. Or to put it another way, the blind men represent us. We are spiritually blind; we do not see spiritual matters as we should. We are also poor, spiritual beggars who have no hope of improving our condition and who have no claim on Jesus. The crowd will not help us either, because the crowd is also blind. It pushes us aside, telling us to be quiet and get out of the way. We have only one hope: that Jesus might be merciful to us. All we can do is cry out, "Lord, Son of David, have mercy on us!" as the blind men did.

But that is precisely why Jesus came—to have mercy, to serve rather than to be served, and to give his life as a ransom for many. When we ask for mercy, Jesus gives it. He does something else too. He opens our eyes to see him as he is, and he frees us from sin so we can tell others about him and what he has done to be our Savior.[2]

PART EIGHT

The King's Final Break with Judaism

47

The Triumphal Entry

Matthew 21:1-11

As they approached Jerusalem and came to Bethphage on the Mount of Olives, Jesus sent two disciples, saying to them, "Go to the village ahead of you, and at once you will find a donkey tied there, with her colt by her. Untie them and bring them to me. If anyone says anything to you, tell him that the Lord needs them, and he will send them right away."

This took place to fulfill what was spoken through the prophet:

> *"Say to the Daughter of Zion,*
> *'See, your king comes to you,*
> *gentle and riding on a donkey,*
> *on a colt, the foal of a donkey.'"*

The disciples went and did as Jesus had instructed them. They brought the donkey and the colt, placed their cloaks on them, and Jesus sat on them. A very large crowd spread their cloaks on the road, while others cut branches from the trees and spread them on the road. The crowds that went ahead of him and those that followed shouted,

> *"Hosanna to the Son of David!"*
> *"Blessed is he who comes in the name of the Lord!"*
> *"Hosanna in the highest!"*

When Jesus entered Jerusalem, the whole city was stirred and asked, "Who is this?" The crowds answered, "This is Jesus, the prophet from Nazareth in Galilee."

The most important life ever lived was that of Jesus Christ, and the most important part of that life was the momentous week that ended it. The week began with Jesus' entry into Jerusalem on

Palm Sunday. It included a second cleansing of the temple, the final teaching, the institution of the Lord's Supper, and the arrest, trial, and crucifixion. It ended with Jesus' resurrection from the dead on Easter Sunday. Eight momentous days in all.

This final week is so important that the Gospels give a disproportionate amount of space to it. Jesus lived thirty-three years. His active ministry occupied three years. But large portions of the Gospels are given over to the events of just the last eight days. Matthew devotes one-fourth of his Gospel to it (chaps. 21–28). Mark uses one-third of his Gospel (chaps. 11–16). Luke gives a fifth of his chapters to the events of this last week (chaps. 19:28–24). Most remarkable of all, John gives half of his Gospel (chaps. 12–21). Taken together, there are eighty-nine chapters in the Gospels, but twenty-nine and a half of these (exactly one-third) recount what happened between the triumphal entry and Jesus' resurrection. Such is the case because these are the climactic events not only of Jesus' life but of all history. They were planned from before the foundation of the world, and our salvation from sin and wrath depends on them.

It is not just the Gospels that emphasize these events either. We can think of the one verse summary of Christianity that Paul gives at the end of Romans 4: "He was delivered over to death for our sins and was raised to life for our justification" (v. 25). Better yet is the outline Paul provides near the start of 1 Corinthians 15:

> For what I received I passed on to you as of first importance: that Christ died for our sins according to the Scriptures, that he was buried, that he was raised on the third day according to the Scriptures, and that he appeared to Peter, and then to the Twelve. After that, he appeared to more than five hundred of the brothers at the same time, most of whom are still living, though some have fallen asleep. Then he appeared to James, then to all the apostles, and last of all he appeared to me also, as to one abnormally born.
>
> verses 3–8

This is the outline followed by the early preachers, whose sermons are preserved in the Book of Acts: "You killed the author of life, but God raised him from the dead. We are witnesses of this" (Acts 3:15).

Final Break with Judaism

From Matthew's perspective, Jesus' entry into Jerusalem also marked the Lord's final break with Judaism. We can remember from earlier studies that the presentation of Jesus as Israel's king is a major theme of the Gospel, which I have highlighted by subdividing the book along these lines: part 1: "The Coming of the King" (chaps. 1–4); part 2: "The Sermon on the Mount" (chaps. 5–7); part 3: "The Power of the Kingdom" (chaps. 8–10); part 4: "Is Jesus Really God's King?" (chaps. 11–12); part 5: "The Parables of the

Kingdom" (chap. 13); part 6: "The Withdrawal of the King" (chaps. 14–17); part 7: "The Citizens of the Kingdom" (chaps. 18–20); and now, part 8: "The King's Final Break with Judaism" (chaps. 21–23).

There will be two more significant divisions after this, part 9: "The Sermon on the Mount of Olives" (chaps. 24–25) and, finally, part 10: "Death and Resurrection" (chaps. 26–28). The death and resurrection of Jesus have already been anticipated by three specific predictions: Matthew 16:21; 17:22–23; 20:17–19.

A Planned Demonstration

This climactic week begins, then, with what we call the triumphal entry of Jesus into Jerusalem on Palm Sunday. Each of the Gospels records this event,[1] and the first significant detail they record is that Jesus arranged what was to happen. In other words, this was not merely a case of some spontaneous outburst of excitement on the part of the people, though there was obviously some spontaneity about it. Rather, it was something about which the Lord himself carefully planned to make a statement.

Matthew says that as Jesus and the disciples were approaching Bethphage, an outlying district of Jerusalem, Jesus sent two of the disciples ahead of them to procure a donkey and her colt. Matthew is the only writer who mentions two animals, and some scholars have suggested, in a manner insulting to Matthew, that he misunderstood the text he is about to cite from Zechariah and invented the extra animal to conform to it. Matthew was not stupid, of course. Jesus did not ride on two animals. He is merely recording a detail the other writers omit, namely, that there was a mother donkey and her foal, on which Jesus actually sat, though the clothes were spread on both. As far as the prophecy is concerned, it is an example of Hebrew parallelism in which two lines say the same thing, which Matthew certainly understood. We could translate, "on a donkey, that is, on a colt, the foal of a donkey."

Matthew records Jesus as saying, "Go to the village ahead of you, and at once you will find a donkey tied there, with her colt by her. Untie them and bring them to me. If anyone says anything to you, tell him that the Lord needs them, and he will send them right away" (vv. 2–3). Mark and Luke say that some people (Luke, "the owners") did ask why the disciples were untying the animal but that they were willing to give it when they learned "the Lord" needed it (Mark 11:4–6; Luke 19:33–34).

Why did Jesus arrange to enter Jerusalem in this way? He did not need to ride. He had already walked the entire distance from Galilee. In fact, this is the only occasion when we hear of Jesus doing anything but walking. Obviously, Jesus wanted to make a statement (as we say) or, to use a biblical way of speaking, a symbolic action. He was acting like Jeremiah when Jeremiah was told to buy and then break a clay jar to symbolize the breaking of the nation (Jer. 19:1–15) or buy a field to symbolize God's commitment to bring

the people back to the land of Israel after their captivity in Babylon (Jer.
32:6–44).

The meaning of what Jesus arranged is found in the quotation of Zechariah
9:9, for Matthew says that this took place "to fulfill what was spoken through
the prophet" (v. 4).

> "Say to the Daughter of Zion,
> 'See, your king comes to you,
> gentle and riding on a donkey,
> on a colt, the foal of a donkey.'"

The quotation is from a section of the book prophesying what was to happen to Israel in the future, and what it prophesies is the coming of God's
King. The quotation does not appear in Mark or Luke. John contains it, but
it is not as complete nor is it emphasized. Matthew is the Gospel of the King,
and this is the point at which Matthew shows Jesus coming to his capital city
as the rightful King of Israel.

But what a king! Not a warlike monarch, arriving on a battle steed to marshall his armies for action. Rather, Jesus comes "gentle and riding on a donkey," as Zechariah says (v. 5). In these far-off days a donkey was not an igno-
ble animal. Kings did ride them. When David appointed Solomon to be his
successor as king of Israel, he had him seated on his personal mule and taken
to Gihon to be anointed by Zadok the priest and Nathan the prophet (1 Kings
1:32–40). Yet the donkey did symbolize that Jesus was coming in peace, not
for war, and that his was to be a gentle, peaceful reign. This is what Jesus
indicated by his action and what Matthew emphasized by retaining the word
gentle in the quote. John omits the line containing *gentle* in his quotation
because he is interested only in the fact that Jesus' riding on a colt fulfilled
the words of Zechariah.

Is Jesus ever going to do battle? Yes, indeed. In Revelation 19 he is
described as arriving on a white horse to judge and make war (v. 11). His
robes are dipped in blood (v. 13), which probably recalls the warlike figure
of Isaiah 63, who comes from Edom with his robes dyed crimson. But that
is for then. For now the King comes humbly and in peace, for his is a peace-
able kingdom. We sing in the hymn "Lead On, O King Eternal,"

> For not with swords loud clashing,
> Nor roll of stirring drums,
> But deeds of love and mercy,
> The heavenly kingdom comes.

Up to this point Jesus had been keeping his messianic claim a secret lest
there be a premature attempt to make him king, and because Jesus was not
the kind of king the people wanted. But now, knowing that the time of his
passion was at hand, Jesus deliberately provoked this demonstration.

The People's Praise

Jesus had sent two disciples for the donkeys. When they arrived, the disciples spread their clothes on both. Jesus sat on the colt, which was probably led by the mother donkey since it was a young animal that had not been ridden before (Mark 11:2; Luke 19:30). The entire band then made its way down the steep descent of the Mount of Olives in full sight of the city of Jerusalem, attracting people as they went. As the crowd came near, others who were in Jerusalem saw what was happening and went out of the city to join the group that was arriving (Matt. 21:9). The people began to cry out,

> "Hosanna to the Son of David!"
> "Blessed is he who comes in the name of the Lord!"
> "Hosanna in the highest!"

Luke adds the cry "Peace in heaven and glory in the highest!" (Luke 19:38), and John adds, "Blessed is the King of Israel!" (John 12:13).

These were spontaneous praise chants, but they were not arbitrary words. Two of these sentences come from Psalm 118. The first is verse 25: "O LORD, save us." The second is verse 26: "Blessed is he who comes in the name of the LORD." In the psalm the words "Blessed is he who comes in the name of the LORD" are found exactly as we have them in our English versions. Verse 25 is quoted differently, but we can see the connection if we know that the words "save us" (from "O LORD, save us" in the first half of the verse) are literally "Save us now" which is the Hebrew word *Hosanna*. This is what the people were shouting when they exclaimed, "Hosanna to the Son of David!" and "Hosanna in the highest!"

The significance of this is that Psalm 118 is the last psalm of the Egyptian Hallel (Psalms 113–118). Hallel means "praise," and the Egyptian Hallel was the collection of praise psalms sung at the great Jewish feasts: the feast of dedication, the feasts of the new moons, and by families at the yearly observance of the Passover. At Passover two of the psalms were sung before the meal and four afterward. In fact, they were probably the psalms sung by Jesus and his disciples in the upper room just before Jesus' arrest and crucifixion (Matt. 26:30; Mark 14:26).

Jesus entered Jerusalem during Passover week, probably at the very time the thousands of Passover lambs were being brought into the city, later to be killed and eaten as part of the Passover observance.[2] It is natural, then, that lines from Psalm 118 were on the people's minds and tongues on this occasion.

Did the people understand that Jesus was the Son of God and that he was coming to save his people from their sins? Of course not, though a few, such as Mary of Bethany, seem to have understood that he was about to die (John 12:7). But whether the masses understood it or not, these verses describe what Jesus was doing and was about to do. He had indeed come "in the name of the Lord" to do the will of his Father in heaven, and what he had been sent to do was save his people from their sins.

Who Is This?

Matthew ends his account of the triumphal entry by telling us that when Jesus entered Jerusalem, "the whole city was stirred," as it had been thirty-three years earlier when the Magi came to inquire, "Where is the one who has been born king of the Jews?" (Matt. 2:2–3). Here they ask, "Who is this?" The crowds answered, "This is Jesus, the prophet from Nazareth in Galilee" (vv. 10–11).

That does not seem to be a very profound answer, but it is probably more significant than it appears. We should remember that the crowd was calling the man who was entering Jerusalem on a donkey the Messiah, for that is what the shouts of praise meant. John tells us that they called him "the King of Israel" explicitly (John 12:13). Therefore, when the people in the city asked, "Who is this?" they meant, "Who is this person you are calling the Messiah?" The answer identified Jesus as the Messiah. The words recorded in Matthew as the crowd's answer seem to mean, "Jesus, the prophet from Nazareth in Galilee, is the messianic Son of David, the King of Israel."

Significant? Yes, but not good enough for two reasons.

First, they were still thinking of a powerful political ruler, the kind who could marshall an army and drive out the occupying Romans. The disciples were thinking along these lines themselves even after the Lord's resurrection (see Acts 1:6).

Second, the people were shallow even in their confession of Jesus as the King and Messiah of Israel. We cannot help but remember that the triumphal entry took place on Sunday, and by the following Thursday (my dating) or Friday (the traditional day for Jesus' execution) they would be singing an entirely different tune as they beseeched Pilate, the Roman governor, "Crucify him! Crucify him!" (Matt. 27:22–23).

What Is Your Answer?

Who is Jesus? This is the time to get your answer to that question straight, in case you have never done it before. Matthew has presented Jesus as God's King. We have seen him rejected by many but believed on by a few. Where do you stand on this issue? Is Jesus the King? Is he the Son of God? Is he the Savior? Have you trusted him for the salvation of your soul?

If you are still hesitating with your answer, let me take you through the possibilities. There are only three of them, once we eliminate the one truly impossible idea that Jesus was merely a good man. Whatever he might be, he was certainly not just a good man, for no good man could honestly make the claims he made. Jesus presented himself as the Savior of the human race, claiming to be God. Is he? If so, he is more than a mere man. If not, then he is at best mistaken (consequently, not "good") and at worst a deceiver. What are we to do with his claims? John R. W. Stott wrote, "The claims are there. They do not in themselves constitute evidence of deity. The claims may have been false. But some explanation of them must be found. We cannot any longer regard Jesus as simply a great teacher, if he was so grievously mistaken in one of the chief subjects of his teaching, namely himself."[3]

C. S. Lewis wrote similarly, "You must make your choice. Either this man was, and is, the Son of God: or else a madman or something worse. You can shut him up for a fool; you can spit at him and kill him for a demon; or you can fall at his feet and call him Lord and God. But let us not come with any patronizing nonsense about his being a great human teacher. He has not left that open to us. He did not intend to."[4]

Thinking of Jesus merely as a good man or a good teacher is impossible, but what are the alternatives? The quotation from C. S. Lewis lists the actual possibilities clearly.

First, Jesus may have been insane or suffering from megalomania. Hitler suffered from megalomania. Napoleon probably did as well. Was Jesus like them? Before we jump too quickly at that explanation, we need to ask whether the total character of Jesus as we know it supports that speculation. Did Jesus act like a person who was crazy? Did he speak like one suffering from megalomania? As we read the Gospels, we see that rather than being mad, Jesus was actually the sanest man who ever lived. He spoke with quiet authority. He was in control of every kind of situation. He will not fit that first, easy classification.

The second possibility is that Jesus was a deceiver, that is, he set out intentionally to fool people. Before we settle on that answer, we need to examine what is involved in it. In the first place, if Jesus was a deceiver, he was the best deceiver who ever lived. Jesus claimed to be God, but that claim was not made in a Greek or Roman environment where the idea of many gods or even half gods was acceptable. It was made at the very heart of monotheistic Judaism. The Jews were ridiculed, even persecuted, for their belief in one God, but they stuck to their conviction fanatically. In that climate Jesus made his claims, and the remarkable thing is that he convinced people to believe in him. Lots of people—men and women, peasants and sophisticates, priests, rulers, eventually even members of his own family.

On the other hand, if Jesus was a deceiver, if he was not God, he should be judged a devil, for he did not merely say, "I am God," and let it go at that. He said, "I am God come to save humanity; I am the way of salvation; trust me with your eternal destiny." Jesus taught that God is holy, that we are separated from him because of our sins, and that he came to be our sin bearer. That is good news, even great news—but only if it is true. If it is not true, then his followers are of all human beings the most miserable, and Jesus should be hated as a devil from hell. If it is not true, Jesus sent generations of gullible followers to a hopeless eternity.

Is he a deceiver? Is that the explanation we have for one who was known for being "meek and lowly," who became a poor itinerant evangelist in order to help the poor and teach those whom others despised? Somehow the facts do not fit. We cannot face the facts of his life and teaching and still call Jesus a deceiver. What then? If he was not a deceiver or insane, only one possibility is left. Jesus is who he said he is. He is the one the Gospels, including Matthew, proclaim him to be. He is the Christ, the Son of God, the Savior. Do you believe that? If you do, now is the time to turn from your sin, trust Jesus for your salvation, and follow him.[5]

48

The Cleansing of the Temple

Matthew 21:12–17

Jesus entered the temple area and drove out all who were buying and selling there. He overturned the tables of the money changers and the benches of those selling doves. "It is written," he said to them, "'My house will be called a house of prayer,' but you are making it a 'den of robbers.'"

The blind and the lame came to him at the temple, and he healed them. But when the chief priests and the teachers of the law saw the wonderful things he did and the children shouting in the temple area, "Hosanna to the Son of David," they were indignant.

"Do you hear what these children are saying?" they asked him.

"Yes," replied Jesus, "have you never read,

"'From the lips of children and infants
you have ordained praise'?"

And he left them and went out of the city to Bethany, where he spent the night.

The twenty-first chapter of Matthew marks the beginning of the end of Jesus' ministry, though we are only two-thirds of the way through the Gospel at this point. Matthew 21 marks this beginning because it records the events leading to Jesus' final break with Judaism. We looked at one of these events in the last study: Jesus' entry into Jerusalem on what we call Palm Sunday (Matt. 21:1–11). Jesus intended it as a presentation of himself to Israel as her Messiah and King. It provoked the praise of the people as well as the hostility of the religious leaders. The second event is the one we come to now: the cleansing of the temple (vv. 12–17).

441

The Day of His Coming

Ten chapters before this (Matt. 11:10), Matthew wrote that Malachi 3:1 was fulfilled by John the Baptist, described as a messenger sent to prepare the way for God's Messiah. But that is not all these verses from Malachi say. Malachi comes at the end of our Old Testament, and the thrust of Malachi 3:1–4 is that God will send the Messiah to purify the temple and his people. These verses say:

> "See, I will send my messenger, who will prepare the way before me. Then suddenly the Lord you are seeking will come to his temple; the messenger of the covenant, whom you desire, will come," says the LORD Almighty.
>
> But who can endure the day of his coming? Who can stand when he appears? For he will be like a refiner's fire or a launderer's soap. He will sit as a refiner and purifier of silver; he will purify the Levites and refine them like gold and silver. Then the LORD will have men who will bring offerings in righteousness, and the offerings of Judah and Jerusalem will be acceptable to the LORD, as in days gone by, as in former years.

These words, as well as other passages similar to them (see Ezekiel 40–48 and Zech. 14:20–21), were well known to the Jews and had led to the belief that the Messiah would purify the temple when he came. Therefore, when Jesus followed his triumphal entry by driving the money changers and those who were buying and selling from the temple, he presented himself as the Messiah acting in this role.[1] Jesus both made a disclosure about who he was and asserted a claim to authority over the religious life of Israel.

Jesus had done this before, at the start of his ministry (see John 2:12–17). But the money changers had turned their tables back up, scooped their scattered coins together, and returned to their business. So here, at the end of his ministry, Jesus cleanses the temple once more.[2]

What Was the Problem?

To get a proper understanding of what was going on, we have to know that the temple was a huge religious complex. The temple itself was relatively small, consisting merely of the Holy Place, where the priests ministered, and the Most Holy Place, which only the high priest could enter once a year. But this comparatively small building was surrounded by several concentric courts, the outermost of which was the very large Court of the Gentiles. This is where the money changing and the selling of sacrificial animals took place because, being the place for Gentiles, it was not thought of as particularly sacred.

Two kinds of business were transacted. The first was the exchange of various national currencies for the temple coins used to pay the temple tax. The temple tax could be paid in the provinces prior to Passover. This is why, several months prior, the tax authorities had asked Peter whether his master had paid the temple tax. As Passover drew near, however, the half shekel tax could be paid only at the temple.

The other kind of trade was the sale of sacrificial animals. Worshipers did not need to buy them at the temple; they could bring their sacrifices with them. But this was inconvenient for pilgrims coming from distant areas of the country or from abroad. Moreover, the law stipulated that the animals had to be without blemish. Whether they were or not was determined by the priests, and there was always a chance that the priests would reject an offering even after it had been brought a long way.

The justification for these practices was not bad. They stressed the holiness of God and the need to offer him the best possible sacrifices. But both were open to abuse. The money changers charged 6 percent for changing money, and if the coin was of greater value than the required half shekel, they charged an additional 6 percent for giving change. The total charge was about half a day's wage for a laboring man. Abuses associated with the sale of the sacrificial animals were worse. A person could bring his own sacrifice, but almost certainly the inspectors would reject any animals not purchased from their concessions, and they were not cheap. For example, a pair of doves could cost fifty times more inside the temple area than outside.

Add to this the fact that at Passover time, which this was, Jerusalem was literally thronged with pilgrims. The city would normally have several thousand residents. But at one Passover season, Josephus, the Jewish historian, reported that 256,500 lambs were taken into the city. When we remember that one lamb was eaten by one household, that the houses were crowded, and that more pilgrims resided in the surrounding villages than in the city itself, as was the case with Jesus and his disciples, we realize that many millions of people crowded the temple courts each day.

Clearly, by the time of the Passover at which Jesus presented himself as Israel's King and Messiah, the temple had become a bazaar.[3]

House of Prayer/Den of Robbers

When Jesus drove the money changers and those who were selling animals for sacrifice from the Court of the Gentiles, he justified his action by a comparison of two Old Testament phrases. In the first, Isaiah referred to the temple as a "house of prayer" (Isa. 56:7). In the second, Jeremiah says that the hypocritical worshipers of his day had caused the temple to become "a den of robbers" (Jer. 7:11). Jeremiah was writing about hypocrisy. Jesus used the word *robbers* to describe the unjust extortion that was going on. But hypocrisy must also have been on his mind, as the story about the barren fig tree that follows shows.

Some have argued that "robbers" may mean something like "nationalist rebels" and that the accusation means the temple had been turned into a "nationalist stronghold," but I think this is unlikely. The real problem was the commercializing of religion. This is also a problem today, especially since we live in a highly commercial age and the ethos of buying and selling impacts the church as much as any other part of modern life. Some years ago in 1979 the Canadian author John White wrote a devastating book about the commercialization of today's church called *The Golden Cow: Materialism in the Twentieth-Century Church*. In this book, White exposes three areas of abuse.

1. *Attachment to things.* I have often made the point, drawing on a famous graduation speech at Harvard University by Aleksandr Solzhenitsyn, that practical Western materialism is as bad and perhaps even worse than the philosophical materialism of communist countries. Communism claims that matter is all that *is*. But Western materialism believes that matter is all that *matters*. White notes this, writing, "No Christian would agree (that is, if the matter were put to him or her as an abstract proposition) that matter is all that matters, for our very faith negates the assertion. Yet if our behavior (as distinct from our verbal profession) is examined, many of us who call ourselves Christians begin to look more like materialists. We talk of heaven but we strive for things."[4]

We see this in denominations in which the only "unforgivable sin" is for a congregation to attempt to leave the denomination with its property. The minister can preach outright heresy and be ignored, sometimes even praised. But if the church tries to leave, the denomination comes down on it with all the legal force at its disposal. A minister friend of mine from Australia says, "The denominations are nothing but real estate holding companies."

But it is not just the older liberal denominations that are enslaved to things. So are countless evangelicals. What else can explain the fact that so many can talk at length about their church building or the budget but have little to offer in a Bible study or a discussion even of such basic Christian doctrines as grace, the atonement, holiness, or serving Christ?

Again, because so many churches and organizations are property centered, their programs become property bound. The problem here is not the property itself. It is useful to have a building in which to meet, and buildings need to be maintained. But instead of assessing the needs of the community and developing plans (including the purchase and use of property) to meet those needs, the work of the church is often confined to the building, and potential ministries are excluded because the building might be harmed.

I know of a church in our city that has a wonderful opportunity for ministry to a nearby university, but it will not get involved with the school because the students do not treat the building with the same respect as the church's shrinking number of elderly members.

2. *Evangelical advertising.* We not only live in a materialistic age, we also live in an age of sophisticated advertising, and the two go hand in hand. We understand how that works with secular companies, though we groan at the sheer volume of catalogs and mail solicitations that come to us on a daily

basis. But what about "Christian junk mail," which is what White calls much of the evangelical literature that comes to his attention?

This is not an easy subject to address, for the majority of people will not give to Christian work unless they are asked to do so, and the intent of much Christian advertising is to present the work and ask for money honestly. But are we trusting God or our motivational techniques? We talk about Hudson Taylor and admire the way he built his mission by prayer alone, not asking for money directly. But we don't believe we can do that today. White says, "We trust in mass advertizing more than we trust in God. We corrode the term prayer support to mean 'financial support.' And while we say we are trusting God to work through the means we are using to 'acquaint the Christian public,' we would feel rather frightened if the means were taken away. Poor old God would be left to stumble along without his crutches."[5]

The problem isn't asking for money, of course. Christian works need money, and Christian workers do not need to be ashamed to request financial help. The problem lies rather in misrepresenting the work that is being done, employing words such as "faith in God alone" to mask requests for money and using secular techniques to manipulate people into giving. Why don't we ask for money honestly? Mike Horton does. On *The White Horse Inn*, his weekly radio program, you will hear Mike say, "Grace is free; radio time is not. We need your gifts to stay on this station."

3. *Crass commercialism.* We come now to exploitation of a different order. Not many laypeople have an opportunity to attend the Christian Booksellers Convention, a trade show so large that only about five cities in the United States have a convention facility large enough to host it. But if you do have an opportunity to go, my advice to you is, "Don't go!" It is one of the most tawdry, offensive, and disillusioning gatherings of evangelical Christians that you can possibly imagine. The publishers are there, many marketing perfectly good books. But so are the hucksters, promoting the worst "Jesus junk" imaginable: T-shirts and bumper stickers ("Honk if you love Jesus") and pencils and plaques and bookmarks, all with some cheap religious saying. The only way to survive the annual booksellers convention is to laugh. If you take it seriously, you will cry.

A recent example of the exploitation of Jesus for profit is the WWJD fad. WWJD stands for "What Would Jesus Do?" and it is found today on bracelets, caps, and other items that evangelical businesses offer for sale. An older man was in a Christian bookstore several months ago and noticed WWJD caps for sale at the checkout counter. They cost $12.95. He asked what WWJD meant. "That means 'What would Jesus do?'" the salesgirl answered sweetly.

The man looked at the cap a bit longer then said, "I don't think Jesus would spend $12.95 for that cap."

Of course, there is nothing wrong with asking, "What would Jesus do?" in any situation. But we might also ask, Who makes these items? And is the goal really to help people live like Jesus or to make a quick, large profit on a fad?

Does something like this honor Jesus? Or does it take God's name in vain? White summarizes: "Local bookstores would not suffer terribly if we boycotted stupid items like 'Honk if you love Jesus' bumper stickers, Jesus sweat shirts, Jesus pencils, bookmarks, praying hands, charismatic jewelry and such sacrilegious garbage. Why don't pastors call on their congregations for such a boycott? [And] how about adult Sunday-school class discussions on 'Modern Moneychangers and How to Overturn Their Tables'?"[6]

Aleksandr Solzhenitsyn saw that the human spirit longs for things higher and purer than a materialistic culture provides and that if we sell out to a lust for mere things, a new Dark Age will have come upon us. John White suggests that "the final Dark Ages are beginning."[7] Judgment is falling on the West. As for the church, the best thing that could possibly happen to it is that Jesus should come again and cleanse it as he intimated he would do one day when he cleansed the Jerusalem temple.

The Blind, the Lame, and Children

Nothing in the Gospel of Matthew is put down randomly. We have noticed that many times already. Now we have two further examples. If religion is not buying and selling—if it is not the thriving religious establishments of the Jewish past or the evangelical present—then what is it? We can hardly miss the answer Matthew gives. He says here that it is two things.

1. *The care of the needy.* This is why he records that although Jesus had driven the changers of money and the sellers of animals from the temple, he welcomed "the blind and the lame" who came to him "at the temple" and that he healed them (v. 14). Matthew is the only Gospel writer to record this. Making the same point in the next chapter, Jesus tells a story about a king whose wedding banquet was ignored by the important people of the day but was attended by people collected from the streets (Matt. 22:8–10). The point is that many who seem to be religious do not get into the kingdom but that the needy come and do get in. We need to seek out and help such people.

James, the Lord's brother, made the point like this: "Religion that God our Father accepts as pure and faultless is this: to look after orphans and widows in their distress and to keep oneself from being polluted by the world" (James 1:27).

Most Jewish authorities of Christ's day forbade the lame, blind, deaf, or otherwise handicapped people from offering sacrifices at the temple, a ruling based on 2 Samuel 5:8. But here, in striking reversal, the handicapped come to Jesus and are healed by him!

2. *The praise of children.* The second answer Matthew gives to the nature of true religion is the praise of Jesus by the children. We can understand how this must have happened on the natural level. When the crowd accompanied Jesus into the temple the day before this, children would have been among them. They would have heard the praises of the people recorded in verse 9 ("Hosanna to the Son of David!" "Blessed is he who comes in the

name of the Lord!" "Hosanna in the highest!"). On the following day they would have been in the temple complex and quite naturally would have begun to repeat what they had heard the adults say earlier (v. 15).

But there is more here than this. On two earlier occasions Jesus used children to illustrate the kind of humility and faith every person must have if he or she is to become a member of Christ's kingdom. "I tell you the truth, unless you change and become like little children, you will never enter the kingdom of heaven," Jesus said (Matt. 18:3). Again, "The kingdom of heaven belongs to such as these" (Matt. 19:14). When we remember this we cannot miss seeing that what we are given in chapter 21 is a picture of what is required. What is needed, the religion God accepts, is not the religion of commercial success or captivating enterprise but of humble, genuine praise of Jesus as the Son of God and the Savior.

What a contrast! Jesus is praised by children, but the chief priests and teachers of the law, who should have been leading that worship, were indignant. They may have had religious objections, of course—"shouting" in the temple area may have seemed irreverent—but what they really hated was that Jesus had gotten the people's attention and that he, rather than accepting and promoting their commercial interests, had upset them.

"Do you hear what these children are saying?" they asked (v. 16).

Jesus had, of course, and his reply was brilliant as always. He quoted from Psalm 8. "Have you never read, 'From the lips of children and infants you have ordained praise'?" The answer did three things: (1) It provided a biblical basis for Jesus' refusal to silence the children; (2) it was a claim to deity, since the words of the psalm are praise directed to God; and (3) it reminded everyone that it is only those who are willing to become like children who perceive the truth about Jesus and are saved.[8]

When Jesus comes to his temple, what he offers is himself, not a pattern for success. If we believe on him, we pass from death to life and become citizens of his kingdom. If we will not have him, what happens is what we discover ominously in verse 17: "He left them and went out of the city to Bethany, where he spent the night." Jesus did this every night, retiring to Bethany, where he and his disciples were staying. But Matthew's words mean more than this. They warn of a final withdrawal by that One whom even many religious people reject. If you will not have Jesus, he will go. But when he does, life, light, and the only hope of salvation go with him.

49

Religion without Fruit

Matthew 21:18-27

Early in the morning, as he was on his way back to the city, he was hungry. Seeing a fig tree by the road, he went up to it but found nothing on it except leaves. Then he said to it, "May you never bear fruit again!" Immediately the tree withered.

When the disciples saw this, they were amazed. "How did the fig tree wither so quickly?" they asked.

Jesus replied, "I tell you the truth, if you have faith and do not doubt, not only can you do what was done to the fig tree, but also you can say to this mountain, 'Go, throw yourself into the sea,' and it will be done. If you believe, you will receive whatever you ask for in prayer."

We are studying a section of Matthew's Gospel that I have titled "The King's Final Break with Judaism," and we should be aware by now of how it is unfolding. We have read about two symbolic actions: (1) the triumphal entry of Jesus into Jerusalem by which the Lord presented himself as Israel's true King, knowing that he would be rejected by both the leaders and the masses of the people; and (2) the cleansing of the temple, which would be no more permanent this time than it had proven to be the first time. In the verses we come to now, we find a third symbolic action: the cursing and withering of the fig tree.

In the Old Testament, Israel is often compared to a fig tree or a vine, and judgment on Israel is compared to its destruction (see Ps. 105:33; Jer. 8:13; Hosea 2:12; 9:10, 16; Micah 7:1–6). Jesus used the image himself in a parable recorded in Luke 13:6–9. In that story, at an earlier point in his ministry, Jesus spoke about a fig tree that was not producing fruit and which the owner was therefore going to cut down. "For three years now I've been coming to

449

look for fruit on this fig tree and haven't found any. Cut it down! Why should it use up the soil?" he said (v. 7).

A servant pleaded for it. "Leave it alone for one more year, and I'll dig around it and fertilize it. If it bears fruit next year, fine! If not, then cut it down" (vv. 8–9). The fruitless fig tree represented the barren religion of Israel as Jesus found it during the three years of his ministry, and its destruction represented God's impending judgment on it.

Similarly, in Matthew 21, Jesus has found the religion of Israel to be barren. Its leaders have turned the temple from "a house of prayer" into a "den of robbers" (v. 13). Jesus has been rejected as king, and the time for judgment has come, which is why Jesus cursed the fig tree, saying, "May you never bear fruit again," and why the fig tree withered. The cursing of the fig tree was a powerful symbolic action. It is also a warning to us of how God views any religion that does not produce genuine spiritual fruit. As John A. Broadus wrote, "That withered fig tree stands as one of the most conspicuous objects in sacred history, an object lesson forever."[1]

Profession without Practice

I know nothing about fig trees, but commentators say that fig trees first produce green figs, which are not very good at this stage but are still edible, and then green leaves immediately after that. Later in the year the figs ripen and are normally picked and eaten. The problem here is that a tree in leaf advertises that it has fruit, but this fig tree had no fruit at all. It was a case of false advertising, which Jesus used as an illustration of hypocrisy in religion.

This is a case of profession without practice, and what a problem it is! It has been a problem all through biblical history. It had been the case in Israel. On the day before the prophet Ezekiel learned of the fall of the city of Jerusalem to the Babylonians, the Lord appeared to him to explain why this was happening, and the explanation was in terms of the people's empty profession. God told Ezekiel:

> Your countrymen are talking together about you by the walls and at the doors of the houses, saying to each other, "Come and hear the message that has come from the LORD." My people come to you, as they usually do, and sit before you to listen to your words, but they do not put them into practice. With their mouths they express devotion, but their hearts are greedy for unjust gain. Indeed, to them you are nothing more than one who sings love songs with a beautiful voice and plays an instrument as well, for they hear your words but do not put them into practice.
>
> Ezekiel 33:30–32

God told Ezekiel that Jerusalem was destroyed the first time because the people wanted merely to be entertained by God's words, not wanting to obey the instructions.

Isaiah said the same thing in words Jesus referred to in Matthew 15:8–9. "The LORD says:

> 'These people come near to me with their mouth
>> and honor me with their lips,
>> but their hearts are far from me.
> Their worship of me
>> is made up only of rules taught by men.'"
>
> Isaiah 29:13

Jesus used this verse to reprove the Pharisees and teachers of the law who made a profession of adhering strictly to God's words when actually they were obeying only their own regulations. Jesus called them "hypocrites" (v. 7) and "blind guides" (v. 14).

This point is made repeatedly in Matthew, several times in the Sermon on the Mount: "So when you give to the needy, do not announce it with trumpets, as the hypocrites do in the synagogues and on the streets, to be honored by men" (Matt. 6:2); "And when you pray, do not be like the hypocrites, for they love to pray standing in the synagogues and on the street corners to be seen by men" (Matt. 6:5); "When you fast, do not look somber as the hypocrites do, for they disfigure their faces to show men they are fasting" (Matt. 6:16); and, "You hypocrite, first take the plank out of your own eye, and then you will see clearly to remove the speck from your brother's eye" (Matt. 7:5).

In chapter 22, when the Pharisees lay plans to trap him in his words, Jesus replies, "You hypocrites, why are you trying to trap me?" (v. 18). Then in the very next chapter, he pronounces a devastating series of woes or judgments on them (Matt. 23:1–39). That chapter ends with the words, "Your house is left to you desolate" (v. 38), which is what Jesus pointed to by the withering of the fig tree in chapter 21.

The Withering of the Fig Tree

Unless we understand this, Jesus' cursing of the fig tree seems entirely out of character at best and petulant or mean at worst. We must not think that Jesus was simply angry at the tree and struck out against it like a child might throw down a cell phone and break it just because he can't make it work. Jesus was not being petulant. He was teaching an important lesson with two points. First, the religion of Israel, focused in her leaders, was not producing fruit. It was a case of blatant hypocrisy. Second, any religion like it will always wither up at last, becoming as dry as a tree that is no longer nourished by its roots.

This is what Israel's official religion had become. It had become dry and useless. Failure to bear genuine fruit was the failure of the leaders who appear in the story immediately before this, wanting Jesus to rebuke the children for their praise, and in the story that follows in which they challenge Jesus' authority and hypocritically decline to answer a question that he puts to them regarding John the Baptist.

But let us not stop here. This is also what will happen to every merely outward church, any gathering of people who show the green leaves of apparent spiritual prosperity but who fail to possess the fruit of the Spirit, which is "love, joy, peace, patience, kindness, goodness, faithfulness, gentleness and self-control" (Gal. 5:22–23).

Jesus addressed this issue in Luke's Gospel. People who were following Jesus made a verbal profession of discipleship. They called him "Lord," which meant they were calling him their Master and were describing themselves as his servants, but they were disregarding his teaching. Jesus showed the impossibility of this intrinsic contradiction by asking pointedly, "Why do you call me, 'Lord, Lord,' and do not do what I say?" (Luke 6:46).

The problem of profession without practice was present in the early church too, as shown in the Epistle of James.

> Do not merely listen to the word, and so deceive yourselves. Do what it says. Anyone who listens to the word but does not do what it says is like a man who looks at his face in a mirror and, after looking at himself, goes away and immediately forgets what he looks like. But the man who looks intently into the perfect law that gives freedom, and continues to do this, not forgetting what he has heard, but doing it—he will be blessed in what he does.
>
> James 1:22–25

The great Anglican evangelical John Ryle wrote:

> Is not every fruitless branch of Christ's visible church in awful danger of becoming a withered fig tree? . . . High ecclesiastical profession without holiness among a people—overweening confidence in councils, bishops, liturgies and ceremonies, while repentance and faith have been neglected—have ruined many a visible church in time past and may yet ruin many more. Where are the once famous churches of Ephesus and Sardis and Carthage and Hippo? They are all gone. They had leaves but no fruit. . . . Let us remember this. Let us beware of church-pride: let us not be high-minded, but fear.[2]

Nothing is so obvious as the truth that religious words without spiritual fruit are worthless. Yet few things are so common. Ryle also wrote, "Open sin, and avowed unbelief, no doubt slay their thousands. But profession without practice slays its tens of thousands."[3] If we belong to Jesus, we will produce spiritual fruit, and if we do not, we do not belong to him. Jesus warned that those who call him "Lord, Lord" but do not obey him will be carried away by life's torrents.

Strong Teaching about Prayer

I do not think Jesus' disciples got the point of what he was saying at this time. If they had understood him, they would more than likely have asked about the failures of the Pharisees or the shallow nature of their religious practices. They did not do this. Instead, they were amazed at the speed with which the fig tree withered and asked him to explain it: "How did the fig tree wither so quickly?" (v. 20).

The disciples' reaction is not surprising since they were always slow to understand what Jesus was teaching, just as we are. What is surprising at first glance is the way Jesus responded to them. Since he had been teaching about the failure of Judaism and would add to that teaching in the parables that conclude this chapter and start the next, we might expect him to have said, "Forget about how quickly the tree withered, and try to understand what I am saying about Judaism." But he didn't do that. Instead, he took the question at face value and replied with some remarkable teaching about prayer: "I tell you the truth, if you have faith and do not doubt, not only can you do what was done to the fig tree, but also you can say to this mountain, 'Go, throw yourself into the sea,' and it will be done. If you believe, you will receive whatever you ask for in prayer" (vv. 21–22).

We have already come across almost the same teaching in Matthew 17:20, where Jesus said, "If you have faith as small as a mustard seed, you can say to this mountain, 'Move from here to there' and it will move. Nothing will be impossible for you." So we have already explored something of what this means. It is not a promise about moving mountains. It is a figure of speech meaning that seemingly impossible things are possible through the power of God, when the people of God take him at his word and pray in a believing way. It is an encouragement to pray often, well, and rightly.

But why did Jesus respond this way here? Perhaps he seized the opportunity to talk about something that was important to him, digressing from his main theme, but perhaps not. Remember that the chapter began with an account of three symbolic acts pointing to the failure of Judaism and it ends with two parables (a third following in chapter 22) that explain the nature of this failure and that a chief failure was the eclipse of prayer by the priests' business interests: "It is written, 'My house will be called a house of prayer,' but you are making it a 'den of robbers'" (v. 13). Suddenly the instruction about prayer fits in and becomes critically important. Jesus is teaching that what is important about genuine religion is not how prosperous our "temples" have become but whether we are actually communing with God and are growing spiritually by it.

Put this over against everything we know about the Pharisees and apply it to ourselves. These men were scrupulous about obeying their legalistic interpretations of God's law, as was Paul, who could say of his younger days as a Pharisee, "as for legalistic righteousness, [I was] faultless" (Phil. 3:6). Their brand of religion had prospered. The temple was an amazingly beautiful and financially successful place. They were highly regarded. Yet this meant nothing to Jesus, who is breaking with Judaism formally in this chapter. He had no interest in the outward show of religion if the hearts of the people were far from him. He counted religion fruitless if financial prosperity had marginalized or eliminated prayer.

If Jesus were speaking to us directly today, would he not say these same things about much of our evangelical religion? Actually, he has said it through Paul, who described religious people of the "last days" as "having a form of godliness but denying its power" (2 Tim. 3:5). Spiritual power comes not through politics or money but through prayer.

The Challenge to Jesus' Authority

These things took place on the way from Bethany to Jerusalem on Tuesday and Wednesday of Passover week (compare Mark 11:12–14, 20). When Jesus entered the city on what was to be his last full day of unhindered teaching, he was approached by the chief priests and elders of the people, who demanded of him: "By what authority are you doing these things? And who gave you this authority?" (v. 23). Mark expands the list to say that Jesus was approached by "the chief priests, the teachers of the law and the elders" (Mark 11:27). These three groups made up the Sanhedrin, so this was probably an official delegation, and what they were making clear, although their words were in the form of a question, is that they had not authorized either Jesus or his teaching. They were the authorities!

Jesus' answer was also in the form of a question. They had asked him about his authority; he would ask them about the authority of John the Baptist, who had preceded him. "John's baptism—where did it come from? Was it from heaven, or from men?" (v. 25). This was a brilliant reply. For one thing, John's ministry was like his own in several important ways. Neither John nor Jesus had studied in the rabbinic schools or been endorsed by the Jerusalem authorities. Both had been accepted by the people. Moreover, John had testified that Jesus was the Christ. Even more, Jesus was "the Lamb of God, who takes away the sin of the world" (John 1:29) and "the Son of God" (v. 34). To acknowledge that John's ministry was from God was to admit the authority of Jesus, for the source of their authority was the same.

Jesus had caught these hypocrites on the horns of a dilemma, and they knew it. They reasoned, "If we say, 'From heaven,' he will ask, 'Then why didn't you believe him?' But if we say, 'From men'—we are afraid of the people, for they all hold that John was a prophet" (vv. 25–26).

There was no way out of that one, so they took the coward's escape, saying, "We don't know." And Jesus responded, "Neither will I tell you by what authority I am doing these things" (v. 27).

This was not an evasion on Jesus' part. It was a brilliant exposure of the leaders' moral bankruptcy. They were asking by what authority Jesus was doing what he did, asserting their ability to judge in his case. But they were forced to confess their inability to make a judgment in the case of John the Baptist and therefore in Jesus' case as well. They knew their own minds, of course. They had refused both John and Jesus because both had criticized them, but they would not admit it. "They preferred to plead ignorance— and to look ridiculous. Their dishonesty had been unmasked."[4]

All Authority Given to Jesus

What of you? You have listened to the testimony of John and the claims of Jesus. You have seen the evidence for his claims. Will you acknowledge that he is the Son of God and the Savior and follow him as your Lord? Will you become a Christian? If you are hesitating, let me tell you a little bit more about the authority of Jesus Christ.

Authority is an important theme in Matthew's Gospel. You may recall that at the beginning, after Jesus had first begun to teach, Matthew said that "the crowds were amazed at his teaching, because he taught as one who had *authority*, and not as their teachers of the law" (Matt. 7:28–29). In chapter 8 the centurion acknowledged his authority, comparing it to his own authority as a military commander: "Just say the word, and my servant will be healed. For I myself am a man under *authority*, with soldiers under me" (vv. 8–9). In chapter 9 Jesus healed the paralyzed man "so that you may know that the Son of Man has *authority* on earth to forgive sins" (v. 6), and the people marveled that "God . . . had given such *authority* to men" (v. 8). In chapter 21, the chapter we are studying now, the word *authority* occurs four times, twice on the lips of Jesus' accusers and twice in his response.

The most important occurrence of the word is at the very end of the Gospel, in the Great Commission, where Jesus says, "All *authority* in heaven and on earth has been given to me. Therefore go and make disciples of all nations, baptizing them in the name of the Father and of the Son and of the Holy Spirit, and teaching them to obey everything I have commanded you. And surely I am with you always, to the very end of the age" (Matt. 28:18–20).

These verses say three important things about Jesus' authority.

1. *Jesus' authority is God's authority.* This is the only thing "all authority in heaven" can mean, for the only ultimate authority in heaven is God's. If Jesus has been given all authority in heaven, this can only mean that he is God and speaks with God's authority. The story about his ability to forgive the sin of the paralyzed man teaches the same truth. The religious leaders thought he was blaspheming on the grounds that only God can forgive sins (Matt. 9:3). The authority of God is the greatest possible authority. We dare not take it lightly.

2. *Jesus' authority validates his teaching.* This is what impressed those who first listened to him, for he did not speak on the authority of those teachers who had gone before him but with intrinsic authority. They knew that all he

said was true and could be trusted absolutely. Have you learned that about Jesus? No one else is that trustworthy. The polls tell us that Americans lie all the time and for no apparent reason. Politicians lie. Only Jesus can be trusted to tell you the truth at all times.

3. *Jesus has authority to forgive sin.* This is the most important point of all, for sin is our greatest problem. Sin keeps us from God. In fact, sin keeps us from the truth, for sin causes us to hide from the truth and cling to our sinful ways at all costs. We need a forgiveness based on the punishment of our sins in another who is able to bear that judgment for us, which is exactly what Jesus did. Jesus died in our place so that he can justly forgive the sin of all who will come to him asking for salvation.

The leaders of Israel would not acknowledge Jesus' authority. They wanted to be the authorities themselves, and the result is that they perished in their sins. Many will perish for exactly the same reason. They cling to their own supposed authority and will not come to Jesus. Why should that be true of you? It need not be. Acknowledge Jesus' authority and ask him to save you from your sins.

50

The Parables of the Two Sons and the Wicked Tenants

Matthew 21:28–46

"What do you think? There was a man who had two sons. He went to the first and said, 'Son, go and work today in the vineyard.'

"'I will not,' he answered, but later he changed his mind and went.

"Then the father went to the other son and said the same thing. He answered, 'I will, sir,' but did not go.

"Which of the two did what his father wanted?"

"The first," they answered.

Jesus said to them, "I tell you the truth, the tax collectors and the prostitutes are entering the kingdom of God ahead of you. For John came to you to show you the way of righteousness, and you did not believe him, but the tax collectors and the prostitutes did. And even after you saw this, you did not repent and believe him. . . ."

When the chief priests and the Pharisees heard Jesus' parables, they knew he was talking about them. They looked for a way to arrest him, but they were afraid of the crowd because the people held that he was a prophet.

Jesus was a superb teacher. He often used a striking action and then, after he had gained the attention of the people, explained what his action meant. We see this frequently in John's Gospel, in which Jesus first performs a miracle and then provides a long discourse

457

to explain the symbolism. The feeding of the five thousand is followed by his teaching on the bread of life, for instance. The raising of Lazarus is followed by his discourse that he is the resurrection.

This pattern has not always been so obvious in Matthew's Gospel, where the teaching tends to stand on its own more than in John. But the pattern is apparent in Matthew 21 and the first part of Matthew 22. In the first half of Matthew 21, Jesus performed three symbolic actions.

1. He entered Jerusalem on Palm Sunday, thereby presenting himself as Israel's true King and Messiah.

2. He cleansed the temple, restoring it to its God-given function as a "house of prayer" rather than a "den of robbers."

3. He cursed the fig tree as a symbol of God's coming judgment on the nation for its failure to produce spiritual fruit.

We understand what those actions meant because we have the Gospel's explanation of them. But they would not have been readily understood by those of Christ's day, not even by the disciples, which is why they are followed by the teaching in the remainder of chapter 21 and the first part of chapter 22. The teaching is in the form of three parables: (1) the parable of two very different sons (Matt. 21:28–32); (2) the parable of the wicked tenant farmers (Matt. 21:33–46); and the parable of the wedding banquet (Matt. 22:1–14). It is obvious that these stories are intended to explain the earlier actions, because the second parable concludes with the judgment, "Therefore . . . the kingdom of God will be taken away from you and given to a people who will produce its fruit" (Matt. 21:43). This is what the withering of the fig tree was about.

The teaching concerning these parables was not lost on the Pharisees and priests who heard it. The chapter ends by saying that "they knew he was talking about them" (v. 45).

Two Very Different Sons

The first story was about two sons. Each was told by his father to go and work in the vineyard. One said he would not, but afterward he repented and went. The other said he would but did not go. Jesus asked, "Which of the two did what his father wanted?" (v. 31).

They answered, "The first."

Jesus then added this conclusion: "I tell you the truth, the tax collectors and the prostitutes are entering the kingdom of God ahead of you. For John came to you to show you the way of righteousness, and you did not believe him, but the tax collectors and the prostitutes did. And even after you saw this, you did not repent and believe him" (vv. 31–32).

The son who said he would obey his father but did not actually do it represents the chief priests and elders; they had a reputation for being God's servants, but they rejected the prophets. The son who rejected his father's command but later did what his father wanted represents the tax collectors and prostitutes, who had been in rebellion against God's standards but who in many instances repented of their particular sins and came to Jesus.

Moreover, since the command of the father was to work in the vineyard, this is a parable not merely of salvation—that is, of believing on Jesus—but also of Christian service. It asks, "Who are those who truly serve?" as well as "Who are God's children?" Or we could put it this way: "What is the fruit of true religion?" Christ's answer is in terms of *doing* or *failing to do* the will of the father, rather than other matters.

Take the case of the second son. He said, "I will, sir," but did not go to the vineyard. A person might reason from this that Jesus suggested it is improper to make promises to God, since we may not keep them. He might conclude, "I will make no promises, no profession of discipleship." That would be wrong, of course. Jesus is not against profession. On the contrary, the Bible links profession to true belief in Jesus. Paul wrote in Romans, "If you confess with your mouth, 'Jesus is Lord,' and believe in your heart that God raised him from the dead, you will be saved. For it is with your heart that you believe and are justified, and it is with your mouth that you confess and are saved" (Rom. 10:9–10). What Jesus denounced is an insincere profession, the profession of one who cries, "Lord, Lord . . . ," but who does not do what Jesus says.

Are you in that category? You cannot answer by saying that you have joined a church, affirmed the creeds, have a reputation as a good Christian, or even that you are a Christian worker or minister. You can do all those things and still be disobedient to God, just as the religious leaders were. They were active in all sorts of religious matters, but they did not believe on Jesus, and they were not working in God's vineyard. They were working in a little vineyard of their own, building their own reputations and erecting their own little kingdom. You can only answer that question properly if you have trusted Jesus as your Savior and are now engaged in the specific work to which he has called you.

There is also the case of the other son. He said no to his father but afterward repented of his disobedience and went to the vineyard to work. We must not think that Jesus approved of everything about him. Jesus did not approve of his initial disobedience. But there was this good thing: Although he had defied his father at first, he later repented and did his father's will.

I mention his early disobedience because people today, often young people, think that it is all right for them to go their own way as long as they go God's way at some later point. They want to have fun now and serve God later—when they are too old to be of much use or when their opportunities for sound preparation are gone. Granted, it is better for them to sin now and repent later than for them to sin now and not repent at all. But the best way is to come to Jesus early and serve him both early and late. It is best to give your entire life to his service.

Besides, if you delay now, you have no guarantee that you will be able to come to Jesus later. You may, but sin takes its toll, and one of the things sin does is trap us so that we cannot get free even if we want to, and usually we do not even want that freedom. If God is speaking to you and you are saying no, you should know that although it may be hard for you to say yes now, it will be even harder to say it the next time around—even assuming that God speaks to you again. The only safe thing is to give prompt and sincere obedience to God's call.

The Story of the Tenants

There is a connection between the parable of the two sons and the parable of the wicked tenant farmers because each has to do with a vineyard, representing God's kingdom or the church. But there is also a progression from the first to the second. In the first parable the fault of the second son is his hypocrisy. He said he would obey but did not. In the story of the tenants the disobedient spirit of the religious leaders is worse than mere hypocrisy. Their spirits are so hardened by evil that they murder the landowner's son, who is obviously Jesus.

The parable of the wicked tenants tells how men who had been selected to manage a vineyard for its owner mistreated the owner's servants and at last killed the owner's son. The father is God; the son is Jesus; the servants are the prophets. The story shows that sinners are so virulent in their hatred of others, including God, that they murder God's servants and would murder God himself if he stooped to place himself within their grasp. What are the two great commandments? The first is, "Love the Lord your God with all your heart and with all your soul and with all your mind." The second is like it: "Love your neighbor as yourself" (Matt. 22:37, 39; see Lev. 19:18; Deut. 6:5). But on the basis of this story, it is correct to say that man in his natural state does precisely the opposite. He hates God with all his heart, with all his soul, and with all his mind, and he hates his neighbor even as he hates himself.

God's Vine

Jesus began by telling how a landowner planted a vineyard, put a wall around it, dug a winepress, and built a watchtower. He was speaking clearly to his Jewish audience. Israel was the "vine" of God, and everything Jesus said in that opening picture was known to have applied to Israel in the Old Testament. Isaiah had written, "My loved one had a vineyard on a fertile hillside. He dug it up and cleared it of stones and planted it with the choicest vines. He built a watchtower in it and cut out a winepress as well" (Isa. 5:1–2). The psalmist had written beautifully, "You brought a vine out of Egypt; you drove out the nations and planted it. You cleared the ground for it, and it took root and filled the land. The mountains were covered with its shade, the mighty cedars with its branches" (Ps. 80:8–10; see also Jer. 2:21 and Ezek. 19:10).

That imagery was so well known to Christ's hearers that when he referred to the vineyard, there could be no doubt in their minds that he was talking about them and those who had the responsibility for their spiritual oversight and development. We may be tempted, therefore, to dismiss the parable, thinking it applies only to them and not to us. But if that is the way we are interpreting it, we are utterly misreading Jesus' words. Jesus told the story in that way because he was speaking to Jews. But would he not have made it equally pointed if he were telling it to us? He may have used another image, or he might simply have said that we too may be compared to vines, as Israel was. Has he not planted us in our lands, whatever they may be? Has he not fenced us in? Has he not watered and cared for us? Has he not built a watchtower for us? Has he not sent his servants to care for us and present our choice fruits to him when he returns for them? He has done all these things. Yet we have not been faithful any more than Israel was faithful. We have also hated God and would destroy him if we could.

We Are Naturally God's Enemies

Years ago the great American theologian Jonathan Edwards developed this theme at length. His sermon was entitled "Men Naturally Are God's Enemies," and it was based on Romans 5:10 ("For if, when we were God's enemies, we were reconciled to him through the death of his Son . . ."). Most of us, when we take a text such as that, focus on the good part—in this case, the wonder of the death of Christ. Edwards did not go about things in that way. He saw that no one could appreciate the death of Christ, the second part of the verse, until he understood that he was an enemy of God, the first part. In this discourse he examined how we are God's enemies until regenerated.

We are God's enemies in several ways, says Edwards: in our judgments, in the natural likes or dislikes of our souls, in our wills, in our affections, and in our practice.

1. *We are God's enemies in our judgments.* We have mean opinions about God. Edwards used an illustration here, asking, What do you do when you are present in some gathering and a friend of yours is attacked? The answer is, you go to his or her defense. And how is it when an enemy is praised? In that case, you introduce negative factors to put down anything in the enemy that might be thought good.

So it is in people's judgments of God, Edwards argues.

> They entertain very low and contemptible thoughts of God. Whatever honor and respect they may pretend, and make a show of toward God, if their practice be examined, it will show that they certainly look upon him as a Being that is but little to be regarded. The language of their hearts is, "Who is the Lord, that I should obey his voice?" (Exod. 5:2), "What is the Almighty, that we should serve him? And what profit should we have if we pray unto him?" (Job 21:15). They count him worthy neither to be loved nor feared. They dare not behave with that slight and disregard towards one of their fellow creatures, when a little raised above them in power and authority, as they dare, and do, towards

God. They value one of their equals much more than God, and are ten times more afraid of offending such, than of displeasing God that made them. They cast such exceeding contempt on God, as to prefer every vile lust before him. And every worldly enjoyment is set higher in their esteem than God. A morsel of meat, or a few pence of worldly gain, is preferred before him. God is set last and lowest in the esteem of natural men.[1]

2. *We are God's enemies in the natural relish of our souls. Relish* is an old-fashioned word that we use today only to refer to condiments for the table. In Edwards's day it meant "likes" or "desires," so what he means here is that we do not naturally like God. In fact, the opposite is the case. By nature we find him and his attributes repugnant. Edwards discusses our hatred of four great attributes of God—his holiness, omniscience, power, and immutability—which I have referred to in other messages, picking up on Edwards's insights. He says of unsaved people:

> They hear God is an infinitely holy, pure, and righteous Being, and they do not like him upon this account; they have no relish of such qualifications; they take no delight in contemplating them. . . . And on account of their distaste of these perfections, they dislike all his other attributes. They have greater aversion to him because his omniscience is a holy omniscience. They are not pleased that he is omnipotent, and can do whatever he pleases, because it is a holy omnipotence. They are enemies even to his mercy, because it is a holy mercy. They do not like his immutability, because by this he never will be otherwise than he is, an infinitely holy God.[2]

That explains why men and women do not want much to do with God, why they try to keep him at such great distance. I had a neighbor once who was so adverse to God that I could not even begin to witness to her. The moment the name of God came up, she cried out, "Don't talk to me about God!" She was even adverse to letting her six-year-old daughter hear God's name mentioned. This is why people will not go with you to church, will not read Christian books, will not pray. It is why even Christian people have such a difficult time with these matters.

3. *We are God's enemies in our wills.* The will of God and our wills are set at cross purposes. What God wills, we hate, and what God hates, we desire. That is why we are so opposed to God's government. We are not God's loyal subjects, as we should be, but are opposed to his rule of us and this world. These rebellious desires were expressed well by the psalmist when he quoted God's enemies as saying, "Let us break [God's] chains . . . and throw off [his] fetters" (Ps. 2:3).

4. *We are God's enemies in our affections.* Our emotions also flare out against God. In prosperous times, when God seems to leave us alone and our plans are not disturbed, we manage for the most part to keep our evil affections hidden. We may even be a bit condescending at such times, as if from the

throne of our own universe we might throw God a tip. But when we are crossed, when something goes wrong, our malice burns against him. "This is exercised in dreadful heart-risings, inward wranglings and quarrelings, and blasphemous thoughts, wherein the heart is like a viper, hissing and spitting poison at God. And however free from it the heart may seem to be, when let alone and secure, yet a very little thing will set it in a rage. Temptations will show what is in the heart. The alteration of a man's circumstances will often discover the heart," Edwards says.[3] He wrote that these hatreds will be seen most clearly when people are cast into hell.

5. *We are God's enemies in our practice.* Here Edwards gets close to the main point of Christ's parable, for he says that although men and women cannot injure God, because he is so much above them, they nevertheless do what they can. They oppose God's honor, persecute his prophets, attempt to thwart his work in this world, and, in general terms, "[en]list under Satan's banner" as willing soldiers.

Judgment Is Coming

What is to be done with such persons? That is the question Jesus asked those who were listening to his parable. He could have given the answer himself, but instead he turned to the very people he was accusing of being the bad tenants and asked them what the owner would do when he returned. He asked them to render judgment. What is the proper response to such wicked and inexcusable behavior? he asked. The people replied rightly, "He will bring those wretches to a wretched end, and he will rent the vineyard to other tenants, who will give him his share of the crop at harvest time" (v. 41). That was correct. It was the only answer anyone could possibly give. However, in rendering that judgment the leaders of the people pronounced their own doom.

What would you say if Jesus asked you that question: "What should the owner of the vineyard do?" Unless you are an utter hypocrite or completely ignorant, you would answer as the Pharisees did, and, like them, you would also render judgment on yourself.

After listening to their answer Jesus concluded, "Have you never read in the Scriptures: 'The stone the builders rejected has become the capstone; the Lord has done this, and it is marvelous in our eyes'? Therefore I tell you that the kingdom of God will be taken away from you and given to a people who will produce its fruit. He who falls on this stone will be broken to pieces, but he on whom it falls will be crushed" (vv. 42–44). The quotation is from Psalm 118:22–23. But when Jesus added to it by speaking of sinners being "crushed" by "this stone," I think he was referring to the vision King Nebuchadnezzar had in the days of the prophet Daniel. Nebuchadnezzar had a dream in which he saw a statue representing four successive world kingdoms. At the end of the vision, a stone that was not cut by human hands came and struck the statue, grinding it to pieces, after which it grew and became a mountain that filled the whole earth (Daniel 2). The stone is Christ. The mountain is his kingdom. Jesus was telling the people of his day, "You can be part of my kingdom and thus grow up in me and fill the earth. That will happen by the decree of God my Father. Or you can stand against me and my kingdom and be broken."

The judgment of God should not be taken lightly, because God should not be taken lightly. God is our Judge. The God who offers salvation now is the God who will judge in righteousness hereafter. Therefore, if you will not have Jesus as your Savior now, in the day of his grace, you will have him as your Judge when you stand before his throne at the final day. Remember that as he spoke those words, Jesus was on the way to the cross to die for such as would believe on him. You can be one of them. Why not come to Jesus now and become a part of his advancing kingdom?[4]

51

The Parable of the Wedding Banquet

Matthew 22:1–14

Jesus spoke to them again in parables, saying: "The kingdom of heaven is like a king who prepared a wedding banquet for his son. He sent his servants to those who had been invited to the banquet to tell them to come, but they refused to come.

"Then he sent some more servants and said, 'Tell those who have been invited that I have prepared my dinner: My oxen and fattened cattle have been butchered, and everything is ready. Come to the wedding banquet.'

"But they paid no attention and went off—one to his field, another to his business. The rest seized his servants, mistreated them and killed them. The king was enraged. He sent his army and destroyed those murderers and burned their city.

"Then he said to his servants, 'The wedding banquet is ready, but those I invited did not deserve to come. Go to the street corners and invite to the banquet anyone you find.' So the servants went out into the streets and gathered all the people they could find, both good and bad, and the wedding hall was filled with guests.

"But when the king came in to see the guests, he noticed a man there who was not wearing wedding clothes. 'Friend,' he asked, 'how did you get in here without wedding clothes?' The man was speechless.

"Then the king told the attendants, 'Tie him hand and foot, and throw him outside, into the darkness, where there will be weeping and gnashing of teeth.'

"For many are invited, but few are chosen."

From time to time in these studies I have acknowledged that a particular parable is difficult to interpret and have mentioned several ways the details of the story might be taken. That problem does not exist with the parables in Matthew 21 and 22: the parable of the two sons, the parable of the wicked tenant farmers, and the

parable of the wedding banquet. On the contrary, they are all too clear—
above all the parable of the banquet! It speaks of God's gracious invitation
in the gospel and of the indifferent and even arrogant way men and women
respond to it. It also refers to hell as the end of those who presume to enter
God's presence without the wedding garment of Christ's righteousness.

This parable is found in Luke as well as in Matthew, though with some
differences. The fullest form is Matthew's; Luke does not mention the guest
who is cast out. But Luke 14:15–24 contains an elaboration of the excuses
made by those who refused the king's invitation.

Those Who Would Not Come

The story begins with a king who has prepared a wedding banquet for his
son and sends servants to those who have been invited to tell them that the
feast is now ready and that they should come. They refuse to come. Their
refusal is an insult, of course. It is dishonoring to the son, the king, and even
to the servants who carried the king's message. But the king is patient at first.
He sends other servants to repeat the invitation: "Tell those who have been
invited that I have prepared my dinner: My oxen and fattened cattle have
been butchered, and everything is ready. Come to the wedding banquet"
(v. 4). But again they refuse. This time, however, they do not merely reject
the invitation, they also mistreat the messengers and kill some of them. The
king sends an army to destroy the murderers and burn their city (vv. 1–7).
After that he invites others.

The reason the parable is so easy to understand is that nearly every part
is discussed in plain terms elsewhere. The king is God, sitting on the throne
of the universe. The son is his Son, the Lord Jesus Christ. The banquet is the
marriage supper of the Lamb. The messengers are the early preachers of
the gospel. Those to whom the invitation was first given are the upright Jews,
and those who eventually come to the banquet are the outcast and poor,
even Gentiles. John 1:11–12 says, "He came to that which was his own, but
his own did not receive him. Yet to all who received him, to those who believed
in his name, he gave the right to become children of God."

John 1:11–12 suggests that on one level at least a number of Jesus' parables deal with the refusal of the Jews to receive Jesus when he first came to
them. This was a major puzzle during the lifetime of the Lord, as well as
afterward, so it is not strange to find parables that either deal with it directly
or allude to it indirectly. The older son in the parable of the prodigal son
represents Israel and her religious leaders particularly. So do the workers in
the vineyard who were hired early but were paid the same as those who came
late. So does the Pharisee in the story of the Pharisee and the tax collector
(Luke 18:9–14). These parables all explore the thinking of those who supposed they had worked long and faithfully for God, unlike the common
people or Gentiles, and were resentful when the grace of God was shown
to people they considered unworthy of it.

The unique element in the parable of the wedding banquet is the willful refusal of those who were invited. It was not that they *could* not come. Rather, they *would* not. The reason for their refusal is not spelled out, but the way the servants were treated suggests what it was. They "seized" the servants, "mistreated them and killed them" (v. 6). If the invited guests felt that way toward the servants, they obviously felt that way toward the king who had sent them and would have seized, mistreated, and killed him if they could have done so. In other words, they would not come because they actually despised the king and were hostile to him.

The leaders of Christ's day bitterly resented this portrait of them, but resent it or not, that is precisely the way these religious leaders thought and acted. In the story immediately before this (Matt. 21:33–46), Jesus told of tenant farmers who beat, killed, and stoned the owner's servants. At last they murdered his son.

In the chapter following (Matthew 23), Jesus pronounces woes on these same people:

> Woe to you, teachers of the law and Pharisees, you hypocrites! You build tombs for the prophets and decorate the graves of the righteous. And you say, "If we had lived in the days of our forefathers, we would not have taken part with them in shedding the blood of the prophets." So you testify against yourselves that you are the descendants of those who murdered the prophets. Fill up, then, the measure of the sin of your forefathers! . . .
>
> I am sending you prophets and wise men and teachers. Some of them you will kill and crucify; others you will flog in your synagogues and pursue from town to town. And so upon you will come all the righteous blood that has been shed on earth, from the blood of righteous Abel to the blood of Zechariah son of Berakiah, whom you murdered between the temple and the altar. . . .
>
> O Jerusalem, Jerusalem, you who kill the prophets and stone those sent to you, how often I have longed to gather your children together, as a hen gathers her chicks under her wings, but you were not willing.
>
> verses 29–37

We know that at the last these rebellious subjects of the King of heaven killed Christ. As Stephen later put it, "Was there ever a prophet your fathers did not persecute? They even killed those who predicted the coming of the Righteous One. And now you have betrayed and murdered him—you who have received the law that was put into effect through angels but have not obeyed it" (Acts 7:52–53).

Today we are not so inclined to kill prophets. If we are honest, however, we will admit that the same spirit is present among many of our contemporaries as they dispose of God's messengers by ridicule or neglect, if not by more violent hostility. Charles H. Spurgeon preached seven sermons on this parable during the course of his long ministry, and he was deeply touched by that fact. He said:

Today this same class will be found among the children of godly parents; dedicated from their birth, prayed for by loving piety, listening to the gospel from their childhood, and yet unsaved. We look for these to come to Jesus. We naturally hope that they will feast upon the provisions of grace, and like their parents will rejoice in Christ Jesus; but alas! How often it is the case they will not come! . . . A preacher may be too rhetorical: let a plain-speaking person be tried. He may be too weighty: let another come with parable and anecdote. Alas! With some of you the thing wanted is not a new voice, but a new heart. You would listen no better to a new messenger than to the old one.[1]

Some who are invited to the gospel banquet do not openly express their hatred of the one who gives it, but they make excuses. They go off "one to his field, another to his business" (v. 5). Jesus elaborates that point in Luke's version: "But they all alike began to make excuses. The first said, 'I have just bought a field, and I must go and see it. Please excuse me.'

"Another said, 'I have just bought five yoke of oxen, and I'm on my way to try them out. Please excuse me.'

"Still another said, 'I just got married, so I can't come'" (Luke 14:18–20). Each of those excuses is trifling. As Jesus tells it, it is not a case of a man being on his deathbed, unable to move, nor a woman being kept at home by a violent husband. Not one of these excuses has any weight at all. So what if a man has just bought a field? There is no reason why he would have to see it on that particular day and miss the banquet. The field could wait. There was no reason why the second person had to try out his oxen. He could have waited a few days. Even the excuse about marriage had no substance. Are we to think that a new bride would be unwelcome at a feast to which her husband was invited?

Besides that, the invitation was not the first they had received. In both versions of the parable Jesus says the invitation was sent to those who had already been invited once. The guests had no excuse for failing to arrange their schedules accordingly. When the final summons came, they should have been eagerly anticipating the banquet.

Many who reject the gospel invitation today have equally flimsy excuses and will rightly incur the King's wrath. They say they are too busy for spiritual things. They say they have fields or patients or bonds or whatever it is that imprisons their souls and keeps them from faith in him who brings salvation. Spurgeon, whom I quoted earlier, tells of a ship owner who was visited by a godly man. The Christian asked, "Well, sir, what is the state of your soul?" to which the merchant replied, "Soul? I have no time to take care of my soul. I have enough to do just taking care of my ships." But he was not too busy to die, which he did a week later.[2]

Do you fit that pattern? Are you more interested in your good credit than in Christ? Do you read the stock quotations more than you read your Bible? You do not have to murder a prophet to miss out. You have only to fritter away your time on things that will eventually pass away and thus let your opportunities for repentance and faith pass by.

Those Who Came

Half the parable (Matt. 22:1–7) is about those who despised the king and would not come to the banquet, but the second half (vv. 8–14) tells of those who did come. The king said, "Go to the street corners and invite to the banquet anyone you find" (v. 9). Luke makes it plain that these persons were drawn from the lower ranks of life. "Go out quickly into the streets and alleys of the town and bring in the poor, the crippled, the blind and the lame. . . . Go out to the roads and country lanes and make them come in, so that my house will be full" (Luke 14:21, 23).

This seems an extraordinary thing for the master to have done or, in Matthew's case, for a king to have done. But when we remember that the master represents God, it seems inevitable. We need to ask questions such as, Is it possible that the King of the universe could ever be dishonored by having no one at the wedding supper of his Son? That no one would be saved? Can the Almighty be vanquished? Disappointed? Can the work of the Lord Jesus Christ be ineffective? Can Jesus have died in vain? Or risen in vain? If Jesus died and no one receives salvation through his completed work, would not God be dishonored? Would Satan not have triumphed? To ask questions such as these is to show the impossibility of such an outcome. God must be honored. Jesus must be effective in his work. Jesus himself said, "All that the Father gives me *will* come to me, and whoever comes to me I will never drive away" (John 6:37, emphasis added).

But surely God is dishonored by the kinds of people who come, someone might say. These are not the important people, not the wise, not the strong, not the mighty. True, and God admits it. Paul wrote, "God chose the foolish things of the world to shame the wise; God chose the weak things of the world to shame the strong. He chose the lowly things of this world and the despised things—and the things that are not—to nullify the things that are, so that no one may boast before him" (1 Cor. 1:27–29). Is God dishonored by dealing with such people? On the contrary, he is highly honored.

How? Let me share Spurgeon's answer to that question:

1. *"The persons who came to the wedding were more grateful than the first invited might have been if they had come.* The richer sort had a good dinner every day. Those farmers could always kill a fat sheep, and those merchants could always buy a calf. 'Thank you for nothing,' they would have said to the king if they had accepted his invitation. But these poor beggars picked off the streets . . . welcomed the fatlings. How glad they were! One of them said to the other, 'It's a long time since you and I last sat down to such a joint as this,' and the other answered, 'I can hardly believe that I am really in a palace dining with a king. Why, yesterday I begged all the day and only had twopence at night. Long live the king, say I, and blessings on the prince and his bride!'

2. *"The joy that day was much more expressed than it would have been had others come.* Those ladies and gentlemen who were first invited, if they had come to the wedding, would have seated themselves there in a very stiff and proper

manner.... But these beggars! They make a merry clatter; they are not muz-
zled by propriety; they are glad at the sight of every dish. . . .

3. *"The occasion became more famous than it would otherwise have been.* If the
feast had gone on as usual it would have been only one among many such
things; but now this royal banquet was the only one of its kind, unique, unpar-
alleled. To gather in poor men off the streets, laboring men and idle men,
bad men and good men, to the wedding of the Crown Prince—this was a
new thing under the sun. Everybody talked of it. There were songs made
about it, and these were sung in the King's honor where none honored kings
before. . . . Dear friends, when the Lord saved some of us by his grace, it was
no common event. When he brought us great sinners to his feet, and washed
us, and clothed us, and fed us, and made us his own, it was a wonder to be
talked of for ever and ever. We will never leave off praising his name throughout eternity. That which looked as though it would defame the King turned
out to his honor, and 'the wedding was furnished with guests.' "[3]

Ultimately, nothing will dishonor God. Unbelievers may despise him and
dishonor him by their rejections of the gospel, but theirs is not the last word.
Their hatred will be overcome by God's good, and the praise of the redeemed
will drown out the cries of the impenitent. To see it we have only to turn to
the last chapters of the Book of Revelation, where we find the wicked being
judged and the redeemed people of God engaged in holy, hearty, heartfelt
praise to him who sits upon the throne and to the Lamb forever.

The Man without a Garment

At this point the parable seems to be over, which is the case in Luke.
But Matthew is not quite finished, and I am glad because here the Lord
gives a much needed warning concerning the man who came to the feast
without a wedding garment. The disadvantaged sometimes possess an
inverse pride. Because they are not rich or famous or powerful but poor
and unknown and weak, they feel they *deserve* the king's bounty and can
come before him in their own character and on the basis of their own
"good" works. Jesus exposed that error by showing how the man who came
to the feast without a garment was at once confronted by the king and then
thrown "outside, into the darkness, where there will be weeping and gnashing of teeth" (v. 13).

What is the wedding garment? It is the righteousness of Jesus Christ, of
course. It is that perfect righteousness that God provides freely to all who
repent of sin and trust in the Lord Jesus Christ alone for their salvation. We
sing about it in a hymn of Nikolaus von Zinzendorf, translated by John
Wesley:

> Jesus, thy blood and righteousness
> My beauty are, my glorious dress;
> 'Midst flaming worlds, in these arrayed,
> With joy shall I lift up my head.

If we are clothed in Christ's righteousness, we will be able to stand before God and rejoice in our salvation, but only if we are so clothed. If we are not clothed in Christ's righteousness, we will be speechless before God and will be cast out.

I am interested in the words "the man was speechless" (v. 12), because that is the same thought Paul expresses in Romans 3:19, when he wraps up his powerful indictment of the human race by concluding that "every mouth [will] be silenced and the whole world held accountable to God."

Early in his ministry, Donald Grey Barnhouse developed a way of presenting the gospel using that text. When Barnhouse was speaking to a person and he wasn't sure whether the person was a Christian, Barnhouse would ask, "Suppose you should die tonight and appear before God in heaven and he should ask you, 'What right do you have to come into my heaven?' what would you say?" He learned from experience that there were only three answers a person could give.

Many would cite their good works, saying, "I'd say I've done the best I can, and I've never done anything particularly bad." This was an appeal to the person's moral record, and Barnhouse would point out that it is our record that has gotten us into trouble in the first place. We have all fallen short of God's moral standard embodied in the law. The Bible flatly declares, "No one will be declared righteous in [God's] sight by observing the law" (Rom. 3:20).

A second group of people would respond as a woman did whom Barnhouse once met on a ship crossing the Atlantic. He asked, "If God demanded of you, 'What right do you have to come into my heaven?' what would you say?"

She responded, "I wouldn't have a thing to say." To put it in other words, she would be "speechless" before God, which is what Paul wrote about in Romans. In Jesus' parable the Lord says this will be the case for all of us when God actually asks that question. In this life we may get by with our excuses or with the delusion that our record is pretty good and God will be satisfied with it. But in that day, when we see God in his glory and understand what true righteousness is, our foolishness will be made apparent to ourselves as well as to all other beings in the universe, and we will be reduced to silence— if we are not clothed with the wedding garment of Christ's righteousness.

Which brings us to the third and only acceptable answer. "What right do you have to come into my heaven?" The only possible answer is, "None at all, so far as I myself am concerned. But Jesus died for my sins and has given me the covering of his own righteousness in which alone I dare to stand before you. I come at your invitation and in that clothing." Will God reject a person who comes in that way? He will not, for it is precisely for such persons that Jesus Christ died. Besides, it is Jesus who has invited us to come to him.[4]

52

Three Attempts to Trap Jesus

Matthew 22:15–40

Then the Pharisees went out and laid plans to trap him in his words. They sent their disciples to him along with the Herodians. "Teacher," they said, "we know you are a man of integrity and that you teach the way of God in accordance with the truth. You aren't swayed by men, because you pay no attention to who they are. Tell us then, what is your opinion? Is it right to pay taxes to Caesar or not?" . . .

That same day the Sadducees, who say there is no resurrection, came to him with a question. "Teacher," they said, "Moses told us that if a man dies without having children, his brother must marry the widow and have children for him. Now there were seven brothers among us. The first one married and died, and since he had no children, he left his wife to his brother. The same thing happened to the second and the third brother, right on down to the seventh. Finally, the woman died. Now then, at the resurrection, whose wife will she be of the seven, since all of them were married to her?" . . .

Hearing that Jesus had silenced the Sadducees, the Pharisees got together. One of them, an expert in the law, tested him with this question: "Teacher, which is the greatest commandment in the Law?"

The die is cast. Jesus has broken with Judaism, and the authorities are seeking a way to get rid of him. They can't just kill him, however; that would be murder. They have to catch him in a teaching they can construe as blasphemy, which was a capital offense. Or at the very least, they have to discredit him before the people. This is what lies behind the three attempts to trap Jesus that we find in Matthew 22. They are expressed as questions: (1) Is it right to pay taxes to Caesar? (2) How can rational persons believe in a physical resurrection? and (3) What is the greatest commandment?

The interesting thing is that Jesus did not merely extricate himself from these little traps, which he had no difficulty doing. The interesting thing is what he teaches on each occasion. In the case of paying taxes, he teaches the legitimate God-given authority of civil government, as well as its limits. In the case of the resurrection, he teaches about the authority of Scripture and the power of God. In the case of the commandments, he summarizes the entire law in terms of our duty to God, on the one hand, and our duty to our fellow human beings, on the other.

The First Attempt: Paying Taxes

The first attempt to trap Jesus was the product of an unholy alliance between the Pharisees, most of whom strongly resented the rule of Rome over their subject nation, and the Herodians, who were more accepting of the foreign power. The Herodians were called Herodians because they supported the ruling house of Herod. Since Herod was supported by the Romans, the Herodians accepted the Roman rule too. Normally the Pharisees would not have worked closely with the Herodians at all. But here these two rival parties team up to ask Jesus a trick question about taxes: "Is it right to pay taxes to Caesar or not?" (v. 17).

They thought that if Jesus said it was right to pay taxes, they could discredit him with the people who hated Rome and for whom these taxes were a much resented burden. He would lose an enormous amount of popular support and could be dismissed as a collaborator. He might even be refused as the Messiah because one of the functions of the Messiah was to drive out any occupying power and establish the Davidic kingdom. On the other hand, if Jesus said they should resist Rome by refusing to pay taxes, then his enemies could denounce him to the authorities as a dangerous insurrectionist.

Jesus asked for a coin. When they produced it, he asked whose portrait was on the coin and whose inscription. "Caesar's," they replied.

"Give to Caesar what is Caesar's," Jesus said, thus laying the basis for the teaching Paul later gave in Romans 13:7, when he wrote, "Give everyone what you owe him: If you owe taxes, pay taxes," and Peter's teaching, when he wrote, "Submit yourselves for the Lord's sake to every authority instituted among men: whether to the king, as the supreme authority, or to governors, who are sent by him to punish those who do wrong and to commend those who do right" (1 Peter 2:13–14). However, as he continued, I think Jesus must have flipped the coin over, exposing the back on which there would have been a portrait of one of the Roman gods or goddesses, making the contrast, "and to God what is God's" (Matt. 22:21).

The first part of Jesus' answer reinforced Caesar's authority, even in such an unpopular matter as taxes. The second part drew limits. Although the state has a God-given and therefore legitimate authority, the authority of God is greater. Therefore, those who know God must worship and obey him even if, in some cases, it means disobeying Caesar.

Four Logical Options

Jesus' answer to the question about taxes suggests four options that are useful in grasping the nature of the state's authority and the rightful limits of a Christian's compliance with it. These options are: (1) God alone as an authority with the authority of Caesar denied, (2) Caesar alone as an authority with the authority of God denied, (3) the authority of both God and Caesar but with Caesar in the dominant position, and (4) the authority of God and Caesar but with God in the dominant position.

1. *God alone as an authority.* The first option is one some Christians have embraced at different periods in history, especially when the state has become excessively oppressive or corrupt. In the early church, persons called anchorites went off into the desert, thereby separating themselves from all social contacts and living, as they believed, solely for the service of God. From that early movement monasticism was born, and for that reason I call this first option *monasticism.*

Yet we must not think of monasticism as something practiced only in the early church or by members of the monastic orders (who do not all agree with it anyway). It is also the essential approach of evangelical Christians who so separate themselves from the world that they withdraw from the surrounding culture, refuse to participate in elections, have only Christian friends, or work only for a Christian company.

2. *Caesar alone as an authority.* The second option is that of most unbelievers and sometimes even of so-called Christians: the choice of Caesar alone. I call this option *secularism.* It was the way chosen by the Jewish leaders at the time of Christ's trial, when they told Pilate, incredibly in light of their past history, "We have no king but Caesar" (John 19:15).

This is the most dangerous of the four options, because if God is left out of the equation, Caesar is left with no ultimate accountability. He has nothing to restrain his whims or cruelty.

In America we recognize the need for checks on governmental power. In fact, this is why we have three main branches of government: the executive branch, the legislative branch, and the judicial branch. Each has a check on the others. The president appoints Supreme Court justices, but if the president gets out of line, the Senate (part of the legislative branch) can impeach him. The president initiates programs, but Congress must fund them. As for Congress, it can make laws, but the president can refuse to sign them (the power of the veto) or the judicial branch can declare them unconstitutional. The Supreme Court is carefully protected out of respect for our laws, but the court cannot initiate legislation. It can only pass judgment on it, and the president has the power to appoint the justices.

We call this a system of checks and balances, and we have it because we recognize that persons in power are untrustworthy. Human rulers regularly conspire against God (Psalm 2). Therefore, if we turn our backs on God, we are at the mercy of our governors.

3. *The authority of God and Caesar but with Caesar in the dominant position.* This is an option many persons claim to hold, but it is the stance of *cowards*. If God's authority is recognized at all, it must be supreme simply because God is supreme by definition. That is what it means to be God. Thus, if anyone claims to obey the state before God or rather than God, while nevertheless still believing in God, it can only be because he is afraid of what Caesar can do to him.

This was the case with Pilate. He knew Jesus was innocent of the charges brought against him. He declared him innocent and even tried to release him. But in the end he gave in and had Jesus crucified. Why? Because he was afraid of Caesar. Toward the end of the trial, when Pilate was holding out against their wishes, the Jewish authorities played their trump card, crying out, "If you let this man go, you are no friend of Caesar" (John 19:12). As a result of that implied threat, Pilate, who feared Caesar and wanted to be Caesar's friend more than anything else in the entire world, gave in and condemned the sinless Son of God.

The irony is that despite his act, Pilate ultimately failed to secure Caesar's friendship. A few years after Christ's trial he was removed from office by the proconsul of Syria and was banished to France, where he died.

4. *The authority of God and Caesar but with God in the dominant position.* The last option is *biblical Christianity*, and it was the position Jesus articulated when he said, "Give to Caesar what is Caesar's, and to God what is God's."

Because Christians recognize the authority of the state, they should be the very best of citizens. They should obey the state in all areas of its legitimate authority. They should obey the speed limits, pay their taxes honestly, vote in elections, support worthy civic endeavors, speak well of their rulers, and support and pray for them. John Calvin expressed this well when he wrote, "We are not only subject to the authority of princes who perform their office toward us uprightly and faithfully as they ought, but also to the authority of all who, by whatever means, have got control of affairs, even though they perform not a whit of the princes' office."[1]

On the other hand, Christians should also be the very best of citizens by opposing the state verbally and even by acts of noncompliance whenever the government strays from its legitimate God-given function or violates the moral law of God. We are to do this chiefly by words, that is, by rational argument, not by coercive power. The power of the sword is the state's, not ours. However, we must resist and even disobey the state when necessary, such as if the state were to forbid us to evangelize, since the command to evangelize has been given to us by Jesus Christ himself. It is also necessary in matters of morality, such as if the state were to command us to do something contrary to the revealed law of God.

The Second Attempt: The Resurrection

The second question was put to Jesus by the Sadducees, the theological liberals of the day, and the question was significant because they did not believe in the resurrection. In fact, they were the materialists of their time and did not believe in any spiritual reality. Acts 23:8 reports that they believed neither in the resurrection nor angels nor spirits. They were also rationalists, and their question was based on what they judged as the logical absurdity of the Pharisees' resurrection doctrines, which they assumed Jesus held. Jesus was known as a conservative in his handling of the Scriptures.

They proposed a hypothetical situation in which a woman had been married to seven men, having been left a widow six times. "Now then," they said, "at the resurrection, whose wife will she be of the seven, since all of them were married to her?" (v. 28). How clever they thought they were. She couldn't belong to all of them, and since she could not, there obviously could be no resurrection.

Jesus silenced them with a simple double rebuke: (1) They did not know the Scriptures or (2) the power of God. Then he quoted from Exodus 3:6: "I am the God of your father, the God of Abraham, the God of Isaac and the God of Jacob." Jesus probably answered with this verse because it is from the Pentateuch. The Sadducees valued the Pentateuch more than they did the other Scriptures, which is why they began their interrogation with a reference to the teaching of Moses about such marriages. Jesus replied on their terms, referring to the Scriptures they accepted, and showed that even the Scriptures they followed contained a doctrine of the afterlife.

Jesus explained that God is "not the God of the dead, but of the living, for to him all are alive" (Luke 20:38). He meant that by the time these words were spoken to Moses, the three great Hebrew patriarchs (Abraham, Isaac, and Jacob) had long since died. Yet God referred to his relationship to them in the present tense, indicating that they must even then be alive in heaven. Jesus refuted the Sadducees by the tense of a single Hebrew verb. Because they did not know the Scriptures and failed to appreciate God's power, they had mistakenly rejected this doctrine as well as other Bible teachings.

God's Word or Man's Word

In his response to the first of his enemies' questions, Jesus provided the classic biblical teaching about the authority of civil government and the right relationship of the believer to the state. In his reply to the second question, Jesus taught the authority and complete reliability of the Bible in everything it teaches. We speak of the Bible's authority, infallibility, and inerrancy, and we ascribe these qualities to it because, as Jesus taught, the Bible is the very Word of God.

There are really only three basic positions in regard to the Bible, and we see them today even as they existed then: (1) The Bible is the Word of God and is infallible, or (2) the Bible is the words of mere men and is not binding on anyone, or (3) the Bible is a combination of both.

The first is *the classic, evangelical doctrine,* held by Christians throughout history. Thus, even when faced with debates about the nature of Jesus Christ, man, or justification, the people involved in those debates always had the Bible to appeal to. Even the heretics regarded the Bible as the Word of God. They disagreed with the church about what it taught and had to be corrected as the church studied the issue, allowing the Holy Spirit to speak through the Word to the people of that day, but everyone believed the Bible is God's Word and is therefore inerrant in whatever it teaches. Only in recent times has this position been abandoned.

Even though we speak of the classic, evangelical view of the Bible and say that the church believes the Bible is the Word of God, we do not deny that it is also expressed in human language. Some people think the Bible was somehow dictated by God. Then they have difficulty explaining how the style of one book differs from the style of another book. That problem is solved when we understand that the Bible also comes to us through human authors, who wrote according to their own style and vocabulary. We acknowledge that in a sense the Bible is also the words of men, though it is more than that. God so guided the human authors that the result, in its whole and in its parts, is what God desired to be expressed. Thus, the Bible is the Word of God from beginning to end and is entirely true because God himself is truthful.

The second view, that the Bible contains the words of men, is *the view of liberalism and neoorthodoxy,* though many of the early neoorthodox theologians had great respect for the Bible and were willing to listen to it. Those who follow neoorthodoxy say that God is so transcendent, so far above us, so separated from where we are that he cannot actually speak in human words. Rather, he reveals himself in ways that we cannot even talk about. The Bible, therefore, was written by men testifying in their own words as to what they believed God said in this real but mysterious and literally nonverbal fashion.

The third position is that *the Bible is the Word of God and the words of men combined.* When you read the Bible, you find things that have certainly come to us from God and are therefore truthful. But we have to admit (so this thinking goes) that when we read the Bible, we also find things that are not truthful, things we know to be in error. Because God does not speak that which is untruthful, these things must have come from human beings and from human beings alone. In other words, the Bible contains a combination of divine words and human words, and it is the task of scholarship to sort them out.

What happens in this framework is that the scholar becomes God. That is, he becomes the authority who tells Christian people what is true and what is not true, what is of God and what is not of God, what they are to believe and what they are not to believe. The result is that because we are sinners (which includes the scholars who, perhaps at this point, are even greater sinners than the rest of us), we tend to weed out what we do not want to hear. The words of God that are given to correct the church, discipline our thinking, and influence our lives are the very parts we decide are errors and get rid of. It was the error the Sadducees had embraced and that Jesus refuted by his teaching in these verses.

The Third Attempt: The Great Commandment

The first and second of these questions were somewhat silly and were easily answered. The third was serious, and we would probably think it an honest question if Matthew had not said, "One of them, an expert in the law, *tested him* with this question" (v. 35, emphasis added).

Apparently, after the Sadducees had been bested by Jesus, the Pharisees got together for one last try. Using their "expert," they asked Jesus a question they probably had debated often in their own circles: "Teacher, which is the greatest commandment in the Law?" (v. 36). It is difficult to guess what they expected to gain by this, but they probably hoped to catch Jesus in a misstatement that they could pounce on and condemn as heresy. At the least, they must have thought this an extremely difficult question. Not long afterward, the Pharisees would make lists of the commandments. They would distinguish 613 commands, 248 of them positive and 365 negative. They thought that ranking and relating these were critical.

Jesus replied simply with a true and unchallengeable answer: "'Love the Lord your God with all your heart and with all your soul and with all your mind.' This is the first and greatest commandment. And the second is like it: 'Love your neighbor as yourself.' All the Law and the Prophets hang on these two commandments" (vv. 37–40). The first of these commandments was from Deuteronomy 6:5. The second was from Leviticus 19:18.

It was a brilliant reply, and Mark records that it produced a favorable reaction from the lawyer who had asked it. "You are right," he said.

Jesus replied by telling him, "You are not far from the kingdom of God" (Mark 12:34). True, but he was not there yet. And the other Pharisees who were in on this terrible attempt to trap Jesus were, for their part, far from the kingdom and heading rapidly in the opposite direction.

Jesus summarized the law by saying, "Love the Lord your God with all your heart and with all your soul and with all your mind" and "your neighbor as yourself" (Matt. 22:37, 39). But as one teacher has said, "Man as sinner [actually] hates God, hates man, and hates himself. He would kill God if he could. He does kill his fellow man when he can. [And] he commits spiritual suicide every day of his life."[2] This is nowhere more obvious than in the plottings of these very men against the Savior. Jesus was love incarnate; he alone loved God the Father with all his heart and with all his soul and with all his mind, and he loves us also. But they, like all sinners, were doing everything they could to eliminate Jesus' presence from their lives.

Everyone should know that true religion consists of a perfect love for God and of other human beings. But none of us can love perfectly. That is why we need a Savior. We need Jesus. You need Jesus. You need to commit yourself to him as the only possible Savior and your rightful Lord.

53

A Question for His Questioners

Matthew 22:41–46

While the Pharisees were gathered together, Jesus asked them, "What do you think about the Christ? Whose son is he?"

"The son of David," they replied.

He said to them, "How is it then that David, speaking by the Spirit, calls him 'Lord'? For he says,

> *"'The Lord said to my Lord:*
> *"Sit at my right hand*
> *until I put your enemies*
> *under your feet."'*

"If then David calls him 'Lord,' how can he be his son?" No one could say a word in reply, and from that day on no one dared to ask him any more questions.

F̲ew things are more deeply instilled into the American way of thinking than the notion of fair play. "It's my turn; you've had the ball long enough," children say when they argue on the playground. "Everyone should pay his fair share," politicians say when they want to raise taxes. Ruth Graham, the wife of evangelist Billy Graham, wrote a book titled *My Turn.*

Well, it was Jesus' turn now. Not that the Pharisees, Sadducees, or other experts in the law wanted to be fair, of course. They were trying to trap him in his words (Matt. 22:15). They had come to him with three sticky questions: "Is it right to pay taxes to Caesar or not?" (v. 17); "Now then, at the resurrection, whose wife will she be of the seven, since all of them were married to her?" (v. 28); and, "Which is the greatest commandment in the Law?" (v. 36). They had trouble with these matters themselves, but Jesus answered their questions easily with words that settled each of these issues forever: (1) Yes, it is right to pay taxes, but it also necessary to pay God what we owe him; (2) yes, there is a resurrection, but it will transcend the physical relationships we know now; and (3) the law is summarized in these words: first, love the Lord your God with all your heart, with all your soul, and with all your mind, and second, love your neighbor as yourself.

But now it was Jesus' turn. Turning to the Pharisees, who were his most persistent interrogators and chief enemies, Jesus asked, "What do you think about the Christ? Whose son is he?"

They thought the answer was easy. "The son of David," they replied. This was a correct response because many Old Testament texts taught that one of David's natural descendants would reign on his throne forever.

But Jesus continued, "How is it then that David, speaking by the Spirit, calls him 'Lord'? For he says,

> "'The Lord said to my Lord:
>   "Sit at my right hand
>   until I put your enemies
>   under your feet.""

If then David calls him 'Lord,' how can he be his son?" (Matt. 22:43–45; see Mark 12:35–37; Luke 20:41–44).

Jesus' words turned an apparently easy question into a profound and searching question. No father calls a son his "lord." Sons are subservient to fathers. Therefore, if David called his natural, physical descendant (the Messiah) his "Lord," it could only be because the One to come would somehow be greater than David was. The only way that could happen was if the Messiah were more than a mere man. He would have to be a divine Messiah, that is, God. This did not fit with the Pharisees' expectation of who the Messiah should be or what he should do, so they were silenced.

The Greatest Messianic Psalm

When Jesus asked the Pharisees his question, he was referring to Psalm 110:1, of course, and he was establishing a pattern for interpreting the Old Testament that his disciples picked up on enthusiastically. The disciples loved to quote this psalm. In fact, they used it so often that it became the psalm most quoted in the New Testament, and verse 1 became the verse most quoted. By my count, Psalm 110:1 is cited directly or alluded to indirectly at least twenty-seven times, the chief passages being Matthew 22:44 (parallel accounts in Mark 12:36; Luke 20:42–43); Acts 2:34–35; 7:56; 1 Corinthians 15:25; Ephesians 1:20; Colossians 3:1; Hebrews 1:3, 13; 12:2; and 1 Peter 3:22.

Verse 4 of Psalm 110, in which Jesus is called "a priest forever, in the order of Melchizedek," is referred to in Hebrews 5:6; 7:17, 21; 8:1; and 10:11–13 and is the dominating idea in those chapters.

Why was Psalm 110 so important to the New Testament writers and to the church? Because Psalm 110 is the greatest and clearest of the messianic psalms.

There are not a large number of messianic psalms. We might include in their number Psalms 2, 22, 45, 72, and 110, plus a few others. But most of these psalms contain only messianic elements while other parts of them are apparently about the earthly king who was reigning at that time. By contrast, Psalm 110 is about a divine king exclusively, a king who has been placed at the right hand of God in heaven and who is presently engaged in extending his spiritual rule throughout the entire earth. Significantly, Psalm 110 also teaches that this divine messianic figure is to be a priest, performing priestly functions, and that additionally he is to be a judge who, at the end of time, will pronounce a final judgment on the nations and peoples of this earth.

Edward Reynolds (1599–1676) was one of the great expositors of Psalm 110, and he wrote that "this psalm is one of the fullest and most compendious prophecies of the person and offices of Christ in the whole Old Testament." He felt that "there are few, if any, of the articles of that creed which we all generally profess, which are not plainly expressed, or by most evident implication couched in this little model." Reynolds believed this psalm taught the doctrines of the divine Trinity; the incarnation, sufferings, resurrection, ascension, and intercession of Jesus Christ; the communion of saints; the last judgment; the remission of sins; and the life everlasting.[1]

Charles H. Spurgeon, the great Baptist preacher of the nineteenth century, taught that Psalm 110 is exclusively about Jesus Christ. David "is not the subject of it even in the smallest degree," he wrote.[2]

"The Lord Says to My Lord"

What about the first verse, the verse Jesus put before his questioners? In Hebrew, which they knew well, the first word of the verse is Jehovah or Yahweh (rendered "Lord"). In our English translations of Psalm 110, "Lord" is printed in capital letters to indicate this.[3] It refers to the God of Israel. The second word for "Lord" is "Adonai." Adonai refers to an individual greater than the speaker. So here is a case of David citing a word of God in which God tells another personage, who is greater than David, to sit at his right hand until he makes his enemies a footstool for his feet. This person can only be a divine Messiah, who is Jesus Christ.

This argument depends on two assumptions, of course. The first is that the psalm was written by David. Otherwise, it could be construed that an inferior member of the court flattered David by calling David "Lord," suggesting that he was to rule by God's special blessing. The second is that David wrote by inspiration so that what he said about this divine figure was true and was an actual prophecy of Jesus Christ. Jesus made both these assumptions when he spoke of "David, speaking by the Spirit."

It is astonishing, therefore, that many commentators, including even some so-called evangelicals, believe Psalm 110 was written by another human writer. They see it as flattery of a merely human king (though with messianic overtones), and they explain Jesus' words as a concession to the widespread but mistaken opinions of his age regarding David's authorship of the psalms.[4] This is a terrible error, and it misses the point of the psalm completely.

Those who deny that the psalm is by David say that "my Lord" refers to a king and that the psalm must therefore be addressed either to David or to one of the kings who followed him. They also argue that much of the psalm is about earthly battles and conquests and that it must therefore refer to an earthly ruler. Additionally, they say, it refers to a figure who is both a king and priest, and, since this is an idea foreign to the Old Testament, the psalm must date not from the time of David or even for hundreds of years after David but from the time of the Maccabees, nearly a thousand years later.[5]

None of these points hold up; the problems with each are transparent. And in any case, in Matthew, Jesus sets his seal upon the Davidic authorship of Psalm 110, even adding that David was speaking by the inspiration of the Holy Spirit when he wrote it.

Don Carson answers the liberal arguments with ten points, showing among other things that (1) the heading of Psalm 110 assigns it to David; (2) the psalm uses such extravagant language ("a priest forever," for example) that it is either a case of the most unbounded hyperbole or about a figure actually greater than David, that is, a Messiah to come; and (3) there is no reason why David, an inspired and insightful writer of others psalms as well, could not have foreseen and written about the Messiah's dual paternity, being both his own descendant and the Son of God. In any case, Jesus attributed the psalm to David and brought this understanding of Psalm 110 into the Christology of the early Christian church.[6]

Derek Kidner expressed the issue well:

> Nowhere in the Psalter does so much hang on the familiar title *A Psalm of David* as it does here; nor is the authorship of any other psalm quite so emphatically endorsed in other parts of Scripture. To amputate this opening phrase, or to allow it no reference to the authorship of the psalm, is to be at odds with the New Testament, which finds King David's acknowledgment of his "Lord" highly significant. For while other psalms share with this one the exalted language which points beyond the reigning king to the Messiah, here alone the king himself does homage to this personage—thereby settling two important questions: whether the perfect king was someone to come, or simply the present ruler idealized; and whether the one to come would be merely man at his best, or more than this.
>
> Our Lord gave full weight to David's authorship and David's words, stressing the former twice by the expression "David himself" and the latter by the comment that he was speaking "in the Holy Spirit" (Mark 12:36ff.), and by

insisting that his terms presented a challenge to accepted ideas of the Messiah, which must be taken seriously.[7]

Peter preached on this text on the Day of Pentecost (Acts 2:34–36), and his conclusion is as valid today as it was then, or when David penned the verse a thousand years before Peter: "'Therefore . . . be assured of this: God has made this Jesus, whom you crucified, both Lord and Christ.' When the people heard this, they were cut to the heart and said to Peter and the other apostles, 'Brothers, what shall we do?' Peter replied, 'Repent and be baptized, every one of you, in the name of Jesus Christ for the forgiveness of your sins'" (Acts 2:36–38). So also should we repent and commit ourselves to Jesus Christ.

"Sit at My Right Hand"

Psalm 110:1 also speaks of the Messiah's position at the right hand of God in heaven and of his lordship over all things in heaven and on earth. Jesus did not elaborate on this part of the verse because his first question had been enough to confound his enemies. But the rest of the verse as well as the psalm as a whole could hardly have been lost on them. Verse 1 is an oracle, that is, a direct and specific word from God—"Sit at my right hand until I make your enemies a footstool for your feet"—and what it tells us is that the Messiah was to reign over all things from heaven. We are familiar with the idea from the Apostles' Creed, which many Christians recite together each week: "He [Jesus] ascended into heaven and is seated on the right hand of God the Father Almighty."

What does it mean to sit at God's right hand? In the ancient world, to sit at a person's right hand was to occupy a place of honor; a seat at the right hand of the host was a place of honor at a dinner. But to sit at a king's right hand was more than mere honor. It was to share in his rule. It signified participation in the royal dignity and power, like a son ruling with his father. This is what Jesus has done since his resurrection and ascension.

Paul wrote about this to the Philippians, saying:

> Therefore God exalted him to the highest place
>   and gave him the name that is above every name,
> that at the name of Jesus every knee should bow,
>   in heaven and on earth and under the earth,
> and every tongue confess that Jesus Christ is Lord,
>   to the glory of God the Father.
>
> Philippians 2:9–11

What a tremendous gulf there is between God's evaluation of his beloved Son and the scorn people had for him when he was on earth, including the scorn of these very Pharisees. When he was on earth, Jesus was despised and rejected, harassed and hated. At last he was unjustly arrested, tried, and cruelly executed. But God reversed all that, for he raised him from the dead and received him into heaven, saying, "Sit at my right hand until I make your enemies a footstool for your feet."

Jesus is at God's right hand today, ruling over all things in heaven and on earth. This is God's doing, so it is not up to us whether Jesus Christ will be Lord or not. Jesus *is* Lord, and God has made him such. We can fight that Lordship and be broken by it—the verse says that Christ's enemies will be made his footstool—or we can submit to his rule in humble obedience with praise.

Most people's image of Jesus is at best that of a baby in a manger. It is a sentimental picture best reserved for Christmas and other sentimental moments. Others picture him hanging on a cross. That too is sentimental, though it is sentimentality of a different, pious sort. Jesus is not in a manger today. That is past. Nor is he hanging on a cross. That too is past. Jesus came once to die and after that to ascend to heaven to share in the fullness of God's power and great glory.

When Stephen, the first martyr, had his vision of the exalted Christ, it was of Jesus "standing at the right hand of God" to receive him into heaven (Acts 7:55). When John had his vision of Jesus on the Isle of Patmos, it was of one who was as God himself. The apostle was so overcome by Jesus' heavenly splendor that he "fell at his feet as though dead" (Rev. 1:17). We need to recover this understanding of who Jesus is and where he is now. If we do, we will worship him better and with greater reverence.

Walter Chantry says:

> Anyone who has caught a glimpse of the heavenly splendor and sovereign might of Christ would do well to imitate the saints of ages past. It is only appropriate to worship him with deep reverence. You may pour out great love in recognition of your personal relationship with him. He is your Lord. You are his and he is yours. However, you are not pals. He is Lord and Master. You are servant and disciple. He is infinitely above you in the scale of being. His throne holds sway over you for your present life and for assigning your eternal reward. A king is to be honored, confessed, obeyed and worshiped.

Indeed, adds Chantry, "Such humble gestures of adoration are the response required in the gospel. 'If you confess with your mouth, "Jesus is Lord," and believe in your heart that God raised him from the dead, you will be saved' (Rom. 10:9)."[8]

Jesus, the Lord

Matthew's account of this incident ends by saying, "from that day on no one dared to ask him any more questions" (v. 46). They were silenced, but they were not convinced. These men did not accept Jesus' teaching, and they eventually had him killed on the charge of blasphemy. But another Pharisee later came to accept what they did not accept and expressed it in classic language. He was Paul, who wrote at the beginning of his letter to the Romans about a gospel "promised beforehand through his prophets in the Holy Scriptures regarding his Son, who as to his human nature was a descendant of David, and who through the Spirit of holiness was declared with power to be the Son of God by his resurrection from the dead" (vv. 2–4).

This is a mature New Testament statement of the points made by Jesus in his confrontation with the Pharisees. To begin with, it contains a contrast between the two natures of the historical earthly Jesus. The first is the human nature. In the Greek text the word is *sarx*, meaning "flesh." But the term is not limited to the fleshly parts of our body as in English. It means "the whole man." This nature is contrasted with Christ's divine nature, which is described as "the Spirit of holiness." The Spirit of holiness does not refer to the Holy Spirit, though many have interpreted it that way, but to Christ's own spiritual or divine nature, which is holy. In other words, the first important thing about this section is its clear recognition of both the human and divine natures of Jesus.

Next, the statement contains a contrast between "descendant of David" and "Son of God." This corresponds to the earlier distinction, because "descendant of David" is linked to Jesus' human nature (it is as a man that he was born into David's family tree) while "Son of God" is linked to his divine nature.

The most important point is the contrast between the word *was*, the verb used in the first part of this descriptive sentence, and *declared*, which is the verb in part two. *Was* is actually the word *became*, and it means that Jesus took on a form of existence that he had not had previously. Before his birth to Mary, at what we call the beginning of the Christian era, Jesus was and had always been God. That is why the other verb that refers to his Godhead is *declared*. He was *declared* to be God, but he *became* man at that particular past point in history by the incarnation. In the short compass of just these twenty-eight Greek words (forty-one in English, vv. 3–4), Paul gave a Christology that unfolds in complete terms what Jesus taught in the question he asked the Pharisees. Jesus is a divine Messiah and Savior; he is both man and God.

The conclusion is that Jesus Christ is the very essence of Christianity. He is the Lord, and because he is, you ought to turn from all known sin and follow him. You may dispute his claims. Millions do. But if they are true, if Jesus is who he claimed to be, there is no reasonable or right option open to you other than your complete allegiance to him. Colonel Robert Ingersoll, a well-known and self-proclaimed agnostic of the last century, was no friend of Christianity, but he said on one occasion, though in a critical vein, "Christianity cannot live in peace with any other form of faith. If that religion be true, there is but one Savior, one inspired book and but one little narrow . . . path that leads to heaven."[9]

That is true, if Jesus is the eternal Son of God who became man to achieve your salvation. Is he? Is he the Son of God? Is he the Savior? If he is, you ought to heed his call for your repentance and faith—it is the demand of the gospel—and follow him.

54

Seven Woes on False Religion

Matthew 23:1-39

Then Jesus said to the crowds and to his disciples: "The teachers of the law and the Pharisees sit in Moses' seat. So you must obey them and do everything they tell you. But do not do what they do, for they do not practice what they preach. They tie up heavy loads and put them on men's shoulders, but they themselves are not willing to lift a finger to move them.

"Everything they do is done for men to see: They make their phylacteries wide and the tassels on their garments long; they love the place of honor at banquets and the most important seats in the synagogues; they love to be greeted in the marketplaces and to have men call them 'Rabbi.'

"But you are not to be called 'Rabbi,' for you have only one Master and you are all brothers. And do not call anyone on earth 'father,' for you have one Father, and he is in heaven. Nor are you to be called 'teacher,' for you have one Teacher, the Christ. The greatest among you will be your servant. For whoever exalts himself will be humbled, and whoever humbles himself will be exalted.

"Woe to you, teachers of the law and Pharisees, you hypocrites!...

"O Jerusalem, Jerusalem, you who kill the prophets and stone those sent to you, how often I have longed to gather your children together, as a hen gathers her chicks under her wings, but you were not willing. Look, your house is left to you desolate. For I tell you, you will not see me again until you say, 'Blessed is he who comes in the name of the Lord.'"

If anyone ever finds himself thinking that in matters of religion all views are relative and any sincere faith and practice will do, that person needs to read Jesus' denunciation of the Pharisees' religion preserved in Matthew 23. People have compared religion to a mountain with heaven on top and with many roads that lead up to it. Or they have thought like Edward Gibbon, the author of *The History of the Decline and Fall of the Roman Empire*, who said that in the days of the empire the various modes of worship that prevailed "were considered by the people as equally true, by the philosophers as equally false, and by the magistrates as equally useful."[1]

Jesus did not accept these easy misconceptions. He was aware of our faults and understood our failures, but he never suggested for a moment that any faith would do. On the contrary, he taught that there is but one way to God, namely, himself (John 14:6), and that any teaching that masks that way or keeps men and women from it is damnable.

Matthew 23, the chapter we come to now, is the fifth of six collections of Jesus' teachings in this Gospel. The others are the Sermon on the Mount (Matt. 5–7); the commissioning of the Twelve (Matt. 10:5–42); the parables of the kingdom (Matt. 13:1–52); teaching about the character of those who will be part of the kingdom (Matt. 18); and the sermon on the Mount of Olives that follows chapter 23 (Matt. 24–25).

Matthew 23 is probably a collection of things Jesus said not only at this time but on other occasions as well. It has a parallel in Luke 11:37–54 from an earlier point in his ministry. Matthew 23 also runs into the longer and last discourse in chapters 24 and 25, though it should be considered separately. It is radically different in its theme, and it is addressed to a different audience, to the crowds and teachers of the law rather than to the disciples exclusively. Moreover, it is a powerful climax to the section of the Gospel that I have called "The King's Final Break with Judaism." Jesus had spoken against the religion of the Pharisees earlier (Matt. 15:7). He had warned his disciples about their harmful teachings (Matt. 16:5–12). Here his exposure and warnings become public. The Pharisees and the teachers of the law had rejected him. They were even then plotting to have him killed. Now he rejects them and warns those he is about to leave behind of the Pharisees' deadly influence.

The Problem with the Pharisees

Matthew Henry, the author of the magnificent six-volume *Commentary on the Whole Bible*, says about some hypocritical preachers: "When in the pulpit, [they] preach . . . so well that it is a pity they should ever come out; but, when out of the pulpit, [they] live . . . so ill that it is a pity they should ever come in."[2] This is what Jesus seems to be saying at the start of the chapter, though his words grow more negative as his exposure of the Pharisees proceeds. These men taught the Scriptures; in that they were right. Their teachings, when accurate, should be obeyed. On the other hand, their practices belied their teaching and should not be imitated.

What was wrong with the Pharisees? We must remember that they were the most highly regarded figures of their day. They believed the Scriptures and had made it their duty to obey them in even the smallest particulars.

Their very name meant "separated," meaning that they were trying to separate themselves from all contaminations of sin. They were not flagrant sexual offenders nor outright thieves nor murderers. When the Pharisee of Jesus' parable said he was neither a robber, nor an evildoer, nor an adulterer and that he fasted twice a week and gave a tithe of all he acquired, he was probably being quite honest. This was the way these men actually lived.

What was wrong with them then? The answer given in verses 4–7 is this: Their character was the exact opposite of that required of the citizens of Christ's kingdom (Matt. 18:1–35), which meant that in spite of their religious professions and stringent legal practices, they did not actually know God and had not been changed inwardly by him. They should have been humble, compassionate, loving, and forgiving, as Jesus was. But they were actually: (1) *hypocritical* ("they do not practice what they preach," v. 3); (2) *indifferent* ("they tie up heavy loads and put them on men's shoulders, but they themselves are not willing to lift a finger to move them," v. 4); and (3) *proud* ("everything they do is done for men to see," v. 5).

These men wanted to be teachers. This is what "Moses' seat" refers to. There was actually a stone seat at the front of most synagogues, and rabbis sat down to teach. Jesus had done this himself when he preached his first sermon in the synagogue at Nazareth (Luke 4:20). We preserve the idea when we speak of a professorial "chair" at a university. The Pharisees had been using their position as teachers to get praise for themselves while making it nearly impossible for those they taught actually to learn the Bible's truths and come to God, and Jesus strongly condemned them for those sins.

A Contrast: Jesus' Teaching

Jesus' teaching was a reversal of the Pharisees' desires for themselves (vv. 8–12). They wanted to be thought important and to be praised by the people for their religious achievements. But Jesus said that his disciples were to be self-effacing and humble, even to the point of declining titles such as "rabbi," "father," and "teacher," and to be servants to other people instead. Jesus did not mean there should never be teachers in the church, for the abilities to pastor and teach were some of the gifts to be given to the church by the risen Lord (Eph. 4:11). He only meant that his followers were not to seek such positions in order to be praised by men.

Verses 11–12 are a reiteration of Jesus' teaching about the character of those who would follow him, already considered in the study of chapter 18: "The greatest among you will be your servant. For whoever exalts himself will be humbled, and whoever humbles himself will be exalted." This seems to have been Jesus' favorite text, since he taught it in various forms and on numerous occasions.

Seven Terrible Woes

In the Sermon on the Mount, Jesus had pronounced multiple blessings on the godly. Here, in the latter half of Matthew 23, he pronounces seven woes on the wicked.[3] This follows an established Old Testament pattern, seen for example in Isaiah 5:8–23, where there are six woes, and in Habakkuk 2:6–20, where there are five. A woe is a lament or wail concerning the final end for evil people. Here each woe is followed by a reason for it.

1. *For making salvation hard for other people (v. 13).* In the first part of chapter 23, Jesus criticized the Pharisees for wanting to be at the top of the religious pyramid, to lead the parade, as we might say. But in their desire to receive the praise of the people, it is as if they had led the parade to the very doors of heaven but then had refused to go in and had effectively blocked the door for others. The kingdom of heaven is Christ's kingdom, of course. So Jesus is saying that the Pharisees were standing in the way of others who, apart from them, might find salvation.

This is a terrible thing to say of religious leaders, but it is a true indictment of many in our day as well as in the time of Jesus. Is it not true of ministers who lead Christian congregations but who never explain the way of salvation through faith in Christ alone? Is it not a just indictment of seminary professors who undermine belief in the authority of the Bible, the deity of Christ, miracles, the efficacy of Jesus' atoning death, and the bodily resurrection, while pretending to serve the church of Christ that pays their salaries? Is it not a proper assessment of professors who write destructive books masquerading as explanations of the Bible's teaching? I know of countless examples of such Pharisaic evils, and I can echo Christ's judgment when he calls down woe on such people for their conduct.

Woe! Woe! A thousand times woe. Would it not be better for such teachers that millstones had been hung around their necks and that they had been cast into the sea rather than have been allowed to lead even one of Christ's little ones to destruction (Matt. 18:6)?

2. *For corrupting converts (v. 15).* The second of Jesus' woes goes beyond the first, for now it is not merely a question of false teachers stopping people from entering Christ's kingdom but of their drawing some into their own corrupt camp and corrupting them by doing so.

Over the centuries the Jews had not been a particularly evangelistic people, since being a Jew was usually defined in ethnic terms. Yet there seems to have been a truly evangelistic fervor during the time of Jesus Christ. We see a reflection of this in the Judaizers who opposed Paul, traveling as far as Galatia to corrupt the fledgling faith of his Gentile converts. Jesus acknowledged the Pharisees' zeal to "travel over land and sea to win a single convert." But what is the value of doing so if the convert becomes "twice as much a son of hell" as those who have converted him? It is an observable fact that people converted to a fanatical position are often more corrupt in their zeal than those who were in the movement from the start.

3. *For trivializing religion (vv. 16–22).* The third accusation deals with the casuistry of these religious professionals. Casuistry involves making minute distinctions in law in order to avoid the true meaning of the law or escape its consequences. In explaining this indictment, Jesus used examples of which he had spoken at other times and in other places, chiefly the way in which lawyers distinguished between legally binding and nonbinding oaths. Their position was that only oaths taken in the name of God were binding. But since the Jews did not usually use the name of God in their speech but rather employed euphemisms such as "heaven," or the "temple," or God's "throne," it became a debatable matter whether a specific oath was in the name of God or not. The Jews would call swearing by the temple invalid, while swearing by the gold of the temple was valid. Swearing by the altar was insignificant, but swearing by the gift that had been placed on the altar counted.

This is a trivialization of truth, and it was countered by Jesus when he said in the Sermon on the Mount, "But I tell you, Do not swear at all. . . . Simply let your 'Yes' be 'Yes,' and your 'No,' 'No'; anything beyond this comes from the evil one" (Matt. 5:34, 37). Jesus called people who handle truth in this useless and corrupting way "blind guides," meaning that they cannot see spiritual issues clearly and therefore not only lead others astray but fall into a pit themselves (Matt. 15:14). Are we to suppose that there is nothing of this in today's religious circles? I suggest that this happens whenever teachers make delicate distinctions about things the Bible teaches, arguing, "This may be sin, but this closely related type of misconduct is not" or, "Jesus may be saying this, but again he may be saying something quite different." They fail to take the Bible's statements at face value and fail to insist not only that truth is truth but that it is always truth and is binding on everyone.

Process theology is especially guilty of this, for it asserts that God himself is changing and that what was true at one time is not necessarily true today and that what was wrong in the days of our fathers may actually be virtuous now. Indeed, we ourselves are changing. We are creating reality, and the values we create for ourselves are as valid as those from any former moment of world history. Ministers are guilty of this failure when they shade the truth of Bible doctrine so as not to offend powerful or wealthy people or merely those who listen to them.

4. *For neglecting what is actually important (vv. 23–24).* Jesus' fourth charge is that the Pharisees fretted over the law's minutia while neglecting matters that were ultimately important. His example is the way the Pharisees handled tithing. The law required tithing of grain, wine, oil, and the firstborn of the flocks (Deut. 14:22–29). Leviticus 27:30 also mentions fruit from trees. But the Pharisees had greatly expanded this to include a tenth of even household spices such as mint, dill, and cumin. These were grown in household plots and existed in small amounts. Jesus' complaint, therefore, is about their preoccupation with mere trivia. He does not say they are wrong to tithe spices. On the contrary, they should not neglect such tithing (v. 23). What was wrong

is that they allowed a concern for minutia to obscure such weightier matters as "justice, mercy and faithfulness" (v. 23).

Do we do the same today? We do if we allow small points of theology or religious practice to crowd out the pursuit of justice for every human being, showing mercy to the poor and helpless, and being faithful to God in living for and serving him. Micah asked, "And what does the LORD require of you?" He answered wisely, "To act justly and to love mercy and to walk humbly with your God" (Micah 6:8).

5. *For self-indulgence (vv. 25–26)*. The Pharisees debated about what it means to keep a kosher kitchen, and the rules they devised were many and complex. William Barclay reports on what some of them were like.

> An earthen vessel which is hollow becomes unclean only on the inside and not on the outside; and it can only be cleansed by being broken. The following earthen vessels cannot become unclean at all—a flat plate without a rim, an open coal-shovel, a grid-iron with holes in it for parching grains of wheat. On the other hand, a plate with a rim, or an earthen spice-box, or a writing-case can become unclean. Of vessels made of leather, bone, wood and glass, flat ones do not become unclean; deep ones do. If they are broken, they become clean.

After a few more examples, Barclay concludes: "The food or drink inside a vessel might have been obtained by cheating or extortion or theft; it might be luxurious and gluttonous; that did not matter, so long as the vessel itself was ceremonially clean."[4]

The obvious application of this is to the concern even most church-going people seem to have for keeping up appearances. As long as we go to church, talk nicely, give a bit of our money to charitable causes, and do our civic duty, it does not seem to matter much whether we are dishonest in business, covetous in money matters, cruel in dealings with our families, selfish, proud, or arrogant. We may even say, "What I do in my own private life does not matter; it's nobody's business but my own." Jesus did not think this way. On the contrary, he said, "You hypocrites! You clean the outside of the cup and dish, but inside they are full of greed and self-indulgence. Blind Pharisee! First clean the inside of the cup and dish, and then the outside also will be clean" (vv. 25–26).

6. *For wickedness within (vv. 27–28)*. The fifth woe leads naturally to the sixth, for having spoken of the dirty insides of their lives, like the contaminated inside of an outwardly polished cup, Jesus added the well-known illustration of whitewashed tombs containing "dead men's bones and everything unclean," a euphemism for decaying human matter.

This was an apt illustration for the moment. This was Passover week, and it was a Jewish practice to use the preceding month of Adar to renew the whitewashing on tombs with the purpose of marking them clearly so the pious who were on their way to Jerusalem for the Passover would not accidentally defile themselves by touching a place where the bodies of the dead were buried. Here Jesus criticizes the Pharisees, first for their hypocrisy, whitewashed without but corrupt within, but also for their fears about outward ceremonial defilement without being profoundly and more rightly troubled by the inward pollution of their lives.

If we are troubled by our equally polluted lives, we will flee to the cross of Christ where alone a true cleansing from sin may be found.

7. *For the murder of God's prophets (vv. 29–36)*. The seventh of these woes is both the climax and the most damning accusation. It was the charge that the Pharisees were the true sons of their ancestral fathers who killed the prophets of God who had been sent to them. Their fathers had murdered all the righteous persons of the past, from Abel, whose death is recounted in the earliest chapters of Genesis, to Zechariah, whose murder is recorded in 2 Chronicles 24:21, the last book of the Hebrew Bible.[5]

Wicked churchmen always kill the righteous. In verse 34, Jesus switches from the past ("shedding the blood of the prophets," v. 30) to the future, saying, "Therefore I am sending you prophets and wise men and teachers. Some of them you will kill and crucify; others you will flog in your synagogues and pursue from town to town. And so upon you will come all the righteous blood that has been shed on earth" (vv. 34–35). This happened. The early gospel preachers were flogged, pursued, and killed. Paul alone is an example. At last a terrible judgment fell on Israel through the destruction of their capital city and nation by the Romans.

Speaking the Truth with Tears

The last verses of Matthew 23 contain Jesus' final lament and prophecy, and they show that his judgments on Israel's leaders were spoken more with tears than with wrath (vv. 37–39). He cried, "O Jerusalem, Jerusalem, you who kill the prophets and stone those sent to you, how often I have longed to gather your children together, as a hen gathers her chicks under her wings, but you were not willing. Look, your house is left to you desolate. For I tell you, you will not see me again until you say, 'Blessed is he who comes in the name of the Lord.'"

We have all known people who like to cry woe and call down wrath on sinners. But no one is ready to speak about judgment who has not first shed tears for those who are affected. Luke says that Jesus literally wept over Jerusalem (Luke 19:41–44). You and I have seen many wrongs. There is much evil in the world. But have we ever really wept for anyone?

PART NINE

The Sermon
on the Mount of Olives

55

Living in the Last Days

Matthew 24:1–28

Jesus left the temple and was walking away when his disciples came up to him to call his attention to its buildings. "Do you see all these things?" he asked. "I tell you the truth, not one stone here will be left on another; every one will be thrown down."

As Jesus was sitting on the Mount of Olives, the disciples came to him privately. "Tell us," they said, "when will this happen, and what will be the sign of your coming and of the end of the age?"

Jesus answered: "Watch out that no one deceives you. For many will come in my name, claiming, 'I am the Christ,' and will deceive many. You will hear of wars and rumors of wars, but see to it that you are not alarmed. Such things must happen, but the end is still to come. Nation will rise against nation, and kingdom against kingdom. There will be famines and earthquakes in various places. All these are the beginning of birth pains.

"Then you will be handed over to be persecuted and put to death, and you will be hated by all nations because of me. At that time many will turn away from the faith and will betray and hate each other, and many false prophets will appear and deceive many people. Because of the increase of wickedness, the love of most will grow cold, but he who stands firm to the end will be saved. And this gospel of the kingdom will be preached in the whole world as a testimony to all nations, and then the end will come."

There are few things as fascinating as prophecy. Or as problematic! Prophecy is fascinating because most people would like to know the future. Some would like to know it out of fear. They would like to be able to avoid life's difficulties or tragedies. Some would like to know what is coming in order to plan for it successfully. If we could know what the stock market will do in the next few months or years, we could all become wealthy. Other people would like to know what is coming out of simple curiosity, to be on the inside track, as it were. Christian speculations about the future are often in this category. In the secular world, horoscopes, fortune-tellers, séances, tarot cards, and the popularity of cult figures such as Jeane Dixon show how fascinated most people are with what is coming.

But prophecy is also difficult. Most prophecies are vague. The famous prophecies of the Greek oracle at Delphi are examples. Once the oracle told a king that if he went into battle, he would destroy a great empire. He assumed it was the empire of the enemy, went to war, and was defeated. The kingdom that was destroyed was his own, but it could just as easily have been the other way around. Most prophecies simply do not come to pass.

Jesus' disciples were curious about the future, and the questions they asked about it provided the occasion for Jesus' famous teaching about the last things recorded in Matthew 24 and 25. It is called the Olivet Discourse because it took place on the Mount of Olives. It is the last of the six collections of Jesus' teachings in this Gospel: chapters 5–7, 10, 13, 18, 23, and 24–25. It is an important part of the Gospel, but it is also a passage that, together with its parallels in Mark 13 and Luke 21, has puzzled and divided commentators throughout the long ages of the church.

Out of this chapter, its parallels, and other specifically prophetic sections of the Bible has come a diversity of eschatological schemes. The major divisions are known as premillennialism, postmillennialism, and amillennialism. But there is also historic premillennialism and a view known as preterism, which is becoming popular in some Reformed circles at the present time. Preterism is the view that all or nearly all the events foretold in Matthew 24 and 25, as well as other passages (such as the Book of Revelation), have already come to pass and that all we have to look forward to is the end of the world and the final judgment.

This is not the place to discuss all these views. But we will touch on some of them as we try to understand what Jesus was teaching in this final collection of teachings in this Gospel.

The Disciples' Two Questions

The place to begin is with the disciples' double question in verse 3: "Tell us," they said, "when will this happen, and what will be the sign of your coming and of the end of the age?"

These were natural queries for them to raise in view of two things they had heard Jesus say. In the first two verses of this chapter, they had called Jesus' attention to the large buildings of the temple complex and had heard Jesus predict Jerusalem's destruction. "Do you see all these things?" he asked. "I tell you the truth, not one stone here will be left on another; every one will be thrown down" (v. 2). Again, just before this, at the end of that terrible list of woes spoken to Jerusalem's religious leaders (reported in Matthew 23), Jesus had spoken of his departure, saying to the citizens of Jerusalem,

"You will not see me again until you say, 'Blessed is he who comes in the name of the Lord'" (Matt. 23:39).

It was natural for the disciples to put those two sayings together. They probably associated Jesus' prediction of the city's destruction with his words about his return. But these were still two separate questions, and they came from separate contexts: When will Jerusalem be destroyed? What will be the sign of your coming and of the end of the age? Jesus answers the questions separately. In fact, that seems to be the main point of the passage. The disciples may have associated the fall of Jerusalem with Christ's coming and the end of the world, but Jesus did not want them to assume that these two matters are necessarily linked. On the contrary, although Jerusalem would fall quickly, within forty or so years of his prediction, the disciples were not to regard either it nor other historical disasters, however terrible, as signs of his coming. His return would be without warning, and they needed to be concerned about being ready for it whenever it took place.

Signs That Are Not Signs

The first part of Jesus' answer has to do with bad things that will happen but which are not in themselves signs of the end. He lists these in verses 4–14, then gives a particularly terrible example of such a bad thing in verses 15–22.

The signs that are not signs are: (1) false messiahs, (2) wars and rumors of wars, (3) famines and earthquakes, (4) persecutions, (5) apostasy, and (6) false prophets. It is easy to give many examples of these from the early years of church history. But that is not the point. The point is that false teachers, natural disasters, persecutions, forsaking of the faith by many, and false teachers will characterize history. We will always have these things. They are painful, and Jesus likens them to "the beginning of birth pains" (v. 8), but they are not signs that the end of the world is near. These things existed in the disciples' days, and they have existed in every age of church history up to and including our own. Indeed, some of them have taken a great deal of time to develop—nation rising against nation and the gospel being preached throughout the whole world, for instance. But the followers of Christ are not to be deceived by false teaching on this subject: "The end is still to come" (v. 6).

The Destruction of Jerusalem

The destruction of Jerusalem (vv. 15–22) is a particularly terrible example of the birth pains Jesus is predicting, and he discusses it in detail, for its own sake—it would be a time of unprecedented suffering—and because of the special significance of Jerusalem in biblical history.

There *was* to be a warning sign of *this* calamity: when "you see standing in the holy place 'the abomination that causes desolation,' spoken of through the prophet Daniel" (v. 15). Those words occur four times in Daniel (8:13; 9:27; 11:31; 12:11), where they seem to refer to the desecration of the temple by Antiochus Epiphanes in 168 B.C. Antiochus erected an altar to Zeus over the altar of burnt offering and sacrificed a pig on it, which was the worst possible affront to Judaism, a true "abomination."[1] But Jesus was not referring to this past event in Matthew 24. He was referring to something like it that would happen before the fall of Jerusalem and would be a warning to his followers to flee the city.

It is not clear to what coming event this actually refers, but it was most likely the approach of the Roman armies and their surrounding of the city during the Jewish War. The standards bore emblems of the legions and images of the emperor and were virtually worshiped by the soldiers. They were erected in the temple area after the city was subdued. The link between these standards and "the abomination that causes desolation" is strongly suggested by the parallel text in Luke 21:20, where "Jerusalem being surrounded by armies" takes the place of "abomination of desolation" found in Matthew.

Josephus describes the destruction of Jerusalem, saying that it was a time of distress unequaled in any previous destruction (*The Jewish War,* V, VI). Eusebius, the Christian historian, and a few other ancient writers say that the Christians fled Jerusalem prior to its fall and found refuge in the town of Pella in Perea (*Ecclesiastical History,* III, v, 3).

The Central Theme

The destruction of Jerusalem would be terrible, but this would still not be the end, which is why verses 23–28 revert to the original point and summarize it. The meaning of these verses goes something like this: "So if anyone says to you, 'Christ is here now,' even then don't be taken in by it; for that one will not be the Christ. Nor will these or any other signs be actual signs of the end. How will you know they are not? It is because the Son of Man will come suddenly, like lightning that is visible in an instant from east to west, and there will be no adequate warning signs of that decisive final coming."

All right, you say, but what should my attitude be in the midst of the terrible things I see occurring now? How should I live between the first coming of Jesus and his second coming, whenever that may be?

The Beginning of World War II

Let me answer the above questions by use of a powerful story. In the summer of 1939, Donald Grey Barnhouse was in Scotland, where he had been preaching. His family had been staying at a small resort on the coast of Normandy in France. He was to be in Belfast, Ireland, the first week in September for meetings, but because he had a free week between the close of the meetings in Scotland and the beginning of the meetings in Ireland, he decided to join his family in France during the interval.

When he handed his passport to the official at the airport in Croyden, he was questioned about his travel plans. He answered that he wanted to return by the end of the week so as to be in Belfast by Saturday night. The official said, "If you want to be in Belfast on Saturday, I strongly urge you not to go to France today." Barnhouse knew that Europe was in turmoil at the time. Hitler had just signed a treaty with Russia and was threatening to march into Danzig. Still, the possibility of actual war seemed remote. Barnhouse decided to go, but the official who stamped his passport did so grimly. "Don't forget that I warned you," he said.

There were soldiers everywhere in France, and the airport buildings had been turned into military barracks. When Barnhouse stopped at the desk to confirm his return reservation for Friday, he was told that no one was sure there would even be a flight on Friday. The flights might be canceled. But the threat seemed unreal with the joy of reunion on his mind.

Leaving the airport, the family drove down the coast a few miles to a peaceful little village. Hundreds of families were there, for this was the height of the French vacation season. From time to time an airplane appeared in the distance, and the beach suddenly became still as it drew closer. But when the vacationers saw that the plane was French, they returned to their activities. Monday went by. Tuesday. Wednesday. Finally, on Thursday morning word came that there would be no more flights to England. If Barnhouse wanted to return to England, he would have to go all the way to Paris and then travel back across France to the coast. Barnhouse left on the next train.

While he was on the train, the French ordered mobilization. In those days every man in France had been through military service, was part of the army, and knew what to do in case of an emergency. As soon as the order was received from Paris, mobilization was announced in every hamlet and village of the country, and there was an instant response.

Moreover, the tocsin sounded. In the Middle Ages, when few people knew how to read, Europe developed a code by which church bells were used to alert the countryside of important events or dangers. The bells would tell when young people were being married, when a child was being baptized, when death had occurred. They also told of war.

This code sounded from every tower in France as the Paris-bound train moved across the green fields. At every stop there were tragic scenes. Men by the hundreds were leaving their weeping wives and children and were boarding the trains that would take them to their particular mobilization centers and then on to fight the Germans. Many would never come back, and the towns through which the train was passing would later crumble under the bombs of the Allies as the Western armies came with their own hard liberation years later.

An hour after Barnhouse reached Paris, he was again on a train, this time speeding toward the coast. In the darkness—for it seemed very dark now—the train pulled up alongside the steamer, and within a few minutes the steamer moved out of the harbor toward England.

On board, the preacher made his way to the bridge and introduced himself to the captain. Together they listened to the radio reports. Hitler had invaded Danzig. The bombing was frightful. Chamberlain had called a meeting of his cabinet. If the Germans were not out of Danzig by eleven o'clock on Sunday morning, Chamberlain had said, war would be declared.

The captain, with British calmness, observed, "This time there will be no turning back. This is it." Barnhouse went to his cabin for a few fitful hours of sleep and then got up again to go ashore in England. It was Friday, September 1, 1939.

Once again it was a beautiful day as the train carried its passengers across Kent to London. At Victoria Station, Barnhouse caught a taxi to take him across the city to the station that serves the north of England. As he drew near he saw thousands of children lined up for immediate evacuation from London. He walked out among the children and saw a pitiful sight—children who in the fear and commotion of the moment were already victims of the war. One little child seemed to sum up the whole picture of this misery. He had been given some chocolate and had managed to smear it all over his face. He had wet his pants. And he had begun to cry, his cries an expression of misery mixed with terror. But nothing could be done. His case was but one little island of misery in the middle of a great continent of misery.

In time the train to the north left London, but it stopped constantly to allow troop trains and trains full of children to go past. The travelers reached Carlisle around midnight, and they spent the night in the crowded lobby of the station hotel. Then there was another train, which took most of Saturday to push on to the coast. That night, when he should have been in Belfast at the dinner that was to open the series of meetings, the preacher stood at the edge of the water and gazed at Ireland across the gray-blue sea.

After dark the ship that was to take him to Ireland set off. The steamer docked at Larne on the coast. Then another train made the run to Belfast, arriving just after three o'clock in the morning. The committee that had arranged the meetings was waiting, and they took Barnhouse through the lightless streets to his hotel. Church was at eleven o'clock, and they would be by to pick him up at 10:30 in the morning. One of them said, "I hope you will have a good sermon. It may be the last that some of the men will ever hear."

Barnhouse stood alone in his room, his luggage piled around him. Slowly he picked up a piece of paper that had been lying on the desk in the room and began to write the outline of his sermon for that morning. He said later, "I stood there and prayed, and suddenly I thought of the perfect text for that hour." Quickly he wrote the text followed by three or four thoughts that would be his subheads.

In the morning his friends came to drive him to St. Enoch's, perhaps the largest church in Ireland. The minister was quite beside himself, shaking the preacher's hand repeatedly. It was a few minutes before eleven o'clock. Chamberlain had announced that he would speak on the radio at that hour, and everyone sensed that he would declare war on Germany. "Thank God, I do not have to preach," the minister said over and over again. "The church will be full of lads who will never come back. I pray God will give you something for them."

As the little group started into the church, it occurred to Barnhouse that everyone would be home listening to the radio and that not many people would be there. But the church was full. Not one seat was empty. The service began. They sang hymns. An elder slipped a note to the pastor, who handed it to Barnhouse. It said, "No reply from Hitler. The prime minister has declared war." A moment later Barnhouse was introduced as the speaker.

He began by telling how he had outlined his sermon in the dim light of his hotel room at four o'clock in the morning, but that, in spite of the circumstances, he had a text for them that was the most wonderful text in the Bible for such a day, September 3, 1939. It was spoken by Jesus Christ, and it was a command: "You will hear of wars and rumors of wars, but see to it that you are not alarmed" (Matt. 24:6).

He then recounted the experiences he had had on his way to Belfast. He told of the horrors, but at each succeeding horror he stopped and repeated the text: *Do not be alarmed.* The tocsin will sound; mobilization will take place. *Do not be alarmed.* Millions of homes will be broken up. *Do not be alarmed.* Children will be torn from their mothers and will represent in their cries all the wails that have been going up from all the world. Jesus said, *Do not be alarmed.*

The tension was mounting in the church. But then, when monstrous grief had been piled on agonizing horror, Barnhouse stopped and said, "These words are either the words of a madman or they are the words of God." He shook his fist toward heaven and cried, "God, unless Jesus Christ is God, these words are the most horrible that could be spoken to men who have hearts that can weep and bowels that can be gripped by human suffering. Men are dying. *Do not be alarmed?* Children are crying in their misery with no beloved face in sight. *Do not be alarmed?* How can Jesus Christ say such a thing?"

But then came the answer. Jesus Christ is God. Jesus is the Lord of history. He is the God of detailed circumstance. Nothing has ever happened that has not flowed in the channel that God has dug for it. There have never been any events that have flamed up in spite of God to leave him astonished or confused. The sin of man has reduced the world to an arena of passion and fury. Men tear at each other's throats. Yet in the midst of the history of which Jesus Christ is Lord, each individual who has believed in him as the Savior will know the power of his resurrection and will learn that events, however terrible, cannot separate us from the love of God.[2]

This is our God, and this is the word of our God. Jesus knew what was to come in the war pits of human history, but he told his disciples, "Do not be alarmed." Wars have come, and they will come again. People will suffer. Men will die. But instead of dismay, we are to serve Jesus faithfully even in the midst of these bad things—until he comes again.

56

The Return of Jesus Christ

Matthew 24:29–35

"Immediately after the distress of those days

> *"'the sun will be darkened,*
> *and the moon will not give its light;*
> *the stars will fall from the sky,*
> *and the heavenly bodies will be shaken.'*

"At that time the sign of the Son of Man will appear in the sky, and all the nations of the earth will mourn. They will see the Son of Man coming on the clouds of the sky, with power and great glory. And he will send his angels with a loud trumpet call, and they will gather his elect from the four winds, from one end of the heavens to the other.

"Now learn this lesson from the fig tree: As soon as its twigs get tender and its leaves come out, you know that summer is near. Even so, when you see all these things, you know that it is near, right at the door. I tell you the truth, this generation will certainly not pass away until all these things have happened. Heaven and earth will pass away, but my words will never pass away."

I do not think there is any great difficulty understanding what Jesus says in the Olivet Discourse up to verse 28 of chapter 24. He has warned the disciples about disruptive world events that will not be signs of his return, and he has predicted the fall of Jerusalem, which, though an exceptionally traumatic event, would be merely another example of the kind of tragedies that will occur throughout history. But the easy part is over. Now we come to the part of the discourse that has given the most trouble to Bible students and commentators.

Was Jesus Mistaken?

The difficulties mostly have to do with timing. Jesus has spoken of the destruction of Jerusalem, which occurred in A.D. 70 by the Roman armies under the command of Titus. But then he continues, "Immediately after the distress of those days 'the sun will be darkened, and the moon will not give its light; the stars will fall from the sky, and the heavenly bodies will be shaken'" (v. 29). This could refer to something in the future, but if that is the case, why did Jesus use the word *immediately,* as in "*immediately* after the distress of those days"? Immediately should mean close in time to the destruction of Jerusalem. But if these portents are tied to the destruction of Jerusalem, we must admit candidly that they do not seem to have happened.

Nor is that all. The next verses begin "at that time" and go on to describe how the Son of Man will come in the clouds, with power and great glory, accompanied by the blast of a trumpet and the appearance of angels to gather the elect from the far corners of the earth. Again, that could be future. Most people have assumed it is. But if that is the case, why does Jesus say, "at that time"? And if he meant what he said, that he would return at the time of or soon after the destruction of Jerusalem, what he predicted did not happen.

We have a nearly identical problem in verse 33, where Jesus says, "When you see all these things, you know that it is near, right at the door." His second coming cannot be the sign of itself. "These things" must refer to things that will precede his return. But what can they be? If they are the tragedies leading up to the fall of Jerusalem, the second coming of the Lord did not follow those events, and Jesus would seem to have been mistaken.

The most apparent and (for some) the worst problem of all is Jesus' solemn affirmation: "I tell you the truth, this generation will certainly not pass away until all these things have happened" (v. 34). What can "this generation" be but the generation then living? Yet if that is what the words mean, Jesus must have been wrong, since many generations have come and gone since that time and Jesus has still not returned. The acclaimed English philosopher and social critic Bertrand Russell said Jesus' teaching about his return was one reason why he could not be a Christian. "He certainly thought that his second coming would occur in clouds of glory before the death of all the people who were living at that time," wrote Russell. But he added, "In that respect, clearly he was not so wise as some other people have been, and he was certainly not superlatively wise."[1]

Attempts at a Solution

There are two easy ways to solve these problems, but they have not been accepted by all commentators.

First, we can place all these events together at one point in time and locate that point at the end of history. One advantage of this view is that we can take the time references literally. The fall of Jerusalem, the signs in the sky, and the return of Jesus occur in tight chronological sequence. All are yet future, and the fall of Jerusalem fits events outlined in other biblical books such as Revelation. This is an understanding common among dispensationalists, for whom the distress of Jerusalem is linked to the great tribulation and precedes the battle of Armageddon and the subsequent reign of Jesus Christ on earth for a thousand years, the millennium. In this view, "this generation" refers to the generation living at the time of the final attack on Jerusalem or is understood to mean "this race," meaning that the Jews will not cease to exist as a race until this happens.

The main reason many people have not been persuaded by this handling of the details of Matthew 24 is that they believe verses 15–22 describe the destruction of Jerusalem by the Romans in A.D. 70. But they also have a problem with "this generation." Most commentators believe this can hardly mean anything other than the generation living at the time Jesus spoke these words.

The other easy way to solve the problem of the time references in Matthew 24 is to put these events together but to place them in the first Christian century in connection with the fall of Jerusalem to the Romans. In this view, the coming of Christ mentioned in verses 30 and 31 refers to his return in judgment on Jerusalem, and the signs of his coming are understood as Old Testament images of historical but earthshaking events. The "end of the age" (v. 3) means the end of the Jewish age, which is followed by the age of the church. This means that nearly everything in Matthew 24 and 25 is about God's judgment on Jerusalem, even Jesus' strong, reiterated warnings to watch and be ready for his return. The same is true for nearly the whole of the Book of Revelation. This view is known as preterism, which means "what has already taken place." Preterism has been affirmed recently in a guarded way by R. C. Sproul,[2] but it has a history of defenders going back quite a few years. One early proponent is J. Stuart Russell, on whose work Sproul largely depends.[3]

Why hasn't everyone accepted this view? One obvious reason is that it is difficult to see how Christ's coming on the clouds, with power and great glory, with the angels gathering his elect from the far corners of the earth, was fulfilled at the time of the destruction of Jerusalem.

There is this problem too—probably the most significant of all. If everything (or nearly everything) in these chapters is about the fall of Jerusalem, then the disciples' question about the end of the age is not really answered, at least not as almost anyone, including the disciples, would have understood it. The chapters most Christians have always looked to for assurance of the Lord's return and encouragement to be ready and watch for it are not about the Lord's future return at all. In fact, Jesus has virtually nothing to say about his second coming. Nor do any of the other biblical writers, including the author of Revelation.

The Flow of the Chapter

How do we solve these difficulties? History suggests that we probably cannot, at least not to everyone's satisfaction, since disagreements about this chapter have existed throughout church history. But let me try anyway, starting with the flow of thought in the chapter.

Verse 3. As I pointed out in the last study, Matthew 24 begins with the disciples' two important questions: (1) "When will this happen?" and (2) "What will be the sign of your coming and of the end of the age?" (v. 3). The first question was about the destruction of Jerusalem, which Jesus had predicted, and the second was about his glorious return, which he had also predicted—two events, though the disciples probably held them together in their minds. Jesus began by answering the second: "What will be the sign of your coming and of the end of the age?"

Verses 4–14. The first thing he told them is that there will be many earthshaking events that might be thought of as signs, but they will not be. The disciples were not to be troubled by them. They will include false messiahs, wars and rumors of wars, famines and earthquakes, persecutions, apostasy, and false prophets. These are "the beginnings of birth pains" (v. 8), but they are not signs of his return. This is because the gospel of the kingdom must be preached in the whole world before the end will come.

Verses 15–22. The next point Jesus makes is that there is going to be one particularly dreadful event, the destruction of Jerusalem, but even this will not be a sign of his return. The disciples should flee the city when they see these things beginning to happen, but this is still not the end.

Verses 23–28. At this point Jesus makes clear that the destruction of Jerusalem is only one example of the bad things that will happen to people in the course of world history. He does so by returning to what he said earlier about false messiahs. They will appear at this time, as at other times. They will not be true messiahs, and the disciples are not to be taken in by them. How will the disciples know that these pretenders are not the true Messiah? By the fact that they will appear in secret ("in the desert" or "in the inner rooms"), while Jesus' appearance will be sudden, unannounced, and immediately visible to all, just like lightning that flashes suddenly and is seen at once by everyone.

Verses 29–35. This leads to Jesus' specific teaching about the second coming. There will be signs in the sky, including "the sign of the Son of Man" (whatever that may be), a loud trumpet call, and the work of angels in gathering the elect from the far reaches of the earth. But the point of these "signs" is not that they will precede Jesus' coming, as if they will be given to enable people to see them and get ready. On the contrary, they will coincide with Christ's coming and will be sudden. If a person is not ready beforehand, there will be nothing he or she will be able to do when Jesus actually returns. Such a person will be lost.

Verses 36–51. In the last section of the chapter, Jesus stresses the sudden-ness of his return by a historical reference and several images. His coming will be like the flood in the days of Noah, or like a thief that enters a house at an unexpected time, or a master who suddenly returns home. Jesus' ser-vants must be ready since "the master of that servant will come on a day when he does not expect him and at an hour he is not aware of" (v. 50).

The Difficult Time References

So far so good. But what about the time references, the problem that has led some commentators to the dispensational or preterist positions? I would argue that these must be fitted to the other statements, namely, that dis-tressful times are not signs of Christ's second coming and that his coming will be so unexpected that no one, not even the angels in heaven nor Jesus himself, can say when it will be. Let's take the references one at a time.

1. What do we do with the words *"immediately after the distress of those days"* *(v. 29)?* The answer is that "the distress of those days" must refer to all the many distressful times throughout history, though perhaps culminating in a time of unusual distress just prior to the Lord's return. Certainly the ear-lier statements about false Christs, false prophets, and apostasy support what other Bible writers have to say about the end of history. In fact, when we read passages such as 2 Peter 3:3–13, we hear deliberate echoes of what Jesus taught in Matthew. And why not? It was from Jesus that Peter and the other writers learned it.

What about the sun being darkened, the moon failing to give light, and the stars falling from heaven? Although preterists rightly point out that this is common Old Testament imagery for any cataclysmic historical event—drawn from texts such as Isaiah 13:9–10; Ezekiel 32:7–8; Joel 2:30, 31; 3:15; Amos 8:9—it is also the case that words such as these occur in New Testament passages where they are clearly associated with Christ's coming at the end of the age. D. A. Carson cites as examples texts such as Matthew 13:40–41; 16:27; 25:31; 1 Corinthians 15:52; 1 Thessalonians 4:14–17; 2 Thessalonians 1:7; 2:1–8; 2 Peter 3:10–12; Revelation 1:7.[4]

Moreover, in the parallel passage in Luke 21, the reference to the sun, moon, and stars is prefaced by the prediction that "Jerusalem will be tram-pled on by the Gentiles until the times of the Gentiles are fulfilled" (v. 24). That must refer to the Gentile domination of Jerusalem from the time of its fall until at least the present age. But it is only after this that Jesus says he will appear the second time. Paul expresses similar ideas about the Gentile age in Romans 11:11–25.

2. *"At that time the sign of the Son of Man will appear in the sky"* (v. 30). I haven't the faintest idea what the sign of the Son of Man is, nor should I. That is something only those who actually see it will know. But if what I have said about the word *immediately* is correct, this particular time reference is not difficult. It simply links the actual appearance of Jesus to the astronomical

irregularities described in verse 29. At the end of the times of distress, which is all of human history, the sun, moon, and stars will be darkened, and at that time Jesus will appear in heaven with his holy angels. That is when the angels will gather the elect.

3. *"When you see all these things"* and *"this generation will certainly not pass away until all these things have happened" (vv. 33–34).* These two references go together because they are part of the same paragraph and occur one right after the other. There is a slight change of tone with verse 32. Jesus has spoken of his sudden return in glory, but now he is giving a lesson for those who will be living in the period between his first coming and his second. They are to learn from the fig tree, which signals summer by developing tender twigs and by putting out leaves. "All these things" are compared to those tender twigs and leaves, which means that the distressful things of verses 2–28 show that the Lord's return is imminent, which it always is!

What about "this generation"? In this view it really is the generation living at the time Christ spoke these words, because that generation actually did see "all these things."[5] They knew of many false Christs, heard of wars and rumors of wars, experienced famines and earthquakes, witnessed apostasy, and heard of false prophets. So has every generation since. Therefore, we have all seen everything we need to see or can see prior to Jesus' return. We have nothing to look forward to except the second coming. The bottom line of this is that we need to be ready, because "no one knows about that day or hour" when the Lord will come (v. 36).

The Lessons to Be Drawn

Let me go back and review the lessons we should draw from the first thirty-five verses of Matthew 24. The coming of Christ and the end of the world are imminent, meaning that they can occur at any moment. Therefore, our present responsibilities must be:

1. *To watch out that no one deceives us (vv. 4, 26).* Jesus has a great deal to say about deception in this discourse. In fact, having warned against false Christs at the very beginning of the chapter, he returns to this same point after speaking of the fall of Jerusalem, saying, "If anyone says to you, 'Look, here is the Christ!' or 'There he is!' do not believe it. For false Christs and false prophets will appear and perform great signs and miracles to deceive even the elect—if that were possible" (vv. 23–24). He repeats this again in verse 26, where he warns against expecting to find the Christ "out in the desert" or "in the inner rooms."

It would be possible to write a history of the church in terms of the errors that have been foisted upon it, sometimes from without but more often from within, and of how believers have either resisted such errors or have been taken in by them. We have deceivers today, but we are warned here not to be fooled by them.

2. *To be settled even in times of war or threats of war (v. 6).* This warning includes all political and historical events and is a reminder that the city of God is distinct from man's city and will survive regardless of what happens in the world. We are not to be unduly encouraged by political events, nor unduly frightened by them. Charles Colson once wisely reminded the delegates to one of the Christian Booksellers conventions after the president of the United States had spoken and they were cheering wildly, "We must remember that the kingdom of God does not arrive on Air Force One."

3. *To stand firm to the end (v. 13).* We speak of the perseverance of the saints, meaning that God perseveres with his people so that none of those he has elected to salvation will be lost. Jesus taught this clearly in John 10, saying, "My sheep listen to my voice; I know them, and they follow me. I give them eternal life, and they shall never perish; no one can snatch them out of my hand" (vv. 27–28). But while it is true that God perseveres with us, it is also true that we must persevere. That is what Jesus is speaking of here. He is encouraging us to keep on keeping on, since there is no promise of salvation for those who abandon the faith or deny Christ.

The apostle Paul certainly believed in and taught the security of every genuine believer, but he also wrote, "If we endure, we will also reign with him. If we disown him, he will also disown us" (2 Tim. 2:12). Those words seem to have been based on Jesus' teaching in Matthew 10:32–33.

4. *To preach the gospel throughout the world (v. 14).* This is the chief task of the church in the present age. The followers of Christ will be persecuted, and the love of many will grow cold. But throughout the ages of church history, however long they may be, Christians must be strong, faithful, and determined in the task of carrying the gospel to the lost. In fact, this is the note on which the Gospel ends. Jesus' last words to his disciples were, "Therefore go and make disciples of all nations, baptizing them in the name of the Father and of the Son and of the Holy Spirit, and teaching them to obey everything I have commanded you. And surely I am with you always, to the very end of the age" (Matt. 28:19–20).

As we read this chapter, rather than wondering about the specific moment when Jesus will return, we should be asking ourselves if we are ready for it, whenever it might be. The next section of the chapter warns us to be ready precisely because we do not know the time of Jesus' return.

57

Keeping Watch and Being Ready

Matthew 24:36–51

"No one knows about that day or hour, not even the angels in heaven, nor the Son, but only the Father. As it was in the days of Noah, so it will be at the coming of the Son of Man. For in the days before the flood, people were eating and drinking, marrying and giving in marriage, up to the day Noah entered the ark; and they knew nothing about what would happen until the flood came and took them all away. That is how it will be at the coming of the Son of Man. Two men will be in the field; one will be taken and the other left. Two women will be grinding with a hand mill; one will be taken and the other left.

"Therefore keep watch, because you do not know on what day your Lord will come. But understand this: If the owner of the house had known at what time of night the thief was coming, he would have kept watch and would not have let his house be broken into. So you also must be ready, because the Son of Man will come at an hour when you do not expect him.

"Who then is the faithful and wise servant, whom the master has put in charge of the servants in his household to give them their food at the proper time? It will be good for that servant whose master finds him doing so when he returns. I tell you the truth, he will put him in charge of all his possessions. But suppose that servant is wicked and says to himself, 'My master is staying away a long time,' and he then begins to beat his fellow servants and to eat and drink with drunkards. The master of that servant will come on a day when he does not expect him and at an hour he is not aware of. He will cut him to pieces and assign him a place with the hypocrites, where there will be weeping and gnashing of teeth."

An important contrast exists between the verses we looked at in the last study and the opening verse of the section of Matthew 24 to which we now come. It is the difference between

515

"you know" in verse 33 and "no one knows" in verse 36. What the disciples were to know is that "when you see all these things" the end will be "near, right at the door." "These things" refer to the terrible characteristics of their age, and ours—false messiahs, wars, earthquakes, famines, persecutions, apostasy, and false prophets. Having seen these things, we should know that the return of Jesus Christ is near, even at the door. That door could be flung open by Christ at any moment.

On the other hand, we do not know when Christ will return. When Jesus said, "No one knows about that day or hour" (v. 36), he did not mean that smart Bible teachers are nevertheless able to calculate the year or the decade. Those who have tried to do so have always been wrong.

This deliberate contrast reinforces what I have been saying about this chapter, namely: (1) that the return of Christ to gather his elect and judge the world is yet future; (2) that we do not know when this will be; and that, therefore, (3) we must keep watch and be ready, since we will be lost and perish if we do not. Jesus said, "He who stands firm to the end will be saved" (Matt. 10:22).

Everything in this last discourse, even the prediction of the fall of Jerusalem, makes these points. Nothing the disciples or we will ever see is a sure sign of the end, for the end will come without warning. As D. A. Carson writes, "The hour remains unknown until it arrives; and then the cleavage is sudden, absolute, and irreversible."[1]

Let me make this point another way. About half of Matthew 24 deals with signs that are not true signs of Christ's return (vv. 4–26, 32–35). A very small section describes the return of Christ itself (vv. 27–31). But a third of chapter 24 (vv. 36–51) and all of chapter 25 (vv. 1–46), a total of sixty-two verses, warn us to get ready since we do not know when that day of final reckoning will be. Or to put it yet another way, Jesus stresses this single essential point with seven historical references, verbal pictures or parables—four in this chapter and three in the next.

The application is clear: Are you watching? Are you ready for Jesus Christ's return?

The Days of Noah

The first story Jesus uses to emphasize the suddenness of his coming and the need to be ready for it is the destruction of the earth by the flood in the days of Noah. This was a well-known example of God's judgment of wickedness, and it is referred to quite naturally by Old Testament prophets such as Isaiah (Isa. 54:9) and Ezekiel (Ezek. 14:14, 20) and by New Testament writers such as the author of Hebrews (Heb. 11:7) and Peter (1 Peter 3:20; 2 Peter 2:5). Jesus refers to it in verses 37–39.

The point of these verses is that the waters of the flood came suddenly and that those who were not prepared drowned. But this also points to a world that will be largely unbelieving at the time of Christ's return. I emphasize this because some hold that Christ's kingdom will eventually triumph in the world. This view is usually referred to as postmillennialism. The word *millennium* refers to the reign of Christ (for a thousand years, if interpreted literally), and *postmillennialism* means that Jesus will return only after his rule has been universally established. According to this view, Jesus reigns in and through the church and will return only after the church's mission is fulfilled.

Postmillennialism was popular in former centuries when the supposedly "Christian nations" were extending their colonial power. It is not as popular today, when the West is in evident decline. True, the mission of the church does not depend on Western Christianity, and a great growth of Christianity is taking place today in the third world. But even when we turn from history and restrict ourselves to explicit scriptural teaching, not much encourages us to think in this falsely optimistic way. On the contrary, those who were taught by Jesus say that there will be terrible wickedness and even widespread apostasy in the church when Christ returns.

Peter wrote of the presence of false prophets in the last days, saying, "They will secretly introduce destructive heresies" (2 Peter 2:1). Again, "In the last days scoffers will come, scoffing and following their own evil desires. They will say, 'Where is this "coming" he promised? Ever since our fathers died, everything goes on as it has since the beginning of creation'" (2 Peter 3:3–4). Almost all of 2 Peter 2 and 3, two-thirds of the letter, describes the evil of the final days.

Jude is almost entirely about such times, and the author seems to echo Peter when he writes, "Remember what the apostles of our Lord Jesus Christ foretold. They said to you, 'In the last times there will be scoffers who will follow their own ungodly desires.' These are the men who divide you, who follow mere natural instincts and do not have the Spirit" (vv. 17–19).

Paul wrote, "The Spirit clearly says that in later times some will abandon the faith and follow deceiving spirits and things taught by demons" (1 Tim. 4:1). Or again, "There will be terrible times in the last days. People will be lovers of themselves, lovers of money, boastful, proud, abusive, disobedient to their parents, ungrateful, unholy, without love, unforgiving, slanderous, without self-control, brutal, not lovers of the good, treacherous, rash, conceited, lovers of pleasure rather than lovers of God—having a form of godliness but denying its power" (2 Tim. 3:1–5).

None of these passages teaches that we are to be pessimistic. We must preach Christ everywhere, knowing that all whom God has elected to salvation will be saved. Not one will be lost. But neither do these passages teach an increasingly successful expansion of the gospel, still less a triumphant expansion of organized Christianity throughout the world. Rather, they encourage a faithful adherence to and preaching of the gospel in spite of the fact that it will not be universally received and in spite of the fact that there will be increasingly entrenched unbelief.

It is such a time Jesus envisioned when he told his disciples, "As it was in the days of Noah, so it will be at the coming of the Son of Man. For in the days before the flood, people were eating and drinking, marrying and giving in marriage, up to the day Noah entered the ark; and they knew nothing about what would happen until the flood came and took them all away. That is how it will be at the coming of the Son of Man" (vv. 37–39).

John Ryle had it right when he wrote, "The world will not be converted when Christ returns," adding that "millions of professing Christians will be found thoughtless, unbelieving, Godless, Christless, worldly, and unfit to meet their Judge."[2] Will you be one of those who perishes in the judgment? Or will you be ready and watching when the Lord returns?

A Sudden Separation

The second picture Jesus paints to describe the nature of things at his return is in verses 40 and 41. "Two men will be in the field; one will be taken and the other left. Two women will be grinding with a hand mill; one will be taken and the other left." Here we find the idea of a sudden separation. Two men working in a field would be coworkers. Two women working with a hand mill would probably be closely related, most likely a mother and daughter or two servants in the same household. Outwardly they would seem to be in identical situations and even identical in their relationships to Christ, but at his return one will be taken and the other left behind.

The verbs *taken* and *left* raise questions that Jesus does not answer in this passage. Does *taken* mean taken away in judgment and *left* mean left behind to prosper? That would not be an unreasonable way to understand these words. Or does *taken* mean taken to heaven when the Lord returns in glory with his angels and *left* mean being left behind on earth? Those who believe in a sudden "rapture" of the saints before a final return of Christ and the final judgment choose this second possibility.

It does seem clear that the idea of being taken to be with Christ at his return best fits the chapter, since Jesus had earlier spoken of sending his angels to "gather his elect from the four winds, from one end of the heavens to the other" (v. 31). Yet the verses do not specify how this will happen, and they certainly do not say when. The point is only that "persons most intimately associated will be separated by that unexpected coming," as John Broadus says.[3]

That alone should encourage serious soul-searching. For one thing, it demolishes any fond hope of universalism, the idea that in the end everyone will be saved since God could never send anyone to hell. No one in the entire Bible speaks of hell as much as Jesus. In fact, he does so in this very chapter, saying in verse 51 that the servant who is found to have been unfaithful when the master returns will be "cut . . . to pieces" and assigned "a place with the hypocrites, where there will be weeping and gnashing of teeth." In the next chapter "weeping and gnashing of teeth" is joined to "darkness," "eternal fire," and "eternal punishment," meaning hell. When Jesus says that "one will be taken and the other left," he means that not all will be saved. Many will be lost. Be sure that you are not among those who perish when Jesus returns.

And there is this point too: No one will be saved simply by being close to or even related to another person who is a Christian. Salvation is not a hereditary matter. On the contrary, *you* must believe on Jesus, and *you* must be ready.

The Need to Be Watching

The third of Jesus' illustrations is of a thief breaking into a house. "But understand this: If the owner of the house had known at what time of night the thief was coming, he would have kept watch and would not have let his house be broken into" (v. 43).

This parable also teaches the sudden and unpredictable coming of the Lord and is used this way in four other New Testament passages. Paul wrote, "The day of the Lord will come like a thief in the night. While people are saying, 'Peace and safety,' destruction will come on them suddenly, as labor pains on a pregnant woman, and they will not escape" (1 Thess. 5:2–3). Peter said, "The day of the Lord will come like a thief. The heavens will disappear with a roar; the elements will be destroyed by fire, and the earth and everything in it will be laid bare" (2 Peter 3:10). Jesus told the church in Sardis, "If you do not wake up, I will come like a thief, and you will not know at what time I will come to you" (Rev. 3:3). He says the same thing later in Revelation: "Behold, I come like a thief" (Rev. 16:15). Each of these verses emphasizes the suddenness of Christ's return.

But the image of a thief adds two additional factors. First, it adds the matter of value, since the thief comes to steal what is worthwhile. Almost everyone values his or her possessions. No one is careless with money, cars, or jewelry. That is why we lock these things up. We have safe-deposit boxes. We install antitheft devices and alarms on our cars. We insure especially valuable possessions. If we take such great care about these items, things that will all be lost to us or decay over time, shouldn't we take at least that much care about things that are eternal? Shouldn't we be at least equally anxious for the salvation of our souls?

Jesus said on an earlier occasion, "What good will it be for a man if he gains the whole world, yet forfeits his soul?" (Matt. 16:26). Obviously, it will be no good at all. Such a person will have lost the only thing that really matters, and in the end he will lose the world as well.

Second, the picture of the thief emphasizes the necessity of being watchful. "Since no one knows at what time, or during what 'watch,' the thief might strike, constant vigilance is required," says D. A. Carson.[4] The need to watch is explicitly stated both in the verse that precedes the words about the thief and in the one that follows. "Therefore keep watch, because you do not know on what day your Lord will come" (v. 42) and, "So you also must be ready, because the Son of Man will come at an hour when you do not expect him" (v. 44).

Are you keeping watch? Are you ready?

The Need to Be Ready

Each of these pictures is alike in stressing the sudden nature and unpredictability of Christ's return, but each also adds its own unique elements. The picture of the flood reminds us that many persons will be lost. The picture of the two men working in the fields and the two women grinding at the mill points to a radical separation and reminds us that we are not saved by knowing or being close to a believer. The picture of the thief reminds us that our souls are valuable and that it is simple prudence for us to be ready.

What about this next picture, the contrast between the two servants? This picture provides an explanation of what being ready means. Being ready means loving, trusting, and waiting for Jesus Christ, of course. The faithful servant is faithful because he is expecting his Lord's return. But it also has to do with faithful service, that is, continuing to carry out what Jesus has left us in this world to do. We find the same idea in two of the three parables in chapter 25. In one parable faithfulness is demonstrated by the wise use of the talents Christ has given (Matt. 25:14–30). In the other it is seen in selfless service to those who are hungry or thirsty or have other pressing needs (Matt. 25:31–46).

How are we to evaluate the service of these two men? Not much is said about the good servant, only that he gave the other servants their food at the proper time. Jesus may be thinking of spiritual food and of the service of ministers in teaching the Bible. On the other hand, a great deal is said about the bad servant. His service is marked by three vices.

1. *Carelessness.* He neglects his work because, he says, "My master is staying away a long time" (v. 48). This reminds us of 2 Peter 3:4, which I referred to earlier: "They will say, 'Where is this "coming" he promised? Ever since our fathers died, everything goes on as it has since the beginning of creation.'" It always seems like that to unbelievers. Jesus has not returned yet, so they are careless. But, says Peter, they "deliberately forget" that God judged the world in ancient times by water and that he has promised to do so again by fire at the final day (vv. 5–7). Besides, "with the Lord a day is like a thousand years, and a thousand years are like a day" (v. 8). What seems delayed to us is not a delay with him. Therefore, says Peter, "Be on your guard so that you may not be carried away by the error of lawless men and fall from your secure position" (v. 17).

2. *Cruelty.* The second vice of the wicked servant is cruelty to his fellow servants, because he began "to beat" them (v. 49). This is like the Pharisees whom Jesus said would pursue, flog, kill, and crucify his servants (Matt. 23:34), only here it is not merely the apostles and missionaries who are beaten. The underservants are beaten, and the one doing the beating is a person who claims to be a servant of the Lord.

3. *Carousing.* Finally, the Lord denounces the wicked servant for his carousing, noting that he has begun "to eat and drink with drunkards" (v. 49). He is behaving like those living in the days of Noah who were "eating and drink-

ing" and "knew nothing about what would happen until the flood came and took them all away" (vv. 38–39).[5]

The passage says of the good servant only that it will be good for him when his master returns. But of the bad servant it says, "The master of that servant will come on a day when he does not expect him and at an hour he is not aware of. He will cut him to pieces and assign him a place with the hypocrites, where there will be weeping and gnashing of teeth" (vv. 50–51).

Are You Ready?

There is an old fable in which three apprentice devils were talking to Satan. The first one said, "I will tell people there is no God." Satan replied, "That will not fool many, because they know there is a God." The second devil said, "I will tell them there is no hell." Satan said, "You will never fool many that way, because they know there is a hell." The third said, "I will tell people there is no hurry." Satan said, "Go, and you will ruin millions."[6]

Lord Shaftesbury, the great English social reformer of the nineteenth century (1801–1885), is reported to have said on one occasion, "I do not think that in the last forty years I have ever lived one conscious hour that was not influenced by the thought of our Lord's return." The anticipation of Jesus' return must have been one of the strongest influences behind Shaftesbury's efforts to assist the poor and advance the cause of foreign missions. Shaftesbury expected to meet Jesus face to face, and he watched for him. He was ready for his master to come.

So I ask again, even as Jesus asks over and over again in these chapters: Are you ready for his return? Are you watching? To be ready when Jesus returns means salvation; not to be ready is to perish.

58

The Parable of the Wise and Foolish Virgins

Matthew 25:1-13

"At that time the kingdom of heaven will be like ten virgins who took their lamps and went out to meet the bridegroom. Five of them were foolish and five were wise. The foolish ones took their lamps but did not take any oil with them. The wise, however, took oil in jars along with their lamps. The bridegroom was a long time in coming, and they all became drowsy and fell asleep.

"At midnight the cry rang out: 'Here's the bridegroom! Come out to meet him!'

"Then all the virgins woke up and trimmed their lamps. The foolish ones said to the wise, 'Give us some of your oil; our lamps are going out.'

"'No,' they replied, 'there may not be enough for both us and you. Instead, go to those who sell oil and buy some for yourselves.'

"But while they were on their way to buy the oil, the bridegroom arrived. The virgins who were ready went in with him to the wedding banquet. And the door was shut.

"Later the others also came. 'Sir! Sir!' they said. 'Open the door for us!'

"But he replied, 'I tell you the truth, I don't know you.'

"Therefore keep watch, because you do not know the day or the hour."

K eep watch, and be ready! You might think I overdid that point in the last study through my examination of Jesus' four illustrations all urging us to be ready. But I cannot have overdone it since in Matthew 25 Jesus continues his teaching on the Mount of Olives by adding three more parables that also warn us to watch and be ready. The first is the parable of the five wise and five foolish virgins (vv. 1–13).

The second is the parable of the talents (vv. 14–30). The third is the story of the separation of the sheep and the goats (vv. 31–46).

Each parable makes its own points, but taken together they intensify and even broaden Jesus' warnings. Instead of speaking of people who are obviously saved or lost, such as those who perished in the flood or the wicked, careless servant, Jesus seems to speak of people who look like believers and who even think they are but who will not be ready when he comes.

Three Points in Common

We are going to be studying each of these parables in turn, looking for the specific teaching of each, but it is helpful to notice that they are also parallel stories and have several important things in common. There are three ways in which the stories are the same.

1. *In each case the return of the Lord is sudden and unexpected.* In the story of the wise and foolish virgins, the cry, "Here's the bridegroom! Come out to meet him!" (v. 6) comes at midnight, when the women are asleep. The cry awakens them, and they rise up suddenly. In the story of the talents, the master returns "after a long time" (v. 19) when he is least expected. In the case of the sheep and the goats, the decisive moment arrives "when the Son of Man comes in his glory, and all the angels with him" (v. 31).

This is the chief point Jesus has been making from the very beginning of the discourse in chapter 24. The disciples wanted to know when Christ would return, and Jesus replied that they could not know. They would see many signs that would not be true signs of his coming: false Christs, wars, famines, earthquakes, persecution, apostasy, and false prophets. When he actually does come, his coming will be so sudden and unexpected that no signs of it can be given. Therefore, they must be ready.

The story of the wise and foolish virgins is connected to the previous chapter because it ends with words that are a deliberate echo of verse 42: "Therefore keep watch, because you do not know on what day your Lord will come." The parable ends, "Therefore keep watch, because you do not know the day or the hour" (Matt. 25:13). The story of the servants expands the much briefer story of the servants in Matthew 24:45–51. The parable of the sheep and the goats wraps up the entire discourse, drawing on words taken from the Lord's description of his return in chapter 24. In this chapter he also speaks of the Son of Man coming in his glory with the angels (v. 31).

2. *In each case the Lord's return results in an unalterable division between two groups of people.* These are stories about the final judgment, and the root meaning of the word *judgment* is "division." The Greek word is *krisis,* which we have retained in English with only a slight change in spelling. A crisis is an event that requires us to turn one way or another, to the right or to the left, forward or back. In this case, the division is between those who are ready when Jesus returns and those who are not ready. In the case of the women, five go into the wedding banquet and five are shut out. In the case of the

servants, two are commended and one is judged. In the case of the sheep and the goats, the sheep inherit the kingdom that has been prepared for them while the goats receive eternal punishment.

3. *In each case the people who are lost are utterly surprised at their rejection.* This is the most striking feature of these stories. The women who are shut out of the banquet can hardly believe that the door has been closed to them. "Sir! Sir!" they say. "Open the door for us!" But the bridegroom does not. The wicked servant thinks he has done right by burying the talent he was given. He expects to be praised and is astonished that he is rebuked and cast out. The goats do not understand the Lord's disapproval. "Lord, when did we see you hungry or thirsty or a stranger or needing clothes or sick or in prison, and did not help you?" (v. 44).

When we think about this feature of the stories, we realize that they are not about people who have no use for Christ or his gospel. They are about people who are part of what we would call the visible church. Like many in our churches today, these people think they are saved and that they are on their way to heaven, but their actual destiny is hell. Is it any wonder the Lord states his warning to "keep watch and be ready" so forcefully?

A Profound and Brilliant Story

The story of the ten virgins is a masterpiece, as Bible students have long recognized. It is realistic in its details and poignant in application, and the deeper a person explores it, the more profound its lessons become.

Jesus tells about ten young women who are invited to a marriage feast. Five are wise and five are foolish. The wise women show their wisdom by planning for the possible delay of the bridegroom. They take extra oil for their lamps so they will be ready when he comes. The foolish women neglect to do so. While the women wait, they all fall asleep. Suddenly a cry goes out that the bridegroom is coming. The wise get up and trim their lamps. The others recognize that they are out of oil and ask to borrow some. "No," say the wise. "There may not be enough for both us and you. Instead, go to those who sell oil and buy some for yourselves" (v. 9). The women who are unprepared start off for more oil, but while they are gone the bridegroom comes, and those who are ready go in with him to the feast. After a while the foolish virgins return and find the door shut.

"Open the door for us!" they cry.

But the bridegroom says, "I don't know you" (v. 12).

The Lord concludes, "Therefore keep watch, because you do not know the day or the hour [of my return]" (v. 13).

How the Women Are Alike

It is not difficult to see the story's main points, especially its chief point, namely, the difference between the wise and the foolish women. Five were ready and five were not. But it is also worth seeing the ways in which the women are alike. There are at least seven similarities.

1. *All had been invited to the banquet.* Each of these women had received an invitation and was anticipating a banquet when the bridegroom came. This feature singles out the people who have heard the gospel invitation. They are not the unreached who have never heard of Christ.

2. *All had responded positively to the wedding invitation.* Some may have disregarded it or scorned it, as the townspeople did in one of Jesus' other parables (Matt. 22:1–14). But that was not the case with these women. They had received the invitation and had responded positively, which they demonstrated by waiting for the bridegroom's appearance.

3. *All were part of what we would call the visible church.* They had joined the fellowship of those who were waiting for the Lord.

4. *All had some affection and even love for the bridegroom.* They were not indifferent participants. This was a happy occasion, and they were happy for the bridegroom. It was their affection for him that had brought them to the point at which the story begins: "Ten virgins . . . took their lamps and went out to meet the bridegroom" (v. 1).

5. *All confessed Jesus as their Lord.* The New International Version translates the word they used to address the bridegroom as "Sir," but it is actually the word *kyrios*, which is usually rendered "Lord." In fact, it is translated "Lord" later in the chapter (vv. 37, 44).

6. *All believed in and in some sense were waiting for Jesus' second coming.* This is all highly commendable. In fact, if most ministers today had a church filled with such people, they would consider themselves greatly blessed. Here were people who had heard the gospel invitation, responded to it, professed love for Christ, joined the church, acknowledged Jesus as Lord, and were now waiting for Christ's return. Could anything be more desirable?

Thomas Shepard was a Puritan preacher who wrote a masterful study of this story called *The Parable of the Ten Virgins Opened and Applied* (1660). He had so many wonderful things to say in praise of the foolish virgins that someone remarked about his description, "Oh, to be one of Shepard's foolish virgins!" He suggested that being like them would be better than being like many of us are now. Still, in spite of their good qualities, the women were shut out.

7. *All were alike in that they became drowsy and fell asleep when the bridegroom's coming was delayed.* Unbelievers sleep, but so do the elect at times. Remember Peter, James, and John in the garden? But suddenly the bridegroom came, and immediately the similarities vanished and the critical difference emerged. Five were ready and five were unprepared.

What It Means to Be Ready

The setting of these chapters is the time leading up to Christ's return. So we must conclude that there will always be people in the church who have heard the gospel invitation, have responded in some sense, and may even have some affection for Jesus, but who are not born again.

Don't be sidetracked by trying to work out the meaning of the oil. Some have identified the oil as the Holy Spirit, because the Spirit is sometimes symbolized by oil in Scripture. But if we do that, we will think that a person can have the Holy Spirit and then run out of him, as it were, or that when one runs out he or she needs to get more. The right thing is to forget about the oil entirely and think only about being ready.

But what does it mean to be ready? Charles H. Spurgeon saw it as an inner change brought about by regeneration or new birth. He wrote, drawing on a good deal of Bible imagery:

> A great change has to be wrought in you, far beyond any power of yours to accomplish, ere you can go in with Christ to the marriage. You must, first of all, be renewed in your nature, or you will not be ready. You must be washed from your sins, or you will not be ready. You must be justified in Christ's righteousness, and you must put on his wedding dress, or else you will not be ready. You must be reconciled to God, you must be made like to God, or you will not be ready. Or, to come to the parable before us, you must have a lamp, and that lamp must be fed with heavenly oil, and it must continue to burn brightly, or else you will not be ready. No child of darkness can go into that place of light. You must be brought out of nature's darkness into God's marvelous light, or else you will never be ready to go in with Christ to the marriage, and to be forever with him.[1]

Which brings us back to the pressing question of these chapters: Are you ready? I do not ask, Have you responded to a gospel invitation? Have you joined a church? Or do you believe in Jesus' second coming? I ask, Have you been born again? Have you believed on Jesus as your Savior from sin? Are you living for Jesus now? Are you truly ready, or are you among those who only seem to be prepared?

A Time of Crisis

Notice that the difference between the wise women and foolish women was revealed by the coming of the bridegroom. That is, it was revealed in the crisis moment. During the days before the wedding or the night leading up to the start of the feast, few would have noticed that five women had adequately prepared for the bridegroom's coming and five had not. But suddenly the bridegroom came, and the difference was immediately disclosed. The same will happen when Jesus Christ returns. Many who have considered themselves true children of God will be shown they are not, and many who have perhaps not even been regarded as his children will be revealed as believers.

How are you to know whether you are in one camp or the other? One answer is whether you are faithful in serving Jesus. Another is whether you are serving others because of your love for Jesus. These are the answers the next two parables suggest. But let me suggest another answer here. If the return of the Lord Jesus Christ and the division it will cause will bring out the true condition of those who profess Christianity but are not actually born again, isn't it also the case that their condition may be revealed by lesser but, nevertheless, real crisis experiences now? If this is so, you can anticipate the results of the final judgment by the way you react to the problems that come into your life day by day.

Here is how one author puts it:

> Nothing will more correctly reveal what is in a man than the coming upon him of some crushing and unlooked-for crisis. Let it be temporal ruin by the failure of his calculations or the disappointment of all his hopes; let it be the entrance of the death-angel into his home and the removal from it of his nearest and dearest earthly friend; let it be his own prostration by some serious illness which puts him face to face with his dissolution, and forthwith the extent of his resources is unfolded, and it is at once discovered both by others and by himself whether he is animated by unfailing faith in the Lord Jesus Christ and sustained by the grace of the Holy Spirit, or whether he has been deceiving himself, all the while relying on some other support. It was a shrewd remark of Andrew Fuller that a man has only as much religion as he can command in trial.
>
> Let us therefore look back upon the past and analyze our experiences at such testing times as those to which I have referred. We have all had them. We have all heard already, in some form or other, this midnight cry, "Behold, the bridegroom cometh"; for in every such surprise as those which I have described, Jesus was coming to us. How did we meet him then? Did our lamps go out? Or were we able to trim them and keep them burning brightly all through? Oh, if by any such event we discovered our utter resourcelessness, let us betake ourselves now to Christ that he may thoroughly renew us by his Holy Spirit and so prepare us for that last and solemnest crisis when over the graves of the slumbering dead the archangel shall cry out, "Behold, the Bridegroom cometh," and all shall arise to stand before his great white throne.[2]

Three More Lessons

The writer of those words was William Taylor, an American minister who wrote around the turn of the nineteenth century, and what he has written is enough to keep most of us examining ourselves for some time. To use Peter's words, Taylor encourages us to make our "calling and election sure" (2 Peter 1:10). But the parable of the wise and foolish virgins contains several more lessons.

1. *The coming of the Lord may be delayed.* This is an unmistakable inference from the story and one that has bearing on whether the events of these chapters are to be understood as having taken place at the time of the destruction of Jerusalem or whether they look forward to an unspecified future moment. Actually, there are several suggestions that Jesus' return may be

delayed, among them Christ's teaching that "this gospel of the kingdom will be preached in the whole world as a testimony to all nations, and then the end will come" (Matt. 24:14).

2. *The Lord will come without warning.* This is why the parable ends with the words: "Therefore keep watch, because you do not know the day or the hour" (v. 13). Jesus will come without warning either at the end of time or on the day of your death, which for you is much the same thing.

Years ago, when I was first studying this parable, I called a pastor who had been a friend of mine in seminary. He had come from Wyoming and had gone back to pastor a church where he had grown up. A woman answered the phone—it turned out to be his mother—and she told me that her son had suffered a sudden stroke just two weeks earlier, had lingered for ten days, and then had died. My friend was a believer. But death had come suddenly, and he was in the presence of his Lord.

3. *Being prepared is not transferable.* I do not mean by this that one saved person may not be used of God to bring the gospel to another, for that is how the gospel normally spreads. Paul speaks of the gospel being passed "from faith to faith" (Rom. 1:17 KJV). I mean that no person can get by on another's faith. You cannot be saved by the life of Christ in someone else.

Many people delude themselves along those lines. They do not have true faith in Christ, but they have been exposed to it over a period of years and suppose that in the time of Christ's judgment they will be able to appeal to God's work in the life of someone close to them.

"What right do you have to come into my heaven?"

"Well, I don't really know how to answer that, Lord. But consider my mother. She was a godly woman, and I learned a lot from her."

"I didn't ask that," the Lord replied. "I asked, What right do *you* have to enter my heaven?"

"Look at my Sunday school teachers, Lord! They were godly people; they certainly went out of their way to teach me. They prayed for me too. Don't forget them!"

Jesus replied, "What right do *you* have to enter heaven?"

This helps us understand why the wise women refused to give their oil to the five who were foolish. Their refusal seems uncharitable. The selfless thing would have been for the wise women to share their oil, even if it meant they themselves would have run out. But the story is not about charity. Rather, the parable reveals that when Christ returns, each person must stand on his or her own. Your mother's faith will not save you. Your wife's faith will not save you. You will not be saved by the spiritual life of your son or daughter. The question will be, Where do *you* stand? Are *you* alive in Christ? Are *you* ready?

4. *Lost opportunities cannot be regained.* The foolish women set out to buy oil, but the bridegroom came, and they were too late. So it will be when Christ returns in judgment. Those who are ready will be taken in to the marriage feast, and those who are not ready will be shut out.

Do not say, "I will turn to Christ later. I will repent after I enjoy a few more years of sin. There is always time for Jesus." You do not know that. Today may be the last time you will hear the gospel. And even if it is not—even if you do hear it again and again—it will be no easier for you to turn to God later. In fact, the opposite is the case. The fact that you have rejected the free offer of God's grace now will harden you so that you will find it much more difficult to repent later. Millions who once heard the gospel and postponed a decision have since perished in their sins. The only wise thing is to come to Jesus now. The Bible says, "Now is the time of God's favor, now is the day of salvation" (2 Cor. 6:2).

59

The Parable of the Talents

Matthew 25:14–30

"Again, it will be like a man going on a journey, who called his servants and entrusted his property to them. To one he gave five talents of money, to another two talents, and to another one talent, each according to his ability. Then he went on his journey. The man who had received the five talents went at once and put his money to work and gained five more. So also, the one with the two talents gained two more. But the man who had received the one talent went off, dug a hole in the ground and hid his master's money.

"After a long time the master of those servants returned and settled accounts with them. The man who had received the five talents brought the other five. 'Master,' he said, 'you entrusted me with five talents. See, I have gained five more.'

"His master replied, 'Well done, good and faithful servant! You have been faithful with a few things; I will put you in charge of many things. Come and share your master's happiness!'

"The man with the two talents also came. 'Master,' he said, 'you entrusted me with two talents; see, I have gained two more.'

"His master replied, 'Well done, good and faithful servant! You have been faithful with a few things; I will put you in charge of many things. Come and share your master's happiness!'

"Then the man who had received the one talent came. 'Master,' he said, 'I knew that you are a hard man, harvesting where you have not sown and gathering where you have not scattered seed. So I was afraid and went out and hid your talent in the ground. See, here is what belongs to you.'

"His master replied, 'You wicked, lazy servant! So you knew that I harvest where I have not sown and gather where I have not scattered seed? Well then, you should have put my money on deposit with the bankers, so that when I returned I would have received it back with interest.'

"'Take the talent from him and give it to the one who has the ten talents. For everyone who has will be given more, and he will have an abundance. Whoever does not have, even what he has will be taken from him. And throw that worthless servant outside, into the darkness, where there will be weeping and gnashing of teeth.'"

I said in our study of the wise and foolish virgins that there are two good ways to consider the question, How do I know I am ready for the Lord's return? (1) Am I serving the Lord? (2) Am I serving others because I love him? The next two parables, the parable of the talents and the parable of the sheep and the goats, address these questions. The parables carry Jesus' warning to watch and be ready a step beyond the first story.

All three are parables of judgment, and each makes similar points. Thus, the cumulative effect is strong. Jesus is about to go to the cross. His disciples will see him no more. But he reminds them that the day is coming when he will return as judge of all men and that they must be ready to face him in that judgment.

Working for the Master

In the parable of the talents, Jesus tells of a rich man who is about to go off on a journey. He calls three of his servants together and gives them money to be used while he is gone. He gives five talents to the first, two talents to the second, and one talent to the third.[1] In Palestine, a talent was not a coin; it was a measure of weight. Because coins could be of copper, silver, or gold, and Jesus does not specify the kind of coinage in his story, it is impossible to calculate how valuable the talents were. It is sufficient to say that each was a large amount. If a talent was six thousand denarii, it would have taken a worker twenty years to earn that much money, so we are thinking here of hundreds of thousands of dollars at least. The footnote in the New International Version specifies "more than a thousand dollars," but this amount is too low.

Yet the amount is unimportant, and so is the fact that the parable is about money. Money is one thing God entrusts to us that we often misuse. But the same is true of many other endowments. John Ryle says rightly, "Anything whereby we may glorify God is 'a talent.' Our gifts, our influence, our money, our knowledge, our health, our strength, our time, our senses, our reason, our intellect, our memory, our affections, our privileges as members of Christ's Church, our advantages as possessors of the Bible—all, all are talents."[2] The point of the story is that waiting for Christ's return and being ready for it are not passive matters. We must work faithfully and energetically for him now.

William Hendriksen has tried to capture the tone of the conversations in this parable. I think he is right that the decisive matter is the way in which the two good servants and the one bad servant related to the master. The faithful servants served well because they loved him and wanted to please him, while the wicked servant failed to serve well because he actually hated and resented his master.

When the master returns for their accounting and the faithful servants tell what they have done, their words do not merely report that they have doubled the amount they were given. The man who was given five talents seems to have come with two bags, each containing five talents, and what he literally says is, "Master, five talents you placed in my hands; look, an additional five talents I have gained." You can almost feel his proper pride in the achievement. Hendriksen comments, "The man's eyes are sparkling. He is bubbling over with enthusiasm, is thoroughly thrilled, and, as it were, invites his master to start counting."[3] The man has been waiting for this moment and is pleased at having done so well. The master is equally delighted. "Well done," he says. We might almost translate his reply as, "Excellent!" "Great!" or "Wonderful!" It is the same with the servant who was given two talents. He says the same thing and receives an identical word of commendation.

By contrast, we can hardly fail to hear the angry, self-justifying, accusing tone of the servant who hid the master's talent in the earth. "Master, I knew that you are a hard man, harvesting where you have not sown and gathering where you have not scattered seed. So I was afraid and went out and hid your talent in the ground. See, here is what belongs to you" (vv. 24–25). This accusation was not true. The master was not a hard man. He had been generous in giving his servants much wealth to work with. But this man hated him. We can hear his contempt as he resentfully throws his talent on the table. "Here is what belongs to you," he says. It was returned exactly as the master had given it, not a bit more and no less.

In response, the master condemns him both for his wickedness and for being lazy—wicked because he accused his master unjustly, and lazy because he did not faithfully use what he was given. The master then gives the talent to the one who has ten, on the principle that "everyone who has will be given more" and "whoever does not have, even what he has will be taken from him" (v. 29). He then has the lazy servant cast "outside, into the darkness" (v. 30).

We must avoid a "do nothing" Christianity, of course. One commentator wrote, "To have done no harm is praise for a stone, not for a man." But the situation here is worse than that. To have done nothing is proof that we do not love Jesus Christ, do not belong to him, and have no share in his kingdom. It is to perish forever.

What other lessons should we learn from this story?

A Coming Judgment

The first clear lesson is that there will be a future day of reckoning for all people. That is so obvious both from this parable and from all the parables in Matthew 25 that it seems almost sophomoric to stress it. Yet it must be stressed, if only because people usually think the opposite. Jesus spoke of judgment being obvious. It was not even open to debate. But the people I am describing consider God's judgment as the most irrational and least anticipated thing in the world.

What do people think of when one speaks of dying? Most probably do not want to think of it at all, of course; they are not certain what, if anything, lies beyond death's door. But if they do speak about it, assuming that something does lie beyond this present life, they think of the afterlife in pleasant terms. At the very least they think of a continuation of life as we know it. If not that, it must be something considerably better. Very few consider that it may be worse. They cannot imagine the Almighty as a God of rigid judgment.

This attitude has caused theologian R. C. Sproul to speak of what he has called the doctrine of "justification by death." Protestants and Catholics used to argue over justification. Protestants said that justification is by faith alone *(sola fide)*. Catholics said that it is by faith plus works *(fide et operae)*. But today many people seem to think that to get to heaven all one has to do is die. One is "justified" by death alone *(sola morte)*.

On this matter our contemporaries are irrational, as they are on most other spiritual matters. This is an evil world. All sins are not judged in this world, nor are all good deeds rewarded. If this is a moral universe, if it is created and ruled by a moral God, then there must be a reckoning hereafter in which those scales are balanced. Evil must be punished.

In most theological volumes on eschatology (the last things), there are three great points of emphasis: the return of Christ, the resurrection of the body, and the final judgment. But of the three, the only one that is truly reasonable is the last. There is no reason why Jesus should return again. He came once and was rejected. If he should write us off and never give so much as a second thought to this planet, it would be understandable. It is the same with the resurrection: "Dust you are and to dust you will return" (Gen. 3:19). If that is all there is, who can complain? We have had our lives. Why should we expect anything more? There is nothing logical in either of those two matters in and of themselves. But judgment? That is the most logical thing in the universe, and every story in this chapter cries out that there will most certainly be a final day of reckoning.

In the first case, it was when the bridegroom came. In the second case, it was when the "master of those servants returned and settled accounts with them" (Matt. 25:19). In the third case, it is when "the Son of Man comes in his glory, and all the angels with him" and the nations are gathered together before him for his judgment (vv. 31–32).

Judgment by Works

The second, somewhat surprising lesson of this parable (and the next as well) is the emphasis on works, indeed, on a judgment by works. That sometimes troubles Protestants, who have been taught that salvation is by grace alone through faith apart from works. In the parable of the talents, however, judgment is based on the use or misuse of the talents. In the second parable, it is based on the care or neglect of those who were hungry, thirsty, strangers, naked, sick, or imprisoned.

We must not forget at this point that in an earlier story the emphasis was on the readiness of the five wise virgins. Their readiness corresponds to the new birth and to faith. Therefore, we cannot believe these accompanying stories teach that faith in Christ is unnecessary. Christians must have faith. Still, these stories round out the picture by showing what kind of faith is needed. It is not a dead faith. A dead faith saves no one.

In this teaching, Jesus is one with the apostle James, who said:

> What good is it, my brothers, if a man claims to have faith but has no deeds? Can such faith save him? Suppose a brother or sister is without clothes and daily food. If one of you says to him, "Go, I wish you well; keep warm and well fed," but does nothing about his physical needs, what good is it? In the same way, faith by itself, if it is not accompanied by action, is dead.
>
> James 2:14–17

Usually James is contrasted with Paul at this point, but remember that Paul also said,

> To those who by persistence in doing good seek glory, honor, and immortality, [God] will give eternal life. But for those who are self-seeking and who reject the truth and follow evil, there will be wrath and anger. There will be trouble and distress for every human being who does evil: first for the Jew, then for the Gentile; but glory, honor and peace for everyone who does good: first for the Jew, then for the Gentile. For God does not show favoritism.
>
> Romans 2:7–11

Does that mean we are saved by works after all? Were the reformers wrong? No, but these passages do reveal the necessity of works following faith—if we are truly born again. There is an unbreakable connection between what we believe and what we do. We believe the gospel because we have been born again, and those who have been born again will always and inevitably begin to live out the superior moral life of Christ within them. The new nature does not manifest itself fully all at once. But if we are justified, we will have it, and it will increasingly and inevitably express itself in faithful and loving service to our Master, Jesus Christ.

We are not justified by works. If we are trying to be justified by works, we are not Christians. But neither can we claim to be Christians if we do not have works. If we are not working for Christ, we are not justified.

There is an additional warning here. When Jesus spoke of the men who were given talents by their master and who used them either wisely or not at all, he said that one was given more than the other and that one was given less. One had five talents; he used them to gain five more. The second had two talents; he used those to gain two more. The last servant was given one. He was judged, but his judgment was not for having failed to gain as much as the two who had been given more. He was judged for failing to use what he had, for hiding his valuable talent in the ground.

We need to remember this parable when we find ourselves making comparisons between Christians. It is true, as this story teaches, that the people of God will work. They will use the talents God has given them, but they will not all do so in the same way or to the same observable degree. Thus, although we know that God will judge the performance or nonperformance of those deeds, it is not our prerogative to do so. We are not all-knowing, as God is, and we are certainly not as wise as he is. Who are we to say that someone else is insufficiently serving or even hiding his talent in the ground? He may not be doing what we are doing, but he may be doing something far greater, which only our own sin blinds us from observing. Remember that Paul said, "Who are you to judge someone else's servant? To his own master he stands or falls. And he will stand, for the Lord is able to make him stand" (Rom. 14:4).

All Mouths Stopped

But I also need to qualify the qualification. The warning applies in our judgment of other people, whom we are not fit to judge. *But it does not apply to us.* On the contrary, we must be rigorous with ourselves. We must not imagine that our poor or nonexistent performance will be excused.

Which brings us to the third clear lesson of the parable: the failure of all excuses before God. The man who was given one talent and hid it in the ground explained that he had not done more because he knew his master's nature too well: "Master, I knew that you are a hard man, harvesting where you have not sown and gathering where you have not scattered seed. So I was afraid and went out and hid your talent in the ground. See, here is what belongs to you" (vv. 24–25). The servant did not actually know his master at all. The servant was only making an excuse. It was a foolish excuse, and it certainly did not fool his master. But many people do the same today. They use the theology of justification to excuse their failure to care for others. They use knowledge of predestination to excuse their failure to evangelize. They use perseverance as an excuse for being lazy.

The master told the servant that if he was right about his character, he should have worked even harder. If the master was hard, the servant should have labored even more to produce a profit for him. The servant was wicked because of his unjustified slander, and he was lazy, which was the real reason for his zero-growth performance. By that standard, what wicked persons must there be in our churches? How lazy must many of us be! D. A. Carson wrote, "It is not enough for Jesus' followers to 'hang in there' and wait for the end. They must see themselves for what they are—servants who owe it to their Master to improve what he entrusts to them. Failure to do so proves they cannot really be valued disciples at all." He then quotes Henry Alford as saying, "The foolish virgins failed from thinking their part too easy; the wicked servant fails from thinking his too hard."[4]

You can get away with giving excuses to other people—to your boss, your parents, your pastor. But do not think you can get away with giving excuses to God. The apostle Paul wrote that in the day of God's judgment "every mouth [will] be silenced and the whole world held accountable to God" (Rom. 3:19). There will not be even a single protest when Judge Jesus takes the bench.

Surprise! Surprise!

I have been to few surprise parties in my life when the guest of honor has been truly surprised. Usually somone spoils the surprise by letting the cat out of the bag. But sometimes the surprise comes off without a hitch. When I read these judgment stories, I think there really will be a surprise for many on the day of judgment, but it will not be pleasant. Many will be startled, shaken, and distressed. The wicked servant thought he had done well. He must have been startled to hear the words, "Throw that worthless servant outside, into the darkness, where there will be weeping and gnashing of teeth" (v. 30).

This will be the end for many who in their lifetime called out, "Lord, Lord," but did not do the things Jesus said. We would not dare to say this if the Lord had not said it first, but on his authority we must say that many who worship in apparently Christian congregations and consider themselves good Christians will be confounded by Christ's judgment.

This last point is very sober. Jesus is speaking of divisions, between the five wise and the five foolish virgins, between the faithful and wicked servants, and in the next parable between the sheep and the goats. But these are not for this life or for a few moments or years after death. They are forever. There is a gulf between heaven and hell, happiness and suffering, misery and the joy of the redeemed. In the next parable, the goats go away "to eternal punishment, but the righteous to eternal life" (v. 46). In the parable of the talents, the faithful are invited to share their master's happiness (vv. 21, 23), while the wicked are cast "outside, into the darkness, where there will be weeping and gnashing of teeth" (v. 30).

What a grim fate that is! *Darkness,* because it is a life without God, who is the source of all light. *Outside,* because it is without God, who is the Creator and center of all things. In that darkness there is no hope, no joy, no love, no laughter. In that outside world there is only weeping and gnashing of teeth forever. Do not go there. Repent of your sin, trust Christ as your Savior, and use your new life in Christ to work for him now.

60

The Parable of the Sheep and the Goats

Matthew 25:31–46

"When the Son of Man comes in his glory, and all the angels with him, he will sit on his throne in heavenly glory. All the nations will be gathered before him, and he will separate the people one from another as a shepherd separates the sheep from the goats. He will put the sheep on his right and the goats on his left.

"Then the King will say to those on his right, 'Come, you who are blessed by my Father; take your inheritance, the kingdom prepared for you since the creation of the world. For I was hungry and you gave me something to eat, I was thirsty and you gave me something to drink, I was a stranger and you invited me in, I needed clothes and you clothed me, I was sick and you looked after me, I was in prison and you came to visit me.'

"Then the righteous will answer him, 'Lord, when did we see you hungry and feed you, or thirsty and give you something to drink? When did we see you a stranger and invite you in, or needing clothes and clothe you? When did we see you sick or in prison and go to visit you?'

"The King will reply, 'I tell you the truth, whatever you did for one of the least of these brothers of mine, you did for me.'

"Then he will say to those on his left, 'Depart from me, you who are cursed, into the eternal fire prepared for the devil and his angels. For I was hungry and you gave me nothing to eat, I was thirsty and you gave me nothing to drink, I was a stranger and you did not invite me in, I needed clothes and you did not clothe me, I was sick and in prison and you did not look after me.'

"They also will answer, 'Lord, when did we see you hungry or thirsty or a stranger or needing clothes or sick or in prison, and did not help you?'

"He will reply, 'I tell you the truth, whatever you did not do for one of the least of these, you did not do for me.'

"Then they will go away to eternal punishment, but the righteous to eternal life."

539

W e come now to the last recorded teaching of Jesus Christ in Matthew's Gospel: the parable of the sheep and the goats. But it is not strictly a parable. It is a dynamic description of the last judgment, using a few symbolic elements: a shepherd, sheep, and goats. This story is unique to Matthew and is an appropriate ending to the chapters in which Jesus speaks of his return.

The story builds on the two previous parables and on the illustrations in chapter 24. The illustrations in chapter 24 and the first of the parables in chapter 25 stressed the need to be ready when Christ returns. The parable of the talents taught the need for faithful work and service, which will be rewarded at the judgment. The final story is of the judgment itself. There is also a progression. In the parable of the wise and foolish virgins, the women who were not ready are only *shut out* from the banquet. In the next parable, the wicked, lazy servant is *thrown out into the darkness*. In the story of the sheep and the goats, those who have ignored the needs of Christ's brothers are *cursed* with an *eternal punishment*.

Interpreting the Passage

We might expect that a story as straightforward as the separation of the sheep and the goats would be easy to interpret, but that does not seem to be the case judging from interpretations given to it by generations of Bible students. There seem to be four main views, depending on how the interpreter understands the words "the least of these brothers of mine" (v. 40).

1. *The words might refer to anyone who is hungry or has other physical needs.* This has been the majority view in church history, and it has led to many sentimental and sometimes fanciful stories. Gregory the Great tells of a monk named Martyrius who came upon a deformed man lying exhausted by the roadside. He carried him to the monastery, and when the abbot saw him coming he called to the other monks, saying, "Open the gates; our brother Martyrius is coming; he is carrying the Lord."[1] Another story concerns Francis of Assisi. Francis was a wealthy, careless man before his conversion. One day he was out riding and saw a loathsome leper. Something moved Francis to dismount and fling his arms around the leper. When he did, the face of the leper changed to the face of Jesus Christ.[2]

Stories such as these are characteristic of medieval piety. But the same view is expressed by persons such as William Barclay, who concluded from these verses, "God will judge us in accordance with our reaction to human need,"[3] or a teacher who wrote, "The Son of Man sees in any wretch his brother."[4]

2. *"The least of these brothers of mine" might mean the Jews.* This is the dispensational view, which understands the judgment to be one of several judgments, this one placed at the close of the great tribulation after Christians have been removed from the world by the rapture. It is usually described as

a judgment of literal nations on the grounds of their treatment of the Jews. Harry Ironside wrote, "'My brethren' . . . are those of Israel who are related to Christ, both according to the flesh and the Spirit, and will be his authoritative witnesses in the coming time of tribulation, when the present church age is ended."[5] This view is possible only if the entire dispensational understanding of prophecy is valid.

3. *"The least of these brothers of mine" could refer to the apostles and other Christian missionaries.* This would mean that the reaction to them and their gospel determines the nation's fate. This is closer to the text than the other ideas, and it has support from Matthew 10:40–42, where Jesus said to the disciples, "He who receives you receives me, and he who receives me receives the one who sent me. . . . And if anyone gives even a cup of cold water to one of these little ones because he is my disciple, I tell you the truth, he will certainly not lose his reward."

Some of these views are better than others, as I have indicated. But the trouble with all of them is that Jesus does not use the word *brothers* in those ways in this Gospel. In Matthew, "brothers" means "disciples," all who follow Christ or all Christians (Matt. 12:48–50; 23:8; 28:10). "Those who are least" also refers to Christ's followers (Matt. 5:19; 11:11; 18:3–6; 18:10–14). This use of the terms means that the next interpretation is the right one.

4. *"The least of these brothers of mine" refers to Christ's disciples or all Christians.* This does not mean that the Bible is unconcerned about the poor and the oppressed. It is. We read about them often. But that is not the thought here. What Jesus means here is that the fate of individuals depends on how they relate to Christ's followers, which means how they also relate to him. John Broadus puts it like this: "Our Lord is not expressly speaking of benevolence to the poor and suffering in general, but of kindness to his poor and suffering 'brethren' for his sake."[6] D. A. Carson says similarly, "True disciples will pass an examination not because they are trying to pass an examination but because they *will* love his brothers and sisters—and therefore Jesus. Goats will fail because, of course, they *will not* particularly care for Jesus' brothers and sisters, and thus will be rejecting the Messiah himself (10:40–42)—just as Saul, in persecuting Christians, was actually persecuting Jesus (see Acts 9:5)."[7]

This understanding of the separation of the sheep and the goats should not surprise us, because it is one of the tests John gives in his first letter as to how we can know we are Christians. He has three tests. The first is whether we believe that Jesus is God come in human flesh (1 John 2:20–23; 4:2–3; 4:15; 5:1). The second is whether we obey Christ's commands (1 John 2:3–6; 3:4–10; 5:2). The third is whether we love other Christians (1 John 2:9–11; 3:14; 4:7–21). This last test is the one on which the story of the separation of the sheep and goats depends, for the issue is whether we love and care for Christ's followers, hence, whether we love Christ. This is what determines our destiny.

Faith and Works

Whether we love others has direct bearing on the relationship of faith and works that bothers some Christians. We know we are saved by faith alone apart from works according to the explicit teaching of the New Testament. Ephesians 2:8–9 says, "For it is by grace you have been saved, through faith—and this not from yourselves, it is the gift of God—not by works, so that no one can boast." But if that is the case, as we believe it to be, how is it that judgment can also be based on works, as in the story of the separation of the sheep and goats or even in the parable of the talents?

The answer, of course, is that passages that speak of judgment based on works are merely saying that it, like all judgments, will be on the basis of demonstrable evidence. The works Christians perform do not save them, but the works are evidence that Christians love and trust Jesus. In other words, this judgment reflects on the highest level what we attempt on a much lower level when we admit people into membership in a particular church. When we do so we look for what we call a "credible profession," meaning a verbal profession of faith in Christ supported by a consistent way of life. An inconsistent life invalidates the profession, however sincerely it may be expressed.

William Hendriksen is on target here when he says, "In the case of any given individual what matters is whether he has during his earthly life given evidence of his faith in the Lord Jesus Christ; therefore, of a life in harmony with Christ's commands and example."[8]

But there is a point worth noting. The evidence of a credible Christian profession is not how many great works have been performed for Jesus, how many churches have been built or sermons preached or millions of dollars given to Christ's cause. The proofs of conversion are not "great" things at all. They are little things, as most people think of them: sharing food with a brother who is hungry, giving water to a sister who is thirsty, welcoming a stranger, offering clothes to one who needs clothing, caring for the sick, or visiting a person who is in prison.

It is because these are little things that the righteous do not even remember having done them. They ask Jesus, "When did we see you hungry and feed you, or thirsty and give you something to drink? When did we see you a stranger and invite you in, or needing clothes and clothe you? When did we see you sick or in prison and go to visit you?" (vv. 37–39).

It is also because these are little things that the unrighteous did not do them. They might have done them if someone important, such as Jesus, had been there. But they hadn't seen anyone like that. "Lord, when did we see you hungry or thirsty or a stranger or needing clothes or sick or in prison, and did not help you?" (v. 44). Of course, they only delude themselves by such comments, because they would not have helped even an important person in a truly selfless way. They would have done it only for what they could have gotten in return.

Let's notice one other thing as well. The wicked are condemned in this story not because of some great positive evil they have done but for their simple neglect of doing good. Or to put it in other terms, the people spoken of here are not the great sinners of the world, like Adolf Hitler or some serial killer. They are the good people who occupy the pews of churches and serve on philanthropic boards. Therefore, when the judgment comes, they are astonished. They are like the foolish virgins who cannot understand why the groom will not open the door for them or the servant who cannot perceive why the Lord is not satisfied by his zero-growth performance.

R. V. G. Tasker says, "As in the previous parables of the ten virgins and of entrusted wealth, so in this picture of the great assize, it is not so much positive wrong-doing that evokes the severest censure, as the utter failure to do good."[9] The desire to do good comes from receiving the life of the Lord Jesus Christ within, which is regeneration.

Hell: How Bad Is It?

We sometimes hear people say that they cannot believe in an Old Testament God who is full of wrath and judgment and that they prefer the God of the gentle Jesus. But they forget that it is Jesus more than any other person in the Bible who speaks most clearly about hell. Matthew 25 is an example. In the parable of the talents, the master cries, "Throw that worthless servant outside, into the darkness, where there will be weeping and gnashing of teeth" (v. 30). In the separation of the sheep from the goats, the King tells the goats, "Depart from me, you who are cursed, into the eternal fire prepared for the devil and his angels" (v. 41). The chapter ends with Jesus' frightening summation: "Then they will go away to eternal punishment, but the righteous to eternal life" (v. 46).

We may not like these statements, but they were spoken by Jesus, the very Son of God, and I think he knew what he was talking about. We would do well to take his warnings seriously. Should we take them seriously? Is hell to be feared? Or can we shrug off our fear with a joke, like the one that tells us not to worry about hell because if we die and go to hell, we'll be so busy shaking hands with old friends that we won't have time to worry?

Jesus described hell this way:

1. *Hell is a total separation*, and not just from those who will be with Christ in heaven. It is separation from God. Jesus expressed it when he quoted the King as saying, "Depart from me, you who are cursed" (v. 41).

It is interesting how most of us divide people. We separate men from women, the haves from the have nots, the privileged from the disadvantaged, the wise from the foolish, rulers from those who are ruled, people who are of our own class from all others. Someone said on one occasion, "The whole world can be divided into two classes, those who divide the world into two classes and those who do not." The ways in which we divide people seem almost endless. Yet the division in Matthew 25 is the only one that really matters—the division between those who will "go away to eternal punishment" and those who will enter into "eternal life" (v. 46), between the saved and the lost. That division is absolute. Charles H. Spurgeon wrote, "Not one goat will be left among the sheep, nor one sheep with the goats. . . . There will be no middle company in that day."[10]

2. *Hell is a bad association.* We learn something interesting about hell in these verses that is not taught explicitly elsewhere. Hell was "prepared for the devil and his angels" (v. 41). If hell was prepared for the devil and his angels—the angels that followed him in his rebellion against God and are now known as demons—we can be certain that they will be in hell some day. And if that is the case, it means that those who have refused Christ and have shown it by their neglect of Christ's followers will be sent there to be with those demons.

Some people think of hell as a place where the devils torment sinners. But Jesus pictures hell as a place where fallen angels and rebellious human beings are together in their suffering. What a terrible association! What a destiny! To spend eternity shoulder to shoulder with an evil being whose one goal has been to defy God and bring others to share in suffering forever. Will the devils not gloat that they have succeeded in bringing people to hell? Will they not gloat over you if you are there?

3. *Hell is suffering.* I suppose the references to hell as a place of "eternal fire" (Matt. 25:41) or "burning sulfur" (Rev. 20:10) are symbolic, if for no other reason than that the demons are disembodied spirits and thus cannot be punished by fire in the literal sense. But what of that? The purpose of imagery is to point beyond what literal language can convey. If a literal burning by fire is bad, the reality of hell's suffering must be immeasurably and inexpressibly worse. Even if the suffering is only mental, internal, or psychological, it is something that produces an eternal "weeping and gnashing of teeth" (Matt. 25:30).

4. *Hell is darkness.* After fire, darkness may not seem so bad, but this is a darkness that shuts off all sight of others, indeed, all sight of everything, even sight of oneself. The only thing that will be left is the conscious, mental self in its rebellion. Can you recall that horrible poem, "Invictus," by William Ernest Henley?

> Out of the night that covers me,
>   Black as the Pit from pole to pole,
> I thank whatever gods may be
>   For my unconquerable soul.

But no one will be thanking God for his soul in hell. Cursing God is more like it. Yet even the cursing will mean nothing, for the punishment is fixed forever and no words or actions will ever change it.

The idea of eternal suffering has been so disturbing to some people that there have been countless attempts to deny it or limit its duration. People have claimed that eternal suffering is inconsistent with the goodness of God, who certainly will never allow any of his creatures to remain in hell forever. But God is a better judge of what is consistent with his goodness than we are, and it is he who says that hell is eternal. Others have argued that an eternal hell is inconsistent with the justice of God, for no sins committed in time could ever deserve such punishment. But what makes sin an infinite evil is that it is against an infinite God. Besides, we must remember that hell's punishments vary in severity according to the nature of the sin (see Matt. 11:22; Luke 12:47–48; 2 Cor. 5:10).

The bottom line is that verse 46 uses the same exact word to describe the duration of the sinner's punishment in hell as it does to describe the duration of the believer's life in heaven. It is the word *eternal*.

John Ryle was no alarmist, but he wrote:

> Who shall describe the misery of eternal punishment? It is something utterly indescribable and inconceivable. The eternal pain of body; the eternal sting of an accusing conscience; the eternal society of none but the wicked, the devil and his angels; the eternal remembrance of opportunities neglected and Christ despised; the eternal prospect of a weary, hopeless future—all this is misery indeed: it is enough to make our ears tingle, and our blood run cold.[11]

"Do These Things"

Why does Jesus say these terrible things? Is he trying to frighten us? No. What good would that do? People are not frightened into heaven. Jesus is warning us, particularly if we suppose that we are right with God when we are not right with him and will not be ready for Jesus when he comes.

When Peter tells us to "make [our] calling and election sure" (2 Peter 1:10), he also explains how it should be done. He says that we must add goodness to faith, knowledge to goodness, self-control to knowledge, perseverance to self-control, godliness to perseverance, brotherly kindness to godliness, and love to brotherly kindness (vv. 5–7). In other words, we must develop Christian character. But then he also adds rightly, "If you *do* these things, you will never fall, and you will receive a rich welcome into the eternal kingdom of our Lord and Savior Jesus Christ" (vv. 10–11, emphasis added). It is only by *doing* them that we show we have the life of Jesus Christ within.

PART TEN

The King's Death and Resurrection

61

Let the Drama Begin

Matthew 26:1-16

When Jesus had finished saying all these things, he said to his disciples, "As you know, the Passover is two days away—and the Son of Man will be handed over to be crucified."

Then the chief priests and the elders of the people assembled in the palace of the high priest, whose name was Caiaphas, and they plotted to arrest Jesus in some sly way and kill him. "But not during the Feast," they said, "or there may be a riot among the people."

While Jesus was in Bethany in the home of a man known as Simon the Leper, a woman came to him with an alabaster jar of very expensive perfume, which she poured on his head as he was reclining at the table.

When the disciples saw this, they were indignant. "Why this waste?" they asked. "This perfume could have been sold at a high price and the money given to the poor."

Aware of this, Jesus said to them, "Why are you bothering this woman? She has done a beautiful thing to me. The poor you will always have with you, but you will not always have me. When she poured this perfume on my body, she did it to prepare me for burial. I tell you the truth, wherever this gospel is preached throughout the world, what she has done will also be told, in memory of her."

Then one of the Twelve—the one called Judas Iscariot—went to the chief priests and asked, "What are you willing to give me if I hand him over to you?" So they counted out for him thirty silver coins. From then on Judas watched for an opportunity to hand him over.

For twenty-five chapters, ever since the introduction of Jesus as the descendant of David in verse 1 of chapter 1, the story of Christ's life has been moving toward a powerful, gripping climax: the murder of the King followed by his resurrection. The story started slowly, but it has been building in intensity throughout the three-year ministry and has now reached the point where the final act of the drama is at hand.[1] The King has come to Jerusalem for the final time, and the leaders of the people, who hate him, are plotting his arrest and execution.

Jesus has been preparing the disciples for his death by teaching them about it in advance. He has done so three times. The first is in Matthew 16:21. "From that time on Jesus began to explain to his disciples that he must go to Jerusalem and suffer many things at the hands of the elders, chief priests and teachers of the law, and that he must be killed and on the third day be raised to life." The second instance is in Matthew 17:22. "When they came together in Galilee, he said to them, 'The Son of Man is going to be betrayed into the hands of men. They will kill him, and on the third day he will be raised to life.'" The third prophecy is in Matthew 20:18. "We are going up to Jerusalem, and the Son of Man will be betrayed to the chief priests and the teachers of the law. They will condemn him to death and will turn him over to the Gentiles to be mocked and flogged and crucified. On the third day he will be raised to life!"

These prophecies grow increasingly detailed: The first merely tells of Jesus' death and resurrection; the second, his betrayal; the third, the involvement of the Gentiles in his mocking, flogging, and specifically his crucifixion. In Matthew 26 Jesus reveals when this will happen; it will be after two days. "As you know, the Passover is two days away—and the Son of Man will be handed over to be crucified" (Matt. 26:2). In all human history, no events have ever been of greater significance or more specifically prophesied than these. This drama is the turning point of history, the very center of Christianity.

Evil in High Places

According to Matthew's arrangement of his material, three events lead up to the arrest and crucifixion: (1) the plot of the Sanhedrin to arrest and kill Jesus (vv. 3–5), (2) the anointing of Jesus in Bethany (vv. 6–13), and (3) the offer of Judas to betray Jesus to the priests (vv. 14–16).

This is not the first time the religious leaders have met to discuss what they should do. They have been opposing Jesus all along. They have tried to catch him in some misstatement. At the end of chapter 21, we are told that "they looked for a way to arrest him" (v. 46). Here they finally get specific. They decide to arrest Jesus secretly, but not during the seven days of Passover, since millions of excitable people are in the city, not a few being Jesus' followers, and they fear a riot.

The leading figure in the plot to arrest and kill Jesus was Caiaphas, the high priest. Caiaphas had been appointed high priest by Valerius Gratus, Pilate's predecessor, in A.D. 18, about twelve years earlier. He was the son-in-law of Annas, the hereditary high priest who had served from A.D. 6–15, until the Romans deposed him. Caiaphas survived until A.D. 36, which means that he held his office for eighteen years. This tells us something important about

him. Between 37 B.C. and A.D. 67, when the last of the high priests was
appointed just before the destruction of the temple, the Romans appointed
and deposed no less than twenty-eight high priests. If Caiaphas survived for
eighteen years, it could only have been because he was a shrewd politician
who wanted to hang on to power at all costs.

This is precisely what the Gospel accounts disclose. In John's Gospel we
are told of a meeting of the leaders at which most were confused as to how
to deal with Jesus. They acknowledged Jesus' miracles, but they were afraid
that if he were allowed to go on as he had been, everyone would believe on
him and the Romans would come and take away their power and their nation
(John 11:47–48). What should they do? Shrewd old Caiaphas had the answer.
"You know nothing at all," he said. "You do not realize that it is better for
you that one man die for the people than that the whole nation perish"
(vv. 49–50). This was a self-serving policy couched in words that falsely suggested his concern was only for the well-being of the Jews.

It is an inescapable irony of the story that Jesus had prophesied his death
in two days while they, who wanted him dead as soon as possible, were plotting a delay of at least nine days—two days until the Passover and seven days
of the feast. Human beings plot, but it is the will of God that is done (Prov.
19:21). It was God's will that Jesus should be killed at the very moment the
Passover lambs were being slain, indicating that Jesus is indeed "the Lamb
of God, who takes away the sin of the world" (John 1:29).

Preparing for the End

At the very time these leaders were plotting to arrest and kill Jesus, another
person was preparing for his death but in an entirely different way and with
a different spirit. This person was Mary of Bethany, though Matthew does
not name her in his account. John records that "Mary took about a pint of
pure nard, an expensive perfume [and] poured it on Jesus' feet and wiped
his feet with her hair" (John 12:3). Matthew says only that "a woman came
to him with an alabaster jar of very expensive perfume, which she poured
on his head as he was reclining at the table" (v. 7).

A great deal has been written about the place and timing of this event.
Some have been troubled by the fact that Luke contains a similar story about
Jesus being anointed by a sinful woman in Galilee (Luke 7:36–38). But the
setting in Luke is different, and the time is earlier. These were distinct events.

A more troubling problem is the placement of this second anointing. John
says that the anointing occurred "six days before the Passover," when Jesus had
first arrived at Bethany (John 12:1), but Matthew and Mark seem to indicate
that at this time the Passover was only two days away (Matt. 26:2; Mark 14:1).

Clearly one or the other of these writers displaced the event for his own
purposes, and commentators come down on different sides of the issue. A
careful reading of the accounts shows that only John is actually dating the
story, however. Matthew and Mark record Jesus' prediction of his passion as

being only two days away. But when they tell the story of the anointing, they say only that it happened "while Jesus was in Bethany" (Matt. 26:6). This is in line with what we know of the Gospel writers. John is precise about his chronology, while Matthew and Mark move and often group material to fit the points they are making. Matthew has not reported that Jesus was in Bethany before this, and he has not had a place to put the story of Jesus' anointing until now. The chapters before this record Jesus' fierce denunciation of the religious leaders (chap. 23) and the Olivet Discourse (chaps. 24–25). Matthew tells of the anointing here because this is the section of the Gospel in which he is beginning to tell how Jesus moved forward to the cross. It is part of the preparation for his sacrifice.

The Gift of Love

Jesus had come with his disciples to Bethany to stay at the home of Mary, Martha, and Lazarus, who were his friends. They gave a supper in Jesus' honor, probably as a thank-you supper for raising Lazarus from the dead. It was a brave thing to do, since the Sanhedrin were seeking to arrest and kill him. What stuck out in everyone's mind, however, as they remembered the dinner, was Mary's extravagant act of anointing Jesus with her valuable perfume. John suggests that Mary had been keeping the ointment for this purpose for some time (John 12:7). She did not act impulsively on a mere whim. Nevertheless, her act was extravagant, since the perfume was worth three hundred denarii, about a year's wages for a working man (John 12:5).

Why did Mary do such an extravagant thing? Jesus gave the answer when he rebuked the disciples who were criticizing her for what they regarded as a waste of money. He explained, "When she poured this perfume on my body, she did it to prepare me for burial" (Matt. 26:12). Perhaps Mary did what she did unwittingly, not understanding its significance, but that does not fit the tone of the story. This was not a meaningless act. She was an amazingly perceptive woman, and the only way to appreciate what she did is to recognize that she alone of all the followers of Jesus understood that he was about to give his life for us on the cross.

Jesus had tried to explain his death to all of them, as I pointed out earlier, but the disciples did not understand. In fact, they were still fighting over who among them should be greatest. Only Mary understood, and she had for some time. Now she poured out her perfume to show Jesus that she understood what he was about to do and loved him for it.

How did Mary come to understand this when the others, particularly the disciples, failed to do so? By being often in the place where we find her now—at Jesus' feet, wiping his feet with her hair. This is where we find her in Luke 10, when Jesus came to visit. Martha was busy with preparations for the meal, but Mary "sat at the Lord's feet listening to what he said" (v. 39). This is where we find her in John 11, when Jesus returned following the death of Lazarus. When Mary came to Jesus "she fell at his feet," saying, "Lord, if you had been here, my brother would not have died" (John 11:32). Every time we see Mary she is at Jesus' feet, worshiping him and learning from him.

May I suggest that if you do not know much about spiritual things, it is because you have not spent time at Jesus' feet. If you want to learn about God and God's ways, you must learn from Jesus. Are you thinking that you cannot literally sit at Jesus' feet today? That is true. But you can do the same thing by studying the Bible. In Hebrew idiom, sitting at the feet of another person means to learn from that person, as a child might learn from a parent, or a pupil from his rabbi. The way we sit at Jesus' feet today is by studying the Bible, for it is there that he speaks to us and instructs us. Do you study the Bible? Many Christians say they wish they knew the Bible better, but they do not put in the necessary work to get to know it. They do not discipline themselves to do what is supremely worthwhile.

Many years ago, when he was just a young boy, Donald Grey Barnhouse was riding on a train with a well-known Bible teacher en route to one of the Bible teacher's meetings. The older man was reading his Bible. Barnhouse was reading the newspaper. At one point the boy looked over at the teacher, saw what he was doing, and said, "I wish I knew the Bible like you do."

"You'll never get to know it by reading the newspaper," the older man said kindly. Barnhouse said later that he got the message, put his paper away, and began to read his own Bible. In time he became a well-known Bible teacher too.[2]

All for Jesus

This story does not merely reveal that Mary sat at Jesus' feet and learned from him, however. That part of the story points to what Jesus gave her, but it is only half of what was going on. Mary also gave herself to Jesus, shown by her act of pouring out her expensive perfume. Mark tells us that she broke her jar to do it (Mark 14:3). She did not merely dip into the perfume a little bit or carefully pour out a small amount. On the contrary, she gave it all.

Many people give themselves to Jesus by offering him little bits of time here, little bits of money there, or little bits of devotion at an appropriate season of the year. They dip and sprinkle and are quite pleased with themselves, but that is because they have never looked deep into Jesus' eyes and grown to know him, as Mary had.

I think I can understand exactly what happened. Mary had sat at Jesus' feet not only to learn from him but also to get to know him. She had looked into his eyes and had seen his sorrow as he thought forward to the cross. She identified with him in his sorrow. She said to herself, "What can I do to show Jesus that I love him and that I understand what he is doing for us?" She thought of her perfume, the most precious possession she had. She gave it, and Jesus understood at once, as he always does. When the disciples objected to the apparent waste, Jesus told them, "Why are you bothering this woman? She has done a beautiful thing to me. The poor you will always have with you, but you will not always have me. When she poured this perfume on my body, she did it to prepare me for burial" (vv. 10–12).

Do not think that if you give Jesus your most precious possession he will overlook it or not know why you have given it. He cherishes the gifts of every yielded heart. Your gift will be different from Mary's. It may be your free time or a bank account or even your children. Would you give your children to the Lord's service if Jesus should call them? Would you give yourself if he should call? Would you give of your wealth to send others? Nothing given out of love will ever be overlooked by Jesus.

A Lasting Memorial and a Life of Infamy

An interesting twist to this story is that Mary anointed Jesus as a memorial for him, in view of his death and burial, though what she did actually became a memorial to her. Jesus' last words declare with solemn emphasis, "I tell you the truth, wherever this gospel is preached throughout the world, what she has done will also be told, in memory of her" (v. 13). So it has been.

Think how many great deeds of the many great kings, generals, tycoons, and other brilliant men of this world have been forgotten. People try to erect great monuments to themselves, but what they have done is hardly remembered by succeeding generations. They are like Ozymandias, about whom Percy Shelley wrote a brilliant poem. A traveler sees an immense but shattered statue in the desert. Nothing is left but the inscription: "My name is Ozymandias, king of kings:/Look on my works, ye Mighty, and despair!" Nothing remained. But Mary's selfless, loving, extravagant act lives on as a memorial to her and a witness to the greatness of her Lord.

Do you want to be remembered? Then do as Mary did. Leave off building monuments; build the lives of other people. Share your possessions, and give yourself to others. Remember that Jesus said, "Whoever wants to save his life will lose it, but whoever loses his life for me will find it. What good will it be for a man if he gains the whole world, yet forfeits his soul?" (Matt. 16:25–26).[3]

This brings us to Matthew's appropriately brief reference to Judas, who, we are told, went to the chief priests and offered to betray Jesus in exchange for thirty silver coins (vv. 14–16). Judas certainly did lose his soul! Jesus called Judas "the one doomed to destruction" (John 17:12), and just a few verses further on in Matthew 26 Jesus says of him, "Woe to that man who betrays the Son of Man! It would be better for him if he had not been born" (v. 24). Clearly Judas perished and his money with him!

What a terrible thing it was to betray Jesus Christ. It was, to use the words Franklin Delano Roosevelt chose to inform the American public of the Japanese attack on Pearl Harbor, "a day that will live in infamy." Judas spent three years in the closest possible association with the only perfect man who ever lived. Yet in the end he turned his back on Jesus and gave him up to be murdered. It was a horrible deed, and Judas experienced a horrible end. But it is not altogether different from the decisions of those who turn their backs on Jesus today and whose end is the same as the betrayer's. Like Judas, many seek the world and its pleasures and forfeit their souls.

What could possibly have induced Judas to betray Jesus to the priests? The only clues we have are his demand for money and the disclosure in John 12 that Judas kept the disciples' purse and stole from it (v. 6). I suppose Judas was worldly in the sense that he evaluated things only by what they were worth in hard currency, and he was probably badly disillusioned when he realized that Jesus was not going to be the kind of Messiah he expected and wanted. Jesus was not going to set up an earthly throne and dispense earthly honors, starting with the faithful Twelve. Judas was probably bitter, believing that he had wasted three years on an utterly hopeless cause.

How could Judas have missed learning what was truly valuable and giving up everything for it? I do not know, but I know that millions are doing just that today. Let me remind you that it is possible to be quite close to Jesus Christ, to sit in a Christian church listening to good sermons, to hear good Bible teaching on radio or television, to have Christian parents or Christian friends who live consistent and effective Christian lives and bear strong testimonies to the gospel of God's grace, and yet fail to love Christ and never reach the point of making a personal commitment to him as one's Lord and Savior. You can be that close to Jesus Christ and yet be lost.

It would be a tragedy for that to be true in your case, but it is not necessary, especially if you have understood who Jesus is and what he came to earth to do. Like Mary, you need to look deeply into his eyes and learn to love him as the one who loves you and gave himself for your salvation.

62

With Jesus in the Upper Room

Matthew 26:17–35

On the first day of the Feast of Unleavened Bread, the disciples came to Jesus and asked, "Where do you want us to make preparations for you to eat the Passover?"

He replied, "Go into the city to a certain man and tell him, 'The Teacher says: My appointed time is near. I am going to celebrate the Passover with my disciples at your house.'" So the disciples did as Jesus had directed them and prepared the Passover.

When evening came, Jesus was reclining at the table with the Twelve. And while they were eating, he said, "I tell you the truth, one of you will betray me."

They were very sad and began to say to him one after the other, "Surely not I, Lord?"

Jesus replied, "The one who has dipped his hand into the bowl with me will betray me. The Son of Man will go just as it is written about him. But woe to that man who betrays the Son of Man! It would be better for him if he had not been born."

Then Judas, the one who would betray him, said, "Surely not I, Rabbi?"

Jesus answered, "Yes, it is you."

While they were eating, Jesus took bread, gave thanks and broke it, and gave it to his disciples, saying, "Take and eat; this is my body."

Then he took the cup, gave thanks and offered it to them, saying, "Drink from it, all of you. This is my blood of the covenant, which is poured out for many for the forgiveness of sins. I tell you, I will not drink of this fruit of the vine from now on until that day when I drink it anew with you in my Father's kingdom."

Not long ago a friend sent me a card with a picture of a small boy wearing a straw hat and floating on an inner tube on a tranquil country pond. His head was thrown back. He was in perfect peace. The caption read: "Each life needs its own quiet place." The verses we come to next in Matthew 26 are like that. They are a quiet place at the center of the storm that is about to break. The rulers of the people are plotting how they might take Jesus' life. Judas has offered to betray Jesus to them at the earliest possible opportunity. Evil is afoot. But while it is gathering, Jesus collects his disciples for one final time of fellowship and teaching before the crucifixion.

The center point of these last moments is the institution of the Lord's Supper, recorded in verses 26–30. But the account is preceded by verses that tell how Jesus arranged for the observance (vv. 17–19), and the words of the institution are bracketed by an announcement of Judas' betrayal in verses 20–25 and a prediction of Peter's denial in verses 31–35.

Jesus Was in Charge

The point of the introduction is that Jesus was in charge of what was happening (vv. 17–19). He was no puppet captured in some unguarded moment but rather a willing voluntary sacrifice who ordered the events leading up to his arrest. He had arranged to eat the Passover in the home of an unnamed man from Jerusalem, and now he sends two of his disciples to make the preparations (Mark 14:13). The secrecy of Jesus' directions was probably designed to prevent a premature arrest since Jesus knew that Judas was looking for a chance to hand him over to the authorities (Matt. 26:16).

The dating of the meal is a puzzle. Matthew says it was on "the first day of the Feast of Unleavened Bread," suggesting that Jesus ate the regular Passover at the prescribed time, which would have been the 15th of the month of Nisan. But John says Jesus ate this meal on the day before the Passover, which would have been the 14th.

John indicates his dating in a number of places, but the clearest is the passage that explains that Caiaphas and the other members of the Sanhedrin would not go into Pilate's palace when they brought Jesus to Pilate for trial because that would have defiled them and kept them from eating the Passover (John 18:28). John also explains that the breaking of the legs of the two thieves who were crucified with Jesus was an act intended to hurry the deaths of these men because the Jews "did not want the bodies left on the crosses during the Sabbath" (John 19:31). In John, the problem facing the Jewish leaders is how to arrest, try, and execute Jesus before the Passover Sabbath begins, since they have been hurried into action by the unexpected offer of Judas to betray his Master.

How is this chronological difficulty resolved? Liberal scholars merely say that either the Synoptic Gospels or John is wrong. The majority of others side with Matthew, Mark, and Luke and try to understand John's time references in alternate ways.[1]

In my judgment, the best and simplest solution is that Jesus knew and no doubt planned that he would be crucified at the very time the Passover lambs were being slain, as John indicates, and therefore arranged to eat this meal with his disciples a day early. This is the view of R. T. France[2] and some others. It explains why there is no mention of the lamb in these accounts, which would be strange if this were an actual Passover celebration, and also why nothing is reported of Jesus' activity on the Wednesday of this week if the meal were on Thursday. In my understanding of the chronology, Jesus arranged for the meal on Wednesday afternoon, ate it with his disciples that evening (the beginning of the 15th of Nisan), was arrested that night, tried and executed by noon the next day (Thursday), and was removed from the cross and buried by Nicodemus and Joseph of Arimathea by nightfall, which was the beginning of the Friday Passover.

I think that the Passover Sabbath, which had begun on Thursday evening and continued into Friday, was followed by the regular Saturday Sabbath, and that Jesus rose from the dead sometime before dawn on Sunday morning, having been in the tomb a literal three days and three nights, as he prophesied (Matt. 12:40). The women came to the tomb on Sunday morning following the two Sabbaths.[3]

"Surely Not I?"

What are we to say about Judas? Only that his betrayal was predicted (vv. 20–25), which showed that Jesus was in control here as well as at other moments, and that Judas's end is clearly stated as a warning.

John Ryle wrote:

> Judas Iscariot had the highest possible religious privileges. He was a chosen apostle and companion of Christ; he was an eye-witness of our Lord's miracles and a hearer of his sermons; he lived in the society of the eleven apostles; he was a fellow-laborer with Peter, James and John. . . . Not one of the eleven seems to have suspected him of hypocrisy. When our Lord said, "One of you shall betray me," no one said, "Is it Judas?" Yet all this time his heart was never changed.[4]

Remember this if you are playing fast and loose with your attachment to Jesus Christ. You can come to church, hear sound preaching, volunteer for Christian work, support Christian causes, even partake of the Lord's Supper, and still perish, if you are not truly born again. And perish Judas did! Judas is in hell today. Jesus' words about Judas's end teach plainly "that it is better never to live at all, than to live without faith and to die without grace," as Ryle states it.[5] It is possible to be as close to Jesus as Judas was and be lost.

The Last Supper

The heart of this passage is Jesus' institution of the Lord's Supper in verses 26–30. Jesus would probably have been following the ritual for the Passover. He may have blessed the bread with the familiar words, "Praise be to you, Yahweh, our God, King of the world, who brings forth bread from the earth."

But suddenly, as he finished the prayer, broke the bread, and began to distribute it around the table, he announced in words that were a sharp break from all that was familiar, "This is my body" (v. 26).

These words were remembered accurately, for they occur in each of the first three Gospels as well as in 1 Corinthians 11. Yet no words in the entire Bible have been fought over more fiercely than these four. There are four main interpretations.

1. *Transubstantiation.* This is the view of Roman Catholicism, which holds that the substance of the bread (but not its accidents) is literally changed into the substance of the body of Jesus Christ. This means that the priests literally handle Christ's body and that the mass is a literal reenactment of Christ's sacrifice. The difference between "substance" and "accidents" comes from Aristotle, whose philosophy governed the thought of the Middle Ages.

2. *Consubstantiation.* This was Martin Luther's view, not that the substance of the bread is changed into the substance of the body of Christ but that the unchanged substance of the bread is united with the substance of Christ's body. Luther knew that the bread is unchanged, but he wanted to preserve a literal understanding of Jesus' words: *Hoc est corpus meus.* The Reformed and Lutheran churches parted over this understanding.

3. *A mere remembrance.* This was the position of Ulrich Zwingli and is held today by most Baptists. It views the sacrament through the words "this do in remembrance of me" (1 Cor. 11:24) and sees the sacrament as a memorial only.

4. *A spiritual presence.* John Calvin's view became the theology of Presbyterians, Methodists, and most Episcopalians. It holds that Jesus is truly present in the communion service, but that he is present spiritually, not in a physical way. The blessing of the communion service is a real blessing linked to the observance of the sacrament, but it is to be received by faith as are all other spiritual blessings. There is nothing automatic or mechanical about its observance.

Nothing anyone says today is likely to budge churches from positions they have held for centuries, but it is worth saying that there is no reason to take the words "This is my body" as a literal statement. The plain meaning of the words "This is my body" is, "This bread represents my body," as also, "This wine represents my shed blood."

There are many reasons for insisting on this. For one thing, the disciples to whom Jesus gave the bread and wine were Jews, and Jews had been taught that it was sinful to eat flesh with the blood in it (Deut. 12:23–25). If they had taken Christ's words literally, they would have been startled or shocked by his words. There is nothing in the narratives to suggest this reaction. The disciples saw no change in the bread or wine, nor would they have expected to. They understood that Jesus' words were figurative, just as many of his other sayings were.

Second, we know that in any communion service (or even the mass) the bread remains bread and the wine remains wine. Our senses are indicators of what is true at this point. The distinction drawn from Aristotle between substance and accidents is artificial and an obvious last resort of persons unwilling to give up the literal sense of the word *is*.

Third, the doctrine of the incarnation teaches that the Son of God took on himself a true human body, and it is the nature of bodies that they cannot be in more than one place or exist in more than one form at the same time. When Jesus instituted the Lord's Supper, he was before the disciples in true bodily form, and if he was present bodily, his body could not have been present in the bread nor his blood in the wine.

Fourth, the statement "This is my body" is no different from numerous similar statements that occur throughout the Bible, such as, "The seven good cows are seven years" (Gen. 41:26); "You are that head of gold" (Dan. 2:38); "The field is the world" (Matt. 13:38); "That rock was Christ" (1 Cor. 10:4); "The seven lampstands are the seven churches" (Rev. 1:20); and Jesus' words, "I am the gate for the sheep" (John 10:7); "I am the true vine" (John 15:1); and so on. Clearly, it is a spiritual feeding on Christ and not a literal eating of his body and a literal drinking of his blood that is intended. We need to do this regularly and with faith.[6]

In some ways, it is a pity that debate about the literal or nonliteral meaning of Christ's words has been so fierce, since it has tended to obscure the equally important (probably far more important) teachings about Jesus' death that we have here. Think how many important doctrines are taught by Jesus' words and this sacrament.

1. *A vicarious atonement.* Jesus died in our place as our substitute, taking our guilt on himself and bearing the punishment for our sins. This was the meaning of the Passover, which was being observed that very week, and it is what is symbolized by the breaking of the bread. As the bread was broken, so would Jesus' body be broken, but not for himself. It would be broken for those who would trust him as their Savior.

2. *A new covenant.* Matthew 26:28 is the only verse containing the word *covenant* in this Gospel. It is an important use of the word and almost certainly a reference to Exodus 24:8, where Moses says, "This is the blood of the covenant that the Lord has made with you."[7] Since Exodus 24 records the establishment of the old covenant, we can hardly miss the contrast between that old covenant and the new covenant that is set in place by Jesus. Matthew and Mark do not use the word *new*, but Luke does (Luke 22:20), and Paul also preserves the word in his transcription of the words, "This cup is the new covenant in my blood; do this, whenever you drink it, in remembrance of me" (1 Cor. 11:25).

Jesus' linking of the old covenant and the new covenant makes clear that his death was the fulfillment and end of the millions of blood sacrifices that had been used to seal and maintain the old covenant. There would be no more need for sacrifices once he had died for our sin. Moreover, although Matthew did not preserve Jesus' use of the word *new*,[8] Jesus apparently said "new," which means that he was also presenting his death as a fulfillment of the promise recorded in Jeremiah 31:

> "The time is coming," declares the LORD,
>   "when I will make a new covenant
> with the house of Israel
>   and with the house of Judah. . . .
> "I will put my law in their minds
>   and write it on their hearts.
> I will be their God,
>   and they will be my people.
> No longer will a man teach his neighbor,
>   or a man his brother, saying, 'Know the LORD,'
> because they will all know me,
>   from the least of them to the greatest,"
>   declares the LORD.
> "For I will forgive their wickedness
>   and will remember their sins no more."
>
>   verses 31, 33–34

The old covenant was a gracious covenant, but the people had not been able to keep it. In the new covenant, God's people would be empowered to keep the law, which would be written on their hearts and minds.

3. *The forgiveness of sins.* The fact that Jesus spoke of the forgiveness of sins is another indication that he was thinking of Jeremiah 31 as well as Exodus 24. But these words make an additional point. To be forgiven by God is our great need, for it is only as our sins are forgiven and we are clothed with the righteousness of Christ that we can stand before a holy God. It is by the blood of Christ alone that we are cleansed from sin's defilement.

4. *Particular redemption.* This passage also contains the doctrine of particular redemption. Jesus did not say that his blood would be poured out for everyone for the forgiveness of their sins, but "for many" (v. 28). It was not poured out for Judas, for he was not saved. If Jesus had died for him, he would have been saved, since even the sin of his betrayal would have been cleansed by Christ's blood. Jesus taught in these few words that his death was for his own people only and that it was effective in saving them and only them from their sins. Jesus' blood made an actual atonement for transgressions. His sacrifice actually propitiated God on their behalf. His death secured their justification, and by his stripes they all were truly healed.

Particular redemption means that Christ's death was not for all, but Jesus' words also teach that it was not merely for a few but for many. Many have come. Many more are yet to come. There are many with whom we have yet to share the gospel.

5. *Eternal security.* Christ's words also teach the truth of eternal security, for he stated as an unchallengeable fact that one day he would drink wine

with his disciples ("with you," v. 29) in his Father's kingdom. How could Jesus be sure? Obviously because his death would accomplish their salvation so completely and perfectly that not even Peter's public denial of the Lord would undermine it.

"I Will Never Disown You"

Which brings us to Peter's denial (vv. 31–35). We do not have to look into Peter's failure in detail here, because we will come to it again at the end of this chapter. But we can say this. There is no doubt that Peter loved Jesus and was fiercely loyal. Peter was earnest when he answered the Lord's predictions by protesting, "Even if all fall away on account of you, I never will" (v. 33) and, "Even if I have to die with you, I will never disown you" (v. 35). But Peter did not know his own weakness, and when the crisis arrived, he fled into the darkness with the others and later denied Jesus as he stood in the courtyard of the priests.

The events had been predicted, of course, and not just by Jesus in these moments before his arrest and crucifixion. A similar prediction is found in Zechariah 13:7, as Jesus understood it: "I will strike the shepherd, and the sheep of the flock will be scattered." Jesus was struck. The sheep were scattered. But it was because Jesus was struck for the disciples that their sins of denial, as well as all their other sins, were forgiven, and it was by the drawing power of Jesus' glorious resurrection that they were eventually brought together again and reestablished as the church, which is Christ's true body on this earth.

It should comfort us to know that Christianity is for people exactly like these weak disciples. Not very often is Christianity for the strong, the powerful, the rich, the successful, or the self-sufficient, because such people do not often think they need Jesus. Paul noticed this and wrote about it in 1 Corinthians 1:26–29. It is difficult to get self-sufficient people to see their need of Christ and come to him. Christianity is most often for those who are weak, ignorant, and often fail but who know their need, turn from sin, and trust Jesus, just as Peter did.

You need to become one of these people. If you do, you will cease to trust in yourself and will trust and love Jesus, and you will know that all the blessings of the gospel are for you.

63

Alone in the Garden

Matthew 26:36-46

Then Jesus went with his disciples to a place called Gethsemane, and he said to them, "Sit here while I go over there and pray." He took Peter and the two sons of Zebedee along with him, and he began to be sorrowful and troubled. Then he said to them, "My soul is overwhelmed with sorrow to the point of death. Stay here and keep watch with me."

Going a little farther, he fell with his face to the ground and prayed, "My Father, if it is possible, may this cup be taken from me. Yet not as I will, but as you will."

Then he returned to his disciples and found them sleeping. "Could you men not keep watch with me for one hour?" he asked Peter. "Watch and pray so that you will not fall into temptation. The spirit is willing, but the body is weak."

He went away a second time and prayed, "My Father, if it is not possible for this cup to be taken away unless I drink it, may your will be done."

When he came back, he again found them sleeping, because their eyes were heavy. So he left them and went away once more and prayed the third time, saying the same thing.

Then he returned to the disciples and said to them, "Are you still sleeping and resting? Look, the hour is near, and the Son of Man is betrayed into the hands of sinners. Rise, let us go! Here comes my betrayer!"

The Bible contains passages that we often handle lightly, thinking either rightly or wrongly that they are not of first importance. But other passages draw us up short and seem to cry out sharply, "Take off your shoes, for the place where you are standing is holy ground."

565

This is especially true of the accounts of Jesus' prayer in the Garden of Gethsemane in which he asked that if it were possible, the cup that he had been given to drink might be taken from him. The account is in each of the first three Gospels (Matt. 26:36–46; Mark 14:32–42; Luke 22:39–46), which indicates that the writers felt this event was of great importance.

Charles H. Spurgeon wrote of this passage, "Here we come to the Holy of Holies of our Lord's life on earth. This is a mystery like that which Moses saw when the bush burned with fire, and was not consumed. No man can rightly expound such a passage as this; it is a subject for prayerful, heart-broken meditation, more than for human language."[1] William Barclay said, "Surely this is a passage we must approach upon our knees."[2] D. A. Carson declared, "As his death was unique, so also was his anguish; and our best response to it is hushed worship."[3]

Yet we are also to learn from this story. That is why it is present in the Gospels. We must learn from it precisely so that we may be moved to prayerful awe and bow before God in hushed worship.

The Lord's Humanity

The first thing we can learn from this story is that the Lord Jesus Christ was fully human. Nowhere else in the Gospel accounts of his life on earth do we see him more pressed down—more vulnerable—than when he took Peter, James, and John, his three closest friends, aside and said to them, "My soul is overwhelmed with sorrow to the point of death. Stay here and keep watch with me" (v. 38).

True, this is not the only place in Scripture where we see the human side of Jesus. We read that he was born of a woman and was laid in a crude manger at his birth. He would have been nursed like other babies. We are told that he "grew in wisdom and stature, and in favor with God and men" (Luke 2:52). Jesus got hungry, especially when he was driven into the wilderness to be tempted by the devil. When he sat at Jacob's well he asked the Samaritan woman for a drink because he was thirsty. He was thirsty on the cross (John 19:28). On one occasion he was so tired that he fell asleep in the stern of a wildly rocking boat in a storm on the Sea of Galilee. When he approached Jerusalem on the day of his triumphal entry, he wept over the city, knowing that the day of its destruction was not distant (Luke 19:41–44). Still, there is no place in which Jesus appears more like us in our humanity than when he experienced sorrow and anguish in the garden.

His was a very great sorrow. It was so great that he wanted to have his closest friends with him in his trouble. He needed to share it with them, which he did by explaining that his grief was so great it was almost killing him. But conversely, it was also so great that he had to bear it alone. He was fulfilling Isaiah 63:3, where the warrior from Bozrah cries, "I have trodden the winepress alone; from the nations no one was with me." Ben H. Price captured Jesus' acute isolation when he wrote:

> It was alone the Savior prayed
> In dark Gethsemane;
> Alone he drained the bitter cup
> And suffered there for me.
> Alone, alone he bore it all alone;
> He gave himself to save his own,
> He suffered, bled, and died alone, alone.[4]

Jesus was like us in his sorrow, but we have to remember too that his sorrow was also *not* like ours. It was greater than anything we will ever bear, since what pressed on him so heavily was the task of bearing the world's sin and its punishment on our behalf. "Cup" is a biblical image for God's wrath, and the wrath of God for sin troubled Jesus when he asked that the cup might be taken from him. Psalm 75:8 reads,

> In the hand of the LORD is a cup
> full of foaming wine mixed with spices;
> he pours it out, and all the wicked of the earth
> drink it down to its very dregs.

Isaiah 51:22 describes the cup as "the goblet of my wrath." Jeremiah 25:15 calls it "the wine of my wrath." Ezekiel 23:31–34 talks about "the cup of ruin and desolation" that was brought upon Samaria. Jesus drank from the cup of God's wrath so we might never have to drink it. In place of that cup we have the communion cup, which is the cup of the new covenant in Christ's blood.

The Importance of Prayer

The second lesson we can learn from this passage is the importance of prayer. Prayer is important at all times. Paul instructed the Thessalonians to "pray continually" (1 Thess. 5:16). He told the Ephesians to "pray in the Spirit on all occasions with all kinds of prayers and requests" (Eph. 6:18). But especially we must pray in times of great sorrow. Jesus did! He prayed at length and fervently. John Ryle said that "prayer is the best practical remedy that we can use in time of trouble."[5] Should we suppose that we have a better cure for it than Jesus?

Hezekiah was one of the godly kings of Judah, who lived in a dangerous age. The kingdom of Assyria had been rising in power, and Shalmaneser, the king of Assyria, had marched against Samaria and destroyed it. His successor, Sennacherib, attacked Judah, captured many of its cities, and shut up Hezekiah and his people in Jerusalem. In a monument erected after the battle, now in the British Museum, he boasted that he had confined Hezekiah in his walled city like a caged bird. Sennacherib sent a letter to the king demanding his surrender. In the midst of this great trouble, Hezekiah took the letter to the temple and "spread it out before the LORD" (2 Kings 19:14).

Hezekiah took his trouble to God, and God answered through the prophet Isaiah, saying that before morning the enemy would be gone. That night an angel of the Lord struck down 185,000 of Sennacherib's soldiers, and the king returned to Nineveh.

That is what you need to do when trouble assails you. Jesus brought his trouble to the Father and was heard. Luke says an angel came and "strengthened him" (Luke 22:43). God will also strengthen you.

How to Pray

The third lesson in these verses is actually a set of lessons, a manual that explains what it really means to pray. There are four things we should learn about prayer from this passage.

1. *True prayer is prayer to God the Father.* I do not mean by this that prayer cannot also be offered to Jesus, who is God the Son, or to the Holy Spirit, who is the Third Person of the Trinity. Prayer to any member of the Trinity is prayer to God. Rather, I mean that true prayer is always prayer to God and that, in addition, it is prayer to the God Jesus said we can address as Father (Matt. 6:9).

The problem here is that probably one prayer in a thousand is a true prayer to God. Prayer to any god other than the God of the Bible is not true prayer, because a god other than the God of the Bible is an imaginary being. He is no true God. Even people who are Christians and who believe they are praying to the Bible's God may actually be praying only as a formality. They are not conscious of being in God's presence; they are often praying merely for show! Their prayers are like the prayer of a fashionable Boston preacher some years ago whose Sunday morning prayer was described by a Boston newspaper as "the most eloquent prayer ever offered to a Boston audience." Reuben Torrey wrote a helpful book about prayer in which he advised, "We should never utter one syllable of prayer either in public or in private until we are definitely conscious that we have come into the presence of God and are actually praying to him."[6]

The other problem is that we do not know God very well and therefore do not pray as we are privileged to pray and should pray. Jesus taught us to pray to God as children coming to our Father in heaven. He did so explicitly in the Lord's Prayer (Matt. 6:9). He does so here by his example.

To call God "father" was a striking, almost blasphemous thing in Jesus' day, when the Jews of the time would not even pronounce God's name (Yahweh or Jehovah), avoiding it out of misplaced reverence. They referred to God as Adonai (Lord) instead. By contrast, Jesus always referred to God as his Father. In fact, he used the endearing term *abba,* which some would translate "daddy." This was so novel that the disciples remembered it and preserved it in their accounts of Jesus' prayers. Mark does so in this account, writing that Jesus prayed, "Abba, Father, everything is possible for you. Take this cup from me. Yet not what I will, but what you will" (Mark 14:36).

2. *Effective prayer is according to God's will.* That brings us to the second lesson about prayer in this passage: Effective prayer is prayer that deliberately submits to God's will. In this account, Jesus' immaculate soul shrank from bearing our sin and experiencing the painful alienation from the Father, which was its punishment. He was not playacting when he said, "If it is possible, may this cup be taken from me." The cross must have been a horror for him infinitely beyond anything you or I can ever imagine. Nevertheless, he prayed, "Not as I will, but as you will."

What does it mean to pray according to God's will? First, it means putting God and his interests first in our lives. Jesus taught us to pray, "Your kingdom come, your will be done on earth as it is in heaven" (Matt. 6:10). Our concern should be for God's kingdom and God's glory rather than our own. If it is, many of the things that trouble us will fade away, and we will even willingly embrace things that are themselves undesirable, difficult, or painful. Jesus accepted the cross and its horrors because he had learned by praying that it was the determined will of God.

Second, praying according to God's will means praying according to what is in the Bible because that is where the will of God is made known to us. Not everything we might want to know is in the Bible. The Bible does not tell us what job we should take, whom we should marry, or where we should live. But it does give us principles that are quite specific. If we are serious about following what is disclosed in the Bible, we will find answers to most of what disturbs or puzzles us.

Are we to suppose that Jesus ignored Scripture during these moments of prayer in the garden? Hardly. His mind was always filled with Scripture, and he would have been thinking through the biblical passages that describe the Messiah's work as he wrestled before his Father with what was coming. We have evidence that he was thinking of Scripture here, because a few moments later, when Peter tried to protect him by striking out at a member of the party that had come to arrest him, Jesus told Peter to put his sword away, saying, "How then would the Scriptures be fulfilled that say it must happen in this way?" (Matt. 26:54).

3. *We must be persistent in some prayers.* The third thing we learn about prayer from this passage is that we must be persistent in our prayers. Some people have argued that we need to offer a specific prayer only once on the grounds that God hears us, will do what is best, and does not need to be badgered into doing what we want. But we can hardly miss the fact that Jesus prayed for the same thing over and over again in this passage. The apostle Paul did the same thing. He told the Corinthians that he had prayed three times for his "thorn in the flesh" to be removed. It was not, but he testified that God gave him grace to bear it (2 Cor. 12:7–9).

That leads to something very important. Persisting in prayer did not get God to change his mind, but it did change Paul's mind so that he saw his weakness differently and was able to praise God for it. He learned that God's power was made perfect in his weakness (v. 9). Was that not also true of Jesus' prayer in the garden? We must be careful that we do not read too much into these accounts, but we can notice a significant progression in Jesus' three requests. In his first prayer, Jesus asked that the cup might be avoided ("may this cup be taken from me," v. 39). In the second prayer, he seems to have recognized that the cup could not be avoided and adds this negative: "If [or since] it is *not* possible for this cup to be taken away unless I drink it" (v. 42, emphasis added). Matthew does not give the wording of the third petition, but we can suppose it was something like this: "Since the cross is your will and since it cannot be avoided, I ask for strength to bear it for your glory." I suggest that Jesus prayed along these lines because of Luke's account. Luke says that "an angel from heaven appeared to him and strengthened him" (Luke 22:43).

How long did this take? We can read these verses in a few seconds, but we have a clue that it took a great deal longer. After Jesus returned the first time he asked, "Could you men not keep watch with me *for one hour?*" (v. 40, emphasis added). Bible references to time are imprecise, of course. No one had watches. But Jesus' question suggests that he prayed for an hour and that he probably did so the second and third times as well. This adds up to several hours of intense prayer. We should not suppose that we can get by with a few short minutes.

4. *We should pray in faith, expecting an answer.* The fourth thing we can learn about prayer from this account is that we need to pray in faith, expecting an answer. The answer will not always be what we anticipate, for God's ways are not our ways nor are his thoughts our thoughts. But we should expect God to answer somehow. The Father answered Jesus because he went to his arrest, trial, and crucifixion with no hint of fear or wavering from this point on. He was settled in his mind and had been given strength for the ordeal. This is also taught by a text in Hebrews that refers to this event. The author of Hebrews wrote, "During the days of Jesus' life on earth, he offered up prayers and petitions with loud cries and tears to the one who could save him from death, and he was heard because of his reverent submission" (Heb. 5:7).

This also seems to be the basis for the challenge to pray that the author of Hebrews gave earlier:

> Therefore, since we have a great high priest who has gone through the heavens, Jesus the Son of God, let us hold firmly to the faith we profess. For we do not have a high priest who is unable to sympathize with our weaknesses, but we have one who has been tempted in every way, just as we are—yet was without sin. Let us then approach the throne of grace with confidence, so that we may receive mercy and find grace to help us in our time of need.
>
> Hebrews 4:14–16

Jesus had more to say about prayer than about almost any other subject, and the point he seems to have made most is simplicity itself: Just pray. There is much about prayer we do not understand and may never understand, but these things we do know: (1) God hears prayer, (2) God answers prayer, (3) we are commanded to pray, (4) prayer matters, and (5) Jesus himself prayed, giving us an example. So pray. Jesus told Peter, "Watch and pray so that you will not fall into temptation" (v. 41).

The Weakness of Our Flesh

That leads to the last lesson we need to draw from this passage, namely, the weakness of our flesh. Did Jesus need to pray? He obviously did, and he was the sinless Son of God. He was the Rock of Ages, an unshakable pillar of strength compared to those around him. But if he needed to pray, how much more do we who are weak and sinful and ignorant and usually oblivious to the temptations that surround us every day?

"The flesh is weak," Jesus said. But not only weak. It is a pit of corruption and rebellion too. The New International Version translates the Greek word *sarx* ("flesh") as "body" in verse 41, but that greatly weakens the word in my opinion. In the New Testament, *flesh* usually means "mere flesh," that is, the whole person as he or she is apart from the regenerating and purifying Spirit of God. Flesh stands for "man the sinner," and man the sinner is more than physically weak. He is corrupt, sinful, and rebellious in his soul.

What is the solution? It is staring us in the face. "Watch and pray," said Jesus. Why? Because apart from prayer we will certainly "fall into temptation" (v. 41). The only way we can stand is in the power of Jesus, who was himself able to stand and who intercedes for us to enable us to stand, even as we pray.

Peter thought he was strong. When Jesus spoke of his impending death, indicating that the disciples would forsake him and scatter, Peter protested. Although that might be true for the others, it would not be true for him since he was willing not only to suffer but even to die for Jesus' sake. Peter meant it. He loved the Lord. He thought he could stand by him. But Peter was weak in the flesh, and he was not able even to keep awake long enough to pray.

Peter also fell into temptation, and he would have fallen away utterly if Jesus had not prayed for him that his faith might be strengthened. Jesus said, "I have prayed for you, Simon, that your faith might not fail. And when you have turned back, strengthen your brothers" (Luke 22:32).

John H. Gerstner suggested at one of the Philadelphia Conferences on Reformation Theology that it must have been Peter who composed the song found in some of today's hymnbooks. It has the recurring chorus line, "Lord, we are able." That is what Peter sang before his fall. But Gerstner suggested that after Peter had fallen and been restored by Jesus, he rewrote his self-confident hymn to read, "Lord, we are *not* able." Peter was not able, and neither are we. In the flesh we will fall, but we can stand in Christ if we come to him and pray, seeking the strength he makes available. So pray. If you have trouble praying, remember that Jesus prayed and that he is praying for you right now.

64

In the Hands of His Enemies

Matthew 26:47–56

While he was still speaking, Judas, one of the Twelve, arrived. With him was a large crowd armed with swords and clubs, sent from the chief priests and the elders of the people. Now the betrayer had arranged a signal with them: "The one I kiss is the man; arrest him." Going at once to Jesus, Judas said, "Greetings, Rabbi!" and kissed him.

Jesus replied, "Friend, do what you came for."

Then the men stepped forward, seized Jesus and arrested him. With that, one of Jesus' companions reached for his sword, drew it out and struck the servant of the high priest, cutting off his ear.

"Put your sword back in its place," Jesus said to him, "for all who draw the sword will die by the sword. Do you think I cannot call on my Father, and he will at once put at my disposal more than twelve legions of angels? But how then would the Scriptures be fulfilled that say it must happen in this way?"

At that time Jesus said to the crowd, "Am I leading a rebellion, that you have come out with swords and clubs to capture me? Every day I sat in the temple courts teaching, and you did not arrest me. But this has all taken place that the writings of the prophets might be fulfilled." Then all the disciples deserted him and fled.

We have been moving toward the arrest, trials, and crucifixion of Jesus of Nazareth for some time, but at last the decisive moment has come. Jesus has prepared his disciples as best they could be prepared, and he has prepared himself by his hours of prayer in the garden. Now the band of armed men who have been sent to seize him and carry him off to the hall of the high priest arrive in Gethsemane, and Jesus goes forward to meet them. In the forefront of the arresting band is Judas, the betrayer.

It is a ludicrous sight. Men with swords pressing forward to arrest the Son of God. Others with torches, as John tells us (John 18:3), coming in the darkness to arrest the one who is the only source of true light.

Why Was Judas Needed?

The last we saw Judas he was in the upper room, where Jesus identified him as the betrayer. He had left after that. Jesus and the eleven disciples left the city for the Mount of Olives, and Jesus prayed about his coming crucifixion. Judas went to the priests and collected the "large crowd" that would take his master into custody.

The real question about Judas's role in the arrest is, Why was he needed at all? Many commentators usually suppose that he needed to show the arresting party where Jesus was. But that is not as obvious as one might suppose. Jesus had not been hiding. He had been guarded in his movements earlier, but not this week. From the Friday preceding his crucifixion when he had arrived at Bethany, he could hardly have been more open. It should have been easy for the crowd to find him and arrest him.

It is usually said at this point that the leaders of the people wanted to arrest Jesus secretly for fear of the people, which clearly was a factor. Even so, there must have been many moments that week when they could have moved against Jesus quietly.

Frank Morison provides an interesting suggestion in his book *Who Moved the Stone?*[1] He argues that the Jewish leaders were afraid of Jesus in two senses. They knew he was popular with the people. If they confronted him openly, there was always the possibility that he would call the crowds to his defense and an uprising would result. They did not want that. Even more disturbing, however, was the matter of Christ's undeniable, supernatural power. They had tried to arrest him on an earlier occasion, but he had simply slipped away from them. On another occasion the soldiers who had been sent to take him prisoner came back with an incredible story: "No one ever spoke the way this man does," they said (John 7:46). What if in the final analysis Jesus was unarrestable?

Besides, there was the problem of doing everything that needed to be done in the available time. This was the day before Passover. Jesus could not be executed on the Sabbath. How could the leaders carry out the arrest and hold the trials—their own trial to secure a verdict of death and the Roman trial necessary to have the execution carried out—all before the Passover Sabbath? We know how they did it. They held their own hurried trial by night, confirming the verdict by an official early morning meeting of the Sanhedrin, and then rushed to Pilate. But the case against Jesus was unprepared and was obviously moving toward an acquittal until the high priest challenged Jesus under oath to testify against himself. Why did they wait so long? Why did they not arrest Jesus several days before this? Or assuming that they had to wait for some reason, why was their case not better thought out? Why did they not have adequate witnesses when they eventually brought Jesus to the judgment hall?

Morison suggests that Judas gave the leaders information that led them to think that, in spite of the difficulties they faced, this was indeed the opportunity they had been waiting for. What might Judas have said? If we recall that Jesus had been talking about his death, trying to prepare the disciples for it, Judas might have said something like this: "Jesus has been talking as if he is about to die. I would say that he is tired and defeated and that the mood of surrender is on him. If you move now, I think he would go with you. But you have to move quickly. He must be arrested tonight. Hurry and make your arrangements. I will lead you to him."

If that is what happened, a quick decision would have followed as to whether the arrangements could be made in time. There had to be an initial hearing in which the accusation could be made. The Sanhedrin would have to be roused from sleep and gathered for an early morning session. Most important, they would have to determine whether the Roman governor would be willing to hold a hearing on what normally would not have been a court day. Meanwhile, the arresting party would have to be set in order. When we see the events in this way, we can understand why so much time elapsed between Judas's departure from the upper room and Christ's arrest in the garden quite possibly three hours later. Judas's arrival in the garden and his betrayal were the climax of many hours of frantic evil activity.

Why did he do it? Millions have asked that question ever since. Was it greed? Did he do it for money? Thirty pieces of silver was not that much money. Was it jealousy? Disappointment that Jesus was not turning out to be the Messiah he expected? Resentment at having wasted three years of his life in what had turned out to be a lost cause? The only explanations we can reject outright are those that attempt to exonerate Judas, such as saying he was only trying to force his Master's hand and get him to seize power boldly.[2]

Judas is a warning to all mere adherents of religion. John Ryle points out that Judas was a chosen apostle, an eyewitness of the miracles, a hearer of the Lord's sermons, a fellow laborer with the eleven, and a reputable professor of religion. Not one of the eleven seems to have doubted him.[3] Yet Judas was no friend of Jesus. He was lost and is now in hell. Learn from Judas how important it is to make your calling and election sure (2 Peter 1:10).

Peter's Attack on Malchus

It is not only from Judas that we learn about failure. We learn from Peter too, though Peter's failure was of a different order. Matthew does not mention Peter, perhaps because Peter was still living when Matthew wrote, and Peter might have been placed in danger. But John, who wrote later, tells us that Peter attacked the servant of the high priest, and the servant's name was Malchus (John 18:10).

What was Peter trying to do? He was trying to cut off Malchus's head, of course. Malchus ducked and lost only an ear, which Luke says Jesus healed (Luke 22:51). But more was going on than this. After Jesus' repeated warnings, Peter probably felt that the critical moment of his testing had arrived. He had been asleep. He awoke suddenly to find the arresting party moving toward Jesus in the garden. He was courageous, and drawing his sword he struck out boldly. But Peter is also pathetic, because his boldness evaporated in a moment when Jesus rebuked his action, and he quickly fled into the darkness with the others. What he did not anticipate was that his real test would come later, when a servant girl would ask him if he had been with Jesus of Nazareth.

It is often that way. We think our tests are physical. Will we have courage to act in some bold way? Actually they are far more likely to come in quiet moments when we need to choose either to speak up for Jesus or deny him.

Jesus taught Peter and the others three things.

1. *Peter's use of his sword was dangerous.* Not to Malchus. Jesus healed him. It was dangerous to Peter since "all who draw the sword will die by the sword" (v. 52). That is not precisely true, of course. Not all who take up arms die in battle. But it is a general principle, and it was a reminder to Peter that he was called to a different way of life.

2. *Peter's use of his sword was unnecessary.* Jesus asked, "Do you think I cannot call on my Father, and he will at once put at my disposal more than twelve legions of angels?" (v. 53). The arresting party could have been no more than a hundred people. A Roman legion was six thousand men. Twelve legions of angels would have been seventy-two thousand angels. Clearly, Jesus did not need to be defended. He was arrested because he was willing to be arrested. He suffered a voluntary death for our sins.

3. *Peter's use of his sword was mistaken.* "How then would the Scriptures be fulfilled that say it must happen in this way?" (v. 54). I do not think it was easy for Jesus to say this. He had wrestled in prayer about what was required of him as God's servant and man's Savior just moments before. But this was what the Bible taught. Isaiah had written of the Messiah, "He was oppressed and afflicted, yet he did not open his mouth; he was led like a lamb to the slaughter, and as a sheep before her shearers is silent, so he did not open his mouth" (Isa. 53:7). This passage does not describe a warrior; it describes a person who willingly died for us.

The words of Psalm 22 also point to the one who would suffer for our sakes.

> Dogs have surrounded me;
> > a band of evil men has encircled me,
> > they have pierced my hands and my feet.
> I can count all my bones;
> > people stare and gloat over me.
> They divide my garments among them
> > and cast lots for my clothing.

verses 16–18

These verses predict details of the crucifixion. They are not about bringing in the kingdom with a sword.

Jesus would also have known the words of Psalm 69:

> I looked for sympathy, but there was none,
>   for comforters, but I found none. . . .
> They put gall in my food
>   and gave me vinegar for my thirst.
>
>   verses 20–21

For Jesus it was more important that Scripture be fulfilled than that he should escape suffering. Indeed, this was the critical point for him because he states it again when he addresses the crowd. "Am I leading a rebellion, that you have come out with swords and clubs to capture me? Every day I sat in the temple courts teaching, and you did not arrest me. But this has all taken place that the writings of the prophets might be fulfilled" (vv. 55–56). The important thing was that the Scriptures might be fulfilled. And they were! They were fulfilled in each detail.

Not with Swords

Let's go back to Peter's attempt to save Jesus with a sword. Christians have sometimes appealed to this text in defense of pacifism, as if Jesus were teaching that his followers can never bear arms. This interpretation fails because it neglects to distinguish between what Augustine termed the city of God and the city of man. The city of God is God's kingdom, the church. The city of man is the world with its institutions. Christians are citizens of both kingdoms. They function in the world, and as citizens of the world they can bear arms. Christians can be soldiers. What is forbidden is the attempt to advance Christianity by forcing other people to be Christians.

Whenever Christians have used force to advance the gospel, the church has always suffered for it. These have been the most terrible periods of church history. Christianity became worldly when it was made the official religion of the Roman Empire under Constantine. The crusades were a horror and disgrace. The worst age of Puritanism occurred when the ministers of Christ gained political power under Oliver Cromwell. Our power is in the Word of God and the gospel, not the sword. Henry Smart's powerful hymn "Lead on, O King Eternal" (1836) expresses it rightly.

> For not with swords loud clashing,
> Nor roll of stirring drums,
> But deeds of love and mercy,
> The heavenly kingdom comes.

John Ryle wrote, "The sword has a lawful office of its own. . . . But the sword is not to be used in the propagation and maintenance of the gospel. . . . Happy would it have been for the church if this sentence had been more frequently remembered."[4]

What are the Christian's weapons? Paul answered, "The weapons we fight with are not the weapons of the world. On the contrary, they have divine power to demolish strongholds. We demolish arguments and every pretention that sets itself up against the knowledge of God, and we take captive every thought to make it obedient to Christ" (2 Cor. 10:4–5). Our battle is not a battle for political power, but of ideas. It is a battle that, as Paul knew, in time changes the world. Paul thought in Christian ways, and he wanted others to think in such ways too.

An example comes from the Reformation period. In 1524, seven years after Martin Luther nailed his Ninety-Five Theses to the door of the Castle Church in Wittenberg, the farmers of Germany rebelled against their feudal lords in what became known as the Peasants' War (1524–1526). The revolt began near Schaffhausen, where Hans Mueller, acting on a suggestion from Thomas Muenzer, organized the peasants into an "Evangelical Brotherhood" that pledged to emancipate the farmers. By the end of that year some thirty thousand farmers were in arms in southern Germany, refusing to pay state taxes, church tithes, or feudal dues.

In March 1525, they circulated a document called the Twelve Articles in which they claimed the right to choose their own pastors, pay only just tithes, be considered free men rather than serfs, enjoy fair rents, and other such reasonable demands. They were also favorable to the Reformation and opposed to the Roman Catholic Church.

The peasants sent a copy to Luther fully expecting his support, and, indeed, Luther's first response was sympathetic. Luther acknowledged the injustices about which the farmers were in arms and blamed the rulers of both state and church for their responsibility. He told them, "We have no one on earth to thank for this mischievous rebellion except you, princes and lords, and especially you blind bishops. . . . You do nothing but flay and rob your subjects, in order that you may lead a life of splendor and pride, until the poor common people can bear it no longer."[5] But Luther did not endorse the rebellion, even though most of its goals coincided with those of the Reformation. Later, when hundreds of monasteries were sacked and many cities overrun, Luther denounced the violence in fierce and characteristically uncompromising terms.

Why did Luther react this way, when nearly everyone expected him to side with the peasants? Luther's justified fear of anarchy was one strong reason. Another was his conviction that God has established the authority of princes. Further, Luther knew that the power of the sword has not been given either to the church or to the individual Christian, and he understood that our weapons are not the weapons of this world. Scriptural arguments alone have power "to demolish strongholds."

According to Luther, the Reformation would proceed *non vi, sed verbo*— not by force, but by the power of God's Word. And so it did! The Peasants' War was a tragic episode. More lives were lost in that war in Germany than in any tumult prior to the Thirty Years' War. Some 130,000 farmers died in battle or afterward as a result of retaliatory punishments. Germany was impoverished. The Reformation itself almost perished. But in the end it did not, because it moved by the power of the Word of God, and God blessed the teaching of that Word by the reformers.

Alone, He Bore It All Alone

The last sentence of this account is a sad one. Despite their protests about standing by him to the end, the disciples fled into the darkness of the garden. The text says, "Then all the disciples deserted him and fled" (v. 56). Jesus had said that the writings of the prophets had to be fulfilled, but here, even before he had fulfilled the most important prophecies by dying, the disciples fulfilled at least one of them by fleeing. Jesus had referred to it on the way to the garden: "I will strike the shepherd, and the sheep of the flock will be scattered" (Matt. 26:31, quoting Zech. 13:7).

Moments before, they had been sleeping rather than praying. Now they were fleeing rather than standing by their Lord. Do you want to know what you are made of, what kind of courage you have? Look at these men in that moment. That is what you are. Like them you are weak and fearful, more concerned for your own well-being than for Jesus. But look at them again a few weeks later, after the resurrection. Look at Peter, who struck with his sword, fled into the darkness, and then told a servant girl he did not even know the Lord. See him at Pentecost as he stands before some of these very people, saying, "Let all Israel be assured of this: God has made this Jesus, whom you crucified, both Lord and Christ" (Acts 2:36). Look at Peter and John before the Sanhedrin, the same judicial body that condemned Jesus to death. They cry, "Salvation is found in no one else, for there is no other name under heaven given to men by which we must be saved" (Acts 4:12).

What a difference the presence and power of Jesus Christ makes. He is able to turn cowards into heroes, foolish persons into those who are wise, and sinners into saints. He will do it for you if you will turn from your foolish self-confidence, embrace the gospel, and lean on him for your daily strength and courage.

65

The Jewish Trial

Matthew 26:57–68

Those who had arrested Jesus took him to Caiaphas, the high priest, where the teachers of the law and the elders had assembled. But Peter followed him at a distance, right up to the courtyard of the high priest. He entered and sat down with the guards to see the outcome.

The chief priests and the whole Sanhedrin were looking for false evidence against Jesus so that they could put him to death. But they did not find any, though many false witnesses came forward.

Finally two came forward and declared, "This fellow said, 'I am able to destroy the temple of God and rebuild it in three days.'"

Then the high priest stood up and said to Jesus, "Are you not going to answer? What is this testimony that these men are bringing against you?" But Jesus remained silent.

The high priest said to him, "I charge you under oath by the living God: Tell us if you are the Christ, the Son of God."

"Yes, it is as you say," Jesus replied. "But I say to all of you: In the future you will see the Son of Man sitting at the right hand of the Mighty One and coming on the clouds of heaven."

Then the high priest tore his clothes and said, "He has spoken blasphemy! Why do we need any more witnesses? Look, now you have heard the blasphemy. What do you think?"

"He is worthy of death," they answered.

Then they spit in his face and struck him with their fists. Others slapped him and said, "Prophesy to us, Christ. Who hit you?"

Most people are fascinated with trials, particularly trials of great men or trials that affect the flow of history. In

1998, millions followed the impeachment trial of President Clinton. While the trial unfolded, people from every walk of life dropped what they were doing to follow the developments on television, and the media seemed to cover almost nothing else.

The same thing happened after the break-in at the democratic campaign headquarters in the Watergate complex in Washington, D.C., in 1972. The chief defendant never came to trial—President Richard Nixon resigned his office, effective August 9, 1974, over two years later—but many of his staff did, and scores were imprisoned. At the peak of the investigations, when the Ervin Committee began televised hearings in the Senate Caucus Room in 1973, businessmen brought television sets to their offices, televisions in bars were tuned to cover the day-by-day deliberations, and the Public Broadcasting System, which reran the days' hearings for the evening audience, enjoyed the greatest response to any programming in its history.

If we think farther back in time, we may recall the trials of Socrates before the leaders of Athens, Charles I before the English Parliament, Aaron Dreyfus in France, Mary Stuart in England, Aaron Burr in America, and the Nazi war criminals in Nuremberg.

These trials have captivated millions. Yet no trial in history has so challenged the human race or so charged our emotions as the trial of Jesus of Nazareth by the Jewish and Roman authorities in Palestine in A.D. 30. Walter Chandler, a former member of the New York bar of lawyers and author of an outstanding book on the trials of Jesus, wrote:

> These [other] trials, one and all, were tame and commonplace, compared with the trial and crucifixion of the Galilean peasant, Jesus of Nazareth. These were earthly trials, on earthly issues, before earthly courts. The trial of the Nazarene was before the high tribunals of both heaven and earth; before the Great Sanhedrin, whose judges were the master-spirits of a divinely commissioned race; before the court of the Roman Empire that controlled the legal and political rights of men throughout the known world.[1]

The Trials of Jesus

No single Gospel writer gives a complete account of Jesus' trial, but we can put what they report together to create a comprehensive picture of what happened. Concisely put, there were four events: (1) the arrest, (2) the Jewish trial, (3) the Roman trial, and (4) the execution. Each of the two trials, the Jewish and the Roman, had three parts.

1. *The Jewish trial.* The first part of the Jewish trial was a preliminary hearing before Annas. This seems to be what John describes in his Gospel (John 18:19–24), though the issue is somewhat confusing because John calls both Annas and Caiaphas "the high priest." The reason he does so is because Annas was the true high priest, appointed for life as high priests were. But the Romans had replaced him with Caiaphas, the son-in-law of Annas, so

that both held the title at the same time. Jesus was questioned at this preliminary hearing to see if there were grounds for bringing a formal charge against him, but the effort was frustrated because Jesus refused to answer questions. This phase of the trial ended when Annas gave up and sent him to Caiaphas.

The part of the trial conducted before Caiaphas was the significant trial. Therefore, Matthew and the other Synoptic writers all reported it (Matt. 26:57–68; Mark 14:53–65; Luke 22:54). At this trial, Jesus was accused of blasphemy, and those present determined that he should be put to death.

The third and last phase of the Jewish trial was a formal hearing before the entire Sanhedrin at daybreak, described in Matthew 27:1; Mark 15:1; and Luke 22:66–71. Such formality was necessary because Jewish law did not allow night trials, and the verdict of the previous evening was inadequate by itself. At this hearing the pertinent questions of the previous night were reiterated and an official judgment was secured. From the stone hall of the Sanhedrin, Jesus was sent to Pilate, whose concurrence was needed if Jesus was to be executed.

2. *The Roman trial.* The Roman trial also had three parts. First, there was a prearranged appearance before Pilate, which is described in all four Gospels (Matt. 27:2, 11–14; Mark 15:1–5; Luke 23:1–5; John 18:28–38). At this appearance the hopes of the Jewish leaders were frustrated, for rather than proceeding with a *pro forma* trial and judgment, which the leaders seem to have expected, Pilate suddenly reopened the case and tried to free the prisoner.

The second phase of the Roman trial occurred when Pilate learned that Jesus was a Galilean and tried to escape responsibility by sending Jesus to Herod, since Herod had jurisdiction over Galilee (Luke 23:6–12).

Herod was not fooled by Pilate's ploy. He sent Jesus back to Pilate, which meant that the third and final phase of the Roman trial was a second appearance before the Roman governor. At this phase of the trial Jesus was condemned to death even though he had done nothing wrong and had already been pronounced innocent by Pilate. John says that Pilate did this three times, declaring, "I find no basis for a charge against him" (John 18:38; 19:4, 6). This was the significant part of the Roman trial, and for this reason, it also is reported by each of the Gospel writers (Matt. 27:15–26; Mark 15:6–15; Luke 23:13–25; John 18:39–19:16).

The Trial before Caiaphas

Many illegalities took place in Christ's trial, among them the arrest and trial by night, the use of a traitor to identify and secure Jesus, the absence of any formal charge, the rushed one-day duration of the trial, the intervention of the high priest in the proceedings, the lack of a defense, and the unanimous verdict. Underneath these many illegalities, however, ran a strong undercurrent of adherence to certain points of law. Most obvious was the calling of witnesses. Matthew indicates what was happening when he records, "The chief priests and the whole Sanhedrin were looking for false evidence against Jesus so that they could put him to death. But they did not find any, though many false witnesses came forward" (vv. 59–60).

If the trial were not so evil and the character of the accusers not so base, one could almost feel sorry for the members of the Sanhedrin who had gathered for this trial. They were clearly unprepared. If they had been prepared, they would have had the charge against Jesus and the witnesses to prove their charge ready. As it was, they seem to have acted suddenly only when Judas unexpectedly offered to betray Jesus to them.

Most problematic was the matter of witnesses. Where in Jerusalem in the middle of the night were they to find witnesses to Jesus' alleged crimes? The judges could not be witnesses themselves. Jewish law excluded this possibility. Witnesses would have to be rounded up from those who might have heard Jesus say something incriminating, but even if witnesses such as this could be found, they would still have to provide evidence according to the strict requirements of Jewish law.

There were three categories of testimony according to the Mishnah: (1) a vain testimony, (2) a standing testimony, and (3) an adequate testimony. A vain testimony referred to accusations that were irrelevant or worthless and could therefore be eliminated at once. In our courts today, such testimony would be "stricken from the record" or the jury would be instructed to "disregard" it. Standing testimony was testimony that had relevance and was permitted to stand until it was either confirmed or disproved. Adequate testimony was relevant testimony on which two or more witnesses agreed. Only testimony in this third category could convict.

Most of the testimony collected at this late hour was vain testimony, though there was much of it. Matthew reports that "*many* false witnesses came forward" (v. 60, emphasis added). But nothing of substance was disclosed. At last two men came with a piece of evidence that at once put the trial on a new and promising footing. Matthew says that they testified, "This fellow said, 'I am able to destroy the temple of God and rebuild it in three days'" (v. 61). This was important because, in the first place, it was apparently true. The fact that two witnesses testified to the same thing pointed to its truthfulness.

In his Gospel, John recalls the incident in which these words were spoken. He says that on the occasion of the first cleansing of the temple, Jesus replied to the demand for a sign by saying, "Destroy this temple, and I will raise it again in three days" (John 2:19). John does not refer to this in his account of the trial, but he indicates that the words were spoken in the courtyard of the temple, therefore, within the hearing of the very types of people who were likely even now to be hanging around the temple in the service of the priests.

This was also a serious bit of testimony because, if substantiated, his words might be construed as sorcery, since no one could destroy the temple and rebuild it except by black magic. Or it could be construed as a threat of sacrilege, since the temple was the most holy place in Israel.

There is something else we should consider, something Frank Morison stresses in his study of Jesus' trial and resurrection.[2] Morison observes that although the saying is reported with variations in wording, the highly unlikely phrase "in three days" occurs in each case. Jesus used this phrase on other occasions in which it was evident that he was prophesying his resurrection, an event that would vindicate his claim to be the unique Son of God. A man as shrewd as Caiaphas could hardly have been unaware of what Jesus' enigmatic saying implied. He must have understood it perfectly, realizing that it was a claim to divinity, even though it was not in a form sufficiently clear to secure a formal condemnation.

The fact that Caiaphas and the others did actually understand Jesus' words in this way is proved by something that happened after the crucifixion. Matthew says that the leaders went to Pilate, saying, "Sir, . . . we remember that while he was still alive that deceiver said, 'After three days I will rise again.' So give the order for the tomb to be made secure until the third day. Otherwise, his disciples may come and steal the body and tell the people that he has been raised from the dead. This last deception will be worse than the first" (27:63–64). These men understood that "after three days" referred to Jesus' predicted resurrection.

So the situation was this: Jesus was accused of having claimed to be God and of saying that he was able to prove it by rising from the dead. It was a fatal accusation. Yet strikingly, important as it was, the testimony of the two witnesses was overthrown. Mark says, "Their testimony did not agree" (Mark 14:59). They may have disagreed about the exact place these words had been spoken, or they may have reported them with minor variations. After all, the incident had occurred three years before.

Caiaphas must have been frustrated and seething with anger. He had taken a chance in arresting Jesus at a late hour during Passover week. He understood what Jesus had been claiming. He had a good case. But he could not secure a legal verdict. He was right. He was close. But the situation was slipping from his grasp.

Caiaphas's Bold Stroke

At this point Caiaphas revealed the shrewdness for which the Romans had undoubtedly made him the chief Jewish ruler. What he did was illegal. The high priest was forbidden to intervene in a capital trial, and he could cast his vote only after the other court members had cast theirs. Nevertheless, what he did was a stroke of political genius. Seeing that the case was dissolving, Caiaphas suddenly turned to the prisoner and demanded on the basis of the most solemn oath in Israel, the Oath of the Testimony, "I charge you under oath by the living God: Tell us if you are the Christ, the Son of God" (v. 63).

This was brilliant for two reasons. First, the wording of the challenge was precise. If Caiaphas had asked only if Jesus was the Messiah, Jesus could have answered yes without jeopardy, for it was not a capital offense to make such a claim. Time would prove it either right or wrong. Again, if Caiaphas had asked only if Jesus was the Son of God, Jesus could also have answered yes without danger, for he had diffused a similar accusation earlier when he reminded his accusers that many Jews were called sons of God (John 10:34–36, quoting Ps. 82:6). However, by combining the two parts as he did, Caiaphas was asking not merely if Jesus was the Messiah or a son of God in some general sense, but whether he was the Messiah who was God. If Jesus said yes to that, he could be convicted of the capital crime of blasphemy.

Second, although Jesus was not obliged to give evidence against himself, as a pious Jew, he would not refuse such a charge. Thus, although he had been silent to this point, Jesus finally spoke up, saying, "Yes, it is as you say. . . . But I say to all of you: In the future you will see the Son of Man sitting at the right hand of the Mighty One and coming on the clouds of heaven" (v. 64).

At this stage of the trial, when there was no point in remaining silent any longer, Jesus not only answered Caiaphas's question by a firm, "Yes, it is as you say," but he also added details as to the kind of Messiah and Son of God he was. He did so by referring to that magnificent passage in Daniel in which the prophet describes a divine figure approaching the Ancient of Days to join in God's judgment.

> There before me was one like a son of man, coming with the clouds of heaven. He approached the Ancient of Days and was led into his presence. He was given authority, glory and sovereign power; all peoples, nations and men of every language worshiped him. His dominion is an everlasting dominion that will not pass away, and his kingdom is one that will never be destroyed.
>
> Daniel 7:13–14

The judges did not misunderstand that reference. "Then the high priest tore his clothes and said, 'He has spoken blasphemy! Why do we need any more witnesses? Look, now you have heard the blasphemy. What do you think?' "'He is worthy of death,' they answered" (vv. 65–66).

The Glaring Omission

Assuming that a *prima facie* case of guilt had been made, as it seems to have been in spite of the fact that the evidence was illegally obtained, what should have been the next step under law? Clearly the Sanhedrin should have begun to inquire diligently into the truth or falsity of the claim. We might think that the very nature of Jesus' claims would have put them beyond any meaningful investigation, but that was not the case. The scribes were masters of the Old Testament. The elders were charged with the defense of anyone in danger of being put to death. They should have asked whether Jesus' claims matched what the Old Testament taught concerning the Messiah. If they had investigated Jesus' case fairly, they might have discovered:

1. According to Scripture, the Messiah was to have been born in Bethlehem, and Jesus was born in Bethlehem (Micah 5:2; Luke 2:1–7).

2. The Messiah was to be virgin born, and Jesus was born of Mary, who was a virgin at the time (Isa. 7:14; Matt. 1:24, 25; Luke 1:26–30).

3. The Messiah was to be of David's line, and Jesus was descended from King David (2 Sam. 7:12, 16; Isa. 11:1–2; Matt. 1:1–16; Luke 3:23–37).

4. The Messiah was to be preceded by a figure like Elijah, and John the Baptist filled that role (Mal. 3:1; 4:5; Matt. 17:12–13; John 1:19–23).

5. The Messiah was to do many great works, and Jesus had performed the works that had been prophesied (Isa. 61:1–2; Matt. 11:1–6; Luke 4:16–21).

6. The Messiah was to make a public entry into Jerusalem riding on a donkey, and Jesus had done this just a few days before (Zech. 9:9; Matt. 21:1–11).

7. The Messiah was to be betrayed by a close friend, and Jesus was so betrayed (Ps. 41:9; Matt. 26:14–15; 27:3–8).

8. The Messiah was to be despised and rejected by his people and to be familiar with suffering, and Jesus was (Isa. 53:2–3).

What about the second part of the accusation, that Jesus claimed to be God's Son? This was a shocking claim to those who were steeped in the Judaism of Christ's day. It must have been deeply abhorrent. But it too should have been investigated in light of Scripture. If the Sanhedrin had done this, they might have observed:

1. There are references in the Old Testament to precisely the kind of unique Son of God Jesus claimed to be (Ps. 2:7; Isa. 9:6).

2. The Old Testament speaks of God becoming flesh (Isa. 7:14).

3. There are Old Testament passages in which Jehovah is said to have appeared among men (Gen. 16:13; 18:13, 17, 26; Dan. 3:25).

These passages contain references to the appearance of God on earth in human form and suggest that Jesus was the one. The Sanhedrin might not have been convinced; they probably would not have been. But this would have been a reasonable defense, and its absence from the trial exposes the closed minds and jealous hearts of those who were Christ's judges.

These leaders were not substantially different from millions of careless people in our day. Christ is proclaimed as God's unique Son, but millions reject that claim and turn their backs on the defense. There is a defense. It is presented regularly in countless Christian churches, on radio and television, in books, magazines, and other forms of communication. But they will not hear it. They will not go to church. They will not read Christian books.

What shall we say of such people? Are they honest? Are they open to the truth? Are they seeking it? No more than Caiaphas.

Yet the important thing is not what they are doing; it is what you are doing. Have you considered Christ's claims? Have you pondered his defense? If not, I challenge you to do so now. In the last analysis, it is not Jesus who is on trial. That is past; it is over. You are the one who is on trial, and the question before you is, What will you do with Jesus?

66

The Temporary Fall of Peter

Matthew 26:69–75

Now Peter was sitting out in the courtyard, and a servant girl came to him. "You also were with Jesus of Galilee," she said.

But he denied it before them all. "I don't know what you're talking about," he said.

Then he went out to the gateway, where another girl saw him and said to the people there, "This fellow was with Jesus of Nazareth."

He denied it again, with an oath: "I don't know the man!"

After a little while, those standing there went up to Peter and said, "Surely you are one of them, for your accent gives you away."

Then he began to call down curses on himself and he swore to them, "I don't know the man!"

Immediately a rooster crowed. Then Peter remembered the word Jesus had spoken: "Before the rooster crows, you will disown me three times." And he went outside and wept bitterly.

We will miss a great deal about Peter's denial of Jesus unless we see it in its context, for Matthew's arrangement of material is never arbitrary, as we have seen many times already. In the case of this account, two matters of context are worth noting.

First, Peter's denial of Jesus stands in contrast to the story of Jesus' trial by the Sanhedrin that precedes it (vv. 57–68). Both are interrogation stories. In the first, Jesus is questioned by the high priests who are his enemies. In the second, Peter is questioned by the high priest's servants. In both stories the speakers affirm the truthfulness of what they are saying by oaths. But Jesus' oath is a proper oath, confirming his true and bold confession, while

Peter's oath is a lie. By taking his stand, Jesus stands for his people and is condemned to death for doing so. By repudiating Jesus, Peter escapes unscathed. Herman Ridderbos points to these parallels, saying, "The juxtaposition of these two stories forms powerful proof that no one other than Jesus, not even Peter, could do the work of the Lord's Suffering Servant. . . . Jesus alone could be faithful; and he won the victory."[1]

The second half of the context is the account of Judas's remorse and suicide that follows Peter's denial (Matt. 27:1–10). It is easy to miss this contrast because of the break between chapters 26 and 27. Both men failed badly and fell, but Peter was a believer whose fall was temporary, while the fall of Judas was permanent. Peter is in heaven. Judas is in hell.

Harmonizing the Accounts

There is no question that the story of Peter's denial of Jesus is a true account, for no Christian writer would record such a damaging story about the church's chief apostle unless it were true. Still, we face problems when matching Matthew's account to what the other writers tell us (Mark 14:66–72; Luke 22:56–62; John 18:15–18, 25–27).

Matthew says that Peter was first accosted in the courtyard by a servant girl who charged that he had been with Jesus of Galilee (Matt. 26:69). After his denial, another girl said to those who were standing in the gateway, "This fellow was with Jesus of Nazareth" (v. 71). Finally, "after a little while" some of those who were standing around said, "Surely you are one of them, for your accent gives you away" (v. 73). Mark's account is similar to Matthew's, varying only in the precise wording of the accusations, and Luke is not far off, though he says that the first accusation came from a servant girl as Peter was sitting by the fire (Luke 22:56) and that the second and third questions came later from unnamed individuals (vv. 58–59).

The biggest problems are with John, who reports that the first question was asked by a servant girl as Peter was coming in the door (John 18:17), the second was asked while he was warming himself by the fire (v. 25), and the third came from one of the high priest's servants, a relative of the man whose ear Peter had cut off. This man demanded, "Didn't I see you with him in the olive grove?" (v. 26).

A great deal of ingenuity has gone into attempts at harmonizing these records, including a heroic effort by Harold Lindsell in *The Battle for the Bible* in which he defends the inerrancy of the accounts by distinguishing six different accusations.[2] But this attempt has problems of its own, since it overlooks Jesus' warning that Peter would deny his Lord not six but three times (Matt. 26:34). Actually, the entire effort is unnecessary. Many people were milling around, and many things must have been said. Besides which, these events transpired in the middle of the night over the course of several hours.

We can visualize it something like this. Peter was brought into the courtyard of the high priest by a disciple who knew the high priest, probably John.

As Peter came in he was recognized by the girl who kept the door, and although she didn't object to Peter's presence initially, she most likely followed him into the courtyard, where he had stopped to warm himself at a fire. She asked her question at that point. John does not actually say she asked her question at the door, only that it was asked by the girl who was "at the door" (v. 17). After this, various questions were asked by different people, at the fire and near the outer gateway, leading to Peter's second denial. Things seem to have settled down then, but sometime after this (Luke says, "about an hour later"), as the trial was drawing to a close, those who were in the courtyard accosted Peter again, among them the relative of the man Peter had attacked, who asked, "Didn't I see you with him in the olive grove?" (John 18:26).

To all these questions Peter replied with increasingly strong denials: "I don't know what you're talking about" (Matt. 26:70), "I don't know the man" (Matt. 26:72, 74), "I don't know this man you're talking about" (Mark 14:71); and to the accusation, "You also are one of them" (Luke 22:58) the response, "I am not" (Luke 22:58; John 18:17, 25). Matthew and Mark say that Peter's later denials were with oaths and cursings.

Each of the Gospels records that at Peter's third denial a rooster crowed, to which Luke adds, "The Lord turned and looked straight at Peter" (Luke 22:61). Presumably Jesus looked at Peter through a window of the upper chamber where the trial was held or as he was being led through the high priest's courtyard to a place of confinement. The first three Gospels say that at that point Peter recognized what he had done and rushed out and wept (Matt. 26:75; Mark 14:72; Luke 22:62). Matthew and Luke add "bitterly."

In Peter's Defense

Peter's denial of Jesus was a terrible failure and a great sin. It was even a frightening sin in light of what Paul wrote to Timothy: "If we endure, we will also reign with him. If we disown him, he will also disown us" (2 Tim. 2:12). At the same time, although it was indeed terrible and great and frightening, it was nevertheless made by a courageous man who genuinely loved Jesus.

What can we say in Peter's defense?

1. *Peter had tried to defend his Master in the garden.* His act was an act of the flesh, of course, and Peter was mistaken about what needed to be done. Jesus corrected him by asking, "Do you think I cannot call on my Father, and he will at once put at my disposal more than twelve legions of angels? But how then would the Scriptures be fulfilled that say it must happen this way?" (Matt. 26:53-54). Still, it was a strong act. Peter had told Jesus that he was willing to die for him, and when he had a chance to prove it, he drew his sword and attacked the man who was leading the arresting column. Would we have been so courageous? Would we have been as bold?

2. *Peter followed Jesus at a distance.* Critics have pointed out that Peter followed "at a distance" (Matt. 26:58), not at Jesus' side, and some have sug-

592 The Temporary Fall of Peter

gested that Peter was motivated by mere curiosity since he "wanted to see the outcome." But Peter at least followed when the other disciples (except possibly John) fled. Since the disciples had been spending each night of the Passover week in Bethany, we are probably correct in thinking they proceeded up and over the Mount of Olives to Bethany, where they hoped to regroup by morning. That was the precise opposite direction from Jerusalem. Peter followed the arresting party not only to Jerusalem but into the courtyard of the high priest.

3. *Peter clearly loved Jesus.* That is the only possible reason why Peter followed Jesus. Like Mary, who is soon to be seen in the garden by the tomb weeping because she loved and missed the Master, Peter did not want to be far from his Lord. True, he wanted "to see the outcome," but this was not idle curiosity. He must have thought he would never be able to live with himself unless he saw this through and knew for certain what would become of Jesus. Peter failed in a situation he would not even have been in had he not loved Jesus greatly.

Yet Peter did fail, and his failure is a lesson for us. Peter was the apparent leader of the disciples. If this had been Nicodemus, we would not be surprised, for Nicodemus had always been afraid of what other people might think. If this had been the rich young ruler, we would not be surprised, for we know that he loved his possessions above everything. We would not be surprised if this had been one who never confessed Jesus openly. Yet this was not Nicodemus or the rich young ruler or some other weak follower. This was Peter! And he fell with such slight provocation! He collapsed before the question of a mere servant girl. If Peter could do that, if he could deny Jesus, so can we. What happened to Peter can happen to the strongest of us, and it may even be the strongest who are in the greatest danger.

Why Did Peter Fall?

The steps of Peter's fall are obvious to anyone who cares enough to study Peter's life. Why should we review it all again, then? Obviously, because we do not learn from Peter's story. We need to hear it again and again. Someone has said, The only thing we learn from history is that we do not learn from history.

There were several steps in Peter's fall.

1. *Peter did not believe Jesus' warning.* Even worse, Peter contradicted Jesus openly. Jesus predicted the disciples' failure, even referring to Zechariah, who had written, "I will strike the shepherd, and the sheep of the flock will be scattered" (Matt. 26:31; Zech. 13:7). He declared, "This very night you will all fall away on account of me" (v. 31). But Peter replied, "Even if all fall away on account of you, I never will" (v. 33). And when Jesus repeated his warning in even stronger terms ("I tell you the truth, this very night, before the rooster crows, you will disown me three times," v. 34), Peter came back with, "Even if I have to die with you, I will never disown you" (v. 35). He was telling

Jesus that he was mistaken, that he was out-and-out wrong. What a foolish thing to do! How absurd to contradict the only person who has never been mistaken, never spoken wrongly, and never told a single lie. Human beings are frequently wrong in their perceptions. Jesus is never wrong, never confused, never mistaken. Nevertheless, Peter did not believe Jesus' warning.

Why are we so much like Peter? Why do we not believe Jesus when he says, "The spirit is willing, but the body is weak" (Matt. 26:41) or, "Apart from me you can do nothing" (John 15:5)? When Jesus said "nothing" he meant nothing. If we believe Jesus when he says these things, we will not be as self-confident as we usually are. We will stay close to Jesus and look to him for direction and strength when temptation comes.

2. *Peter looked down on the other disciples.* Peter probably would have denied that he looked down on the others. He probably would have said, "We are all in this together, boys." But deep in his heart Peter thought he was the most upright, the most perceptive, and the most courageous one. That is why he responded to Jesus' warning about the pending failure of the other disciples as he did. Jesus told them, "This very night you will all fall away on account of me," but Peter answered, "Even if all fall away on account of you, I never will" (v. 33). He meant that he could see the others failing; they were weak, after all. But he could not imagine that he would do the same. Peter looked down on the others and imagined himself to be stronger and more faithful.

He was not, of course! And neither are we. It is easy for us to look at other Christians, find some point at which we can judge ourselves superior, and pat ourselves on the back. But we are not stronger, and there is no sin that any other believer has committed that we are not capable of committing under the same circumstances. God does not look at us and find any one of us superior to another. He looks at us all, sees "how we are formed," and "remembers that we are dust" (Ps. 103:14).

3. *Peter had an inflated opinion of himself.* This goes along with his previous error, for the only reason we look down on others is if we think we are somehow better or stronger than they are. "Others may fall away, but I will never fall away! Not me, not Peter." But Peter did fall away. He was not as strong as he thought he was. In fact, he was actually cowardly and weak, and his failure was worse even than that of the other disciples because they did not deny Jesus.

4. *Peter failed to pray.* True, it was the middle of the night, hours after the sun had gone down. It had been a difficult day, and prayer is difficult especially when we are tired. But Jesus would have been tired too. We know that he got tired, so tired that on one occasion he fell asleep in the stern of a boat that was rocking wildly in a storm on the Sea of Galilee. Besides, Jesus had urged the disciples to pray. "Watch and pray so that you will not fall into temptation," he said (Matt. 26:41). Peter had been told to pray, but he did not. He fell asleep like the others, did not receive the strength through prayer that Jesus did, and then denied Jesus in the courtyard of the high priest before mere servants.

How many of our failures are a result of our failure to pray? Paul told the Thessalonians to "pray continually" (1 Thess. 5:17). But do we? Most of us do not pray for more than just a few minutes daily, if that, not to mention continually and in every circumstance of life.

Much of Jesus's teaching was about prayer, and the bottom line was that we need to pray. He told about a man who was visited at night by a friend. The man had nothing to give his friend to eat, but he went to a neighbor who lived next door and asked for three loaves of bread. And the neighbor gave them, not merely because he was his friend, said Jesus, but because of the man's boldness in asking. Jesus then encouraged us to ask of God in the same manner. "Ask and it will be given to you; seek and you will find; knock and the door will be opened to you. For everyone who asks receives; he who seeks finds; and to him who knocks, the door will be opened" (Luke 11:9–10). The only reason we do not pray is because we are far from God and do not believe that he actually likes to hear our prayers and answer them.

5. *Peter thought he could be safe in bad company.* The people in the courtyard were not Jesus' friends. On the contrary, they were his sworn enemies, and they would not encourage Peter to remain faithful to his Lord.

David knew the danger of bad company, which is why he spoke so often of avoiding evildoers. We are often uneasy when we read such passages, because they sound self-righteous, judgmental, and harsh. But the reason David did not want to associate with evildoers is not because he thought he was better than they were but because he was so much like them. He could not afford to be in their company if he wanted to live an upright life. We say, "Hate the sin, but love the sinner!" Fine. But it is not always easy to do since love of the sinner, if we are not careful, often leads to love of the sinner's vices. David was not sure he could successfully love one and hate the other, so he decided to separate himself as much as possible from those who love and do evil. He prayed,

> Search me, O God, and know my heart;
>   test me and know my anxious thoughts.
> See if there is any offensive way in me,
>   and lead me in the way everlasting.
>
> Psalm 139:23–24

If you want to lead a Christian life, you must not spend too much time with Jesus' enemies.

About sixty years ago, Clarence Macartney, who was at that time minister of the First Presbyterian Church of Pittsburgh, wrote a book on Peter in which he drew two wise lessons from Peter's failure. First, "in human nature [he meant even in a Christian's nature] there is a stubborn hostility to Christ and all that is of Christ." Second, "not only is there in my nature that which is hostile to Christ and makes war upon my better self which declares for

Christ, but that, so far as my own strength and skill are concerned, that worst anti-Christian self will get the victory."[3] Those are two good things to know. Remember that Peter had been with Jesus. He had taken communion. His resolve was never stronger. Yet he fell. And so will we unless Jesus prays for us, supports us, and protects us from the devil.

Why Peter Did Not Fall Away

This is precisely what Jesus did for Peter. In fact, he had told Peter about it that very evening: "Simon, Simon, Satan has asked to sift you as wheat. But I have prayed for you, Simon, that your faith may not fail. And when you have turned back, strengthen your brothers" (Luke 22:31–32).

Are you aware that Jesus has also prayed for you and continues to pray for your perseverance? In John 17, Jesus prayed not only for the original twelve disciples but also "for those who will believe in me through their message," that is, for us (v. 20). He prayed, "Father, I want those you have given me to be with me where I am, and to see my glory, the glory you have given me because you loved me before the creation of the world" (v. 24). We also read in Hebrews that Jesus "is able to save completely those who come to God through him, because he always lives to intercede for them" (Heb. 7:25).

Other people pray for us. That is good. To intercede for someone else is a privilege and is immensely important. Yet our prayers are weak at best, and those who pray for us come and go over time. Only Jesus "always lives to intercede" for those who are his own.

This is the last story in Matthew about Peter. Peter is not mentioned again, and the last thing we read about him is that he "went outside and wept bitterly" (v. 75). Sad? Yes, but it is encouraging too, for Peter's tears meant that he still truly loved Jesus and were a sign of his genuine remorse and true repentance. Jesus had told Peter, "When you have turned back, strengthen your brothers." Because Jesus prayed, Peter was converted and was later used by God to strengthen others. At Pentecost this same Peter, who had denied his Lord even with oaths, preached the first great sermon of the Christian era, and three thousand people believed. If Christ did that with Peter, there is hope for all of us.

67

The Permanent Fall of Judas

Matthew 27:1–10

Early in the morning, all the chief priests and the elders of the people came to the decision to put Jesus to death. They bound him, led him away and handed him over to Pilate, the governor.

When Judas, who had betrayed him, saw that Jesus was condemned, he was seized with remorse and returned the thirty silver coins to the chief priests and the elders. "I have sinned," he said, "for I have betrayed innocent blood."

"What is that to us?" they replied. "That's your responsibility."

So Judas threw the money into the temple and left. Then he went away and hanged himself.

The chief priests picked up the coins and said, "It is against the law to put this money into the treasury, since it is blood money." So they decided to use the money to buy the potter's field as a burial place for foreigners. That is why it has been called the Field of Blood to this day. Then what was spoken by Jeremiah the prophet was fulfilled: "They took the thirty silver coins, the price set on him by the people of Israel, and they used to buy the potter's field, as the Lord commanded me."

The twenty-seventh chapter of Matthew begins with the Jewish rulers handing over Jesus to the Gentiles in the person of Pilate, the Roman governor. This was a fulfillment of Old Testament prophecy as well as of Jesus' own predictions of his death. He had warned the disciples, "We are going up to Jerusalem, and the Son of Man will be betrayed to the chief priests and the teachers of the law. They will condemn him to death and will *turn him over to the Gentiles* to be mocked and flogged and crucified. On the third day he will be raised to life!" (Matt. 20:18–19,

597

emphasis added). Before Matthew recounts those events, however, he pauses to record the fate of Judas, the betrayer. Matthew is the only one of the four Gospel writers to do this.[1]

As I have said several times before, Judas's end is a warning to us that it is possible to spend much time in Jesus' company, hearing the best of sermons, and even witnessing an abundance of miracles, and still perish. It is an encouragement to do what Peter, aware of his own weakness, urged his hearers to do: "Therefore, my brothers, be all the more eager to *make your calling and election sure*. For if you do these things, you will never fall, and you will receive a rich welcome into the eternal kingdom of our Lord and Savior Jesus Christ" (2 Peter 1:10–11, emphasis added).

Remorse Is Not Repentance

What did Judas experience as a result of his heinous betrayal of Jesus Christ? He felt terrible remorse, even a profound self-loathing. But remorse, even accompanied by self-loathing, is not biblical repentance leading to true faith and salvation. Matthew may have indicated this by dropping the word usually employed for repentance *(metanoeo)*, using *metamelomai* instead. Even without this change of words, however, it is clear that Judas's repentance was utterly unlike Peter's. Peter's was a true repentance. Peter was crushed and wept shameful, bitter tears. Judas did not weep. He knew that he had done wrong and regretted his mistake, but his remorse did not drive him to repentance. Repentance would have turned him to Jesus. His sense of unatoned guilt only drove him farther away.

Judas's inadequate confession had two parts.

1. *Judas confessed he was a sinner.* "I have sinned," he said plainly (v. 4). True enough. But many have confessed themselves sinners without their confession making the slightest difference in their lives. True repentance involves a full 180-degree turn, half of it away from sin and half of it to Jesus. That is the only sure path to salvation.

I heard a particularly striking example of this. Dr. Walter C. Kaiser Jr., the president of Gordon-Conwell Theological Seminary, was speaking, and he told of a man he had counseled years before. The man had been a distinguished surgeon, but he had made a wreck of his life. He had begun to drink heavily and had lost his job, his income, his home, and his wife and family. He had turned to Kaiser for help, and Kaiser had told him to pray and ask God for forgiveness. "I don't know how to pray," he said.

"Just talk to God like you are talking to me now," Kaiser answered.

The man began, "Hello, God. It's me. I guess you know I've made a mess of my life. I've made a mess of everything." He went on to tell all the bad things he had done and all the terrible mistakes he had made. He prayed like that for fifteen minutes. Kaiser was delighted. He had never heard a confession as full and forthright as that from anyone. But suddenly the man stopped.

"Go on," said Kaiser. "That's good. What you need to do now is ask God for forgiveness and trust Jesus as your Savior."

The man startled him by suddenly drawing himself upright, squaring his shoulders, and literally shouting out, "No! That is one thing I will never do. I will never ask forgiveness for anything." According to Kaiser, the man had made a ninety-degree turn, but he would not turn to Jesus. He recognized his sin, but he would not turn from it enough to seek the Savior.

2. *Judas confessed that Jesus was innocent.* "I have betrayed innocent blood," was his testimony (v. 4). Once again, a true statement. It was a powerful testimony to Jesus' flawless character and a harsh indictment of the wicked character of the men who had condemned Jesus and to whom Judas spoke. But confessing the innocence of Jesus by itself never saved a single soul. Pilate did the same. In fact, he confessed Jesus was innocent three times over during the course of the Roman trial: "I find no basis for a charge against him" (John 18:38), "I find no basis for a charge against him" (John 19:4), "I find no basis for a charge against him" (v. 6). But Pilate still turned him over to be crucified. Even the crowds that stood by and witnessed the crucifixion exclaimed, "Surely he was the Son of God!" (Matt. 27:54). But it is not recorded that any of them passed from spiritual death to spiritual life through faith in Christ.

What Judas was trying to do is what many people try to do in one way or another: He was trying to make atonement for his sin. But he could not do so for the simple reason that no mere man can do so. Only one person in the entire universe can make atonement, and that is Jesus Christ, who though he is man is also more than man. He is the God-man, and it is only by his shed blood that atonement is made for any sin.

Let me give you two contrasting illustrations. The first is the picture Shakespeare has given us of Lady Macbeth washing her hands after she and her husband murdered Duncan, Scotland's king. She had gotten blood on her hands on the night of the murder, and though she and Macbeth had blamed the deed on their servants, in her imagination she saw the incriminating blood whenever she looked at her hands. She washed and washed them, but washing didn't get the stains out. "What, will these hands ne'er be clean?" she asks. The answer is, they will not. "Here's the smell of blood still; all the perfumes of Arabia will not sweeten this little hand," she confesses weakly (*Macbeth,* act 5, scene 1). Even her husband asks,

> Will all great Neptune's ocean wash this blood
> Clean from my hand? No, this my hand will rather
> The multitudinous seas incarnadine,
> Making the green run red. (act 2, scene 2)

Nothing Macbeth nor Lady Macbeth could do could make atonement for their sin. The guilt of their crime clung to them. But there is one who can make atonement for sin, freeing us from guilt, and he did. That person is Jesus, and that is precisely what he was doing even at the moment when Judas was turning from him to his own despairing act.

That brings me to the second illustration, from a poem by Robert Herrick, who wrote half a generation or so after Shakespeare. Herrick was a Christian, and he thought of his salvation in comparison with a task set for the ancient mythical hero Hercules. He had to clean out the enormous, filthy stables of King Augeias, which he did by diverting a large river into the stables. Herrick compared the stables to his heart, saying,

> Lord, I confesse that Thou alone art able
> To Purifie this my Augean stable:
> Be the Seas water, and the Land all Sope,
> Yet if Thy Bloud not wash me, there's no hope.[2]

That is it exactly. Apart from Jesus' death for us, which paid the penalty for our sin, there is no hope for anyone. But Jesus died, and there is salvation for all who will come to him. Augustus Toplady wrote rightly,

> Rock of Ages, cleft for me,
> Let me hide myself in thee;
> Let the water and the blood,
> From thy riven side which flowed,
> Be of sin the double cure,
> Cleanse me from its guilt and power.

"What can wash away my sin? Nothing but the blood of Jesus." Because he had turned his back on Jesus, who was his only hope, Judas plunged into the dark pit of terminal despair and died by his own foul hand.

Two Perplexing Problems

But how exactly did Judas die? And how should we understand Matthew's strange reference to Jeremiah to explain the priests' decision to buy the potter's field with Judas's blood money? "Then what was spoken by Jeremiah the prophet was fulfilled: 'They took the thirty silver coins, the price set on him by the people of Israel, and they used them to buy the potter's field, as the Lord commanded me'" (vv. 9–10).

1. *How did Judas die?* Matthew is the only Gospel writer to give an account of Judas's death, but Luke refers to it in Acts and seems to say something quite different: "With the reward he got for his wickedness, Judas bought a field; there he fell headlong, his body burst open and all his intestines spilled out. Everyone in Jerusalem heard about this, so they called that field in their language Akeldama, that is, Field of Blood" (Acts 1:18–19).

On the surface this seems entirely different from what Matthew tells us, not only that Judas died by falling rather than by hanging but also that it was he who bought the field. But this is merely a case of our having insufficient data to put the entire picture together. We can conjecture that Judas hanged himself, that his body fell into a ravine somewhat later, and that the field was purchased either beforehand, Judas seeking it out for his suicide, or afterward as a place the priests now judged to be polluted. As for Judas having bought it, the purchase would have been understood that way by the authorities who wanted nothing to do with his money and would have considered the money to belong to Judas even after he threw it down in the temple.

2. *Where is the verse in Jeremiah?* The second problem is a bit more substantial. To begin with, there is no verse in Jeremiah like the one Matthew cites. Zechariah 11:12–13 is something like it. Zechariah's verses concern a potter, thirty pieces of silver, and Zechariah throwing the money into the house of the Lord. But the verses are not about a person who betrays the Messiah, and they say nothing about buying a field. On the other hand, Jeremiah 19 describes a symbolic action in which Jeremiah buys and then breaks a potter's jar, symbolizing the destruction of the nation, and chapter 32 describes the purchase of a field. Yet there is no apparent connection between Jeremiah's two chapters or between the words or actions in Jeremiah and Zechariah.

Most people assume that the closest verbal reference is to Zechariah and explain Matthew's attribution in various ways: Matthew made a mistake, a copyist made an error ("Jeremiah" was written instead of "Zechariah"), Matthew knew of another book by Jeremiah now lost, Jeremiah actually wrote words that Zechariah borrows, or the scroll Matthew refers to was the scroll of Jeremiah to which the minor prophets were attached. None of these are satisfactory explanations. The best explanation is probably that Matthew was pulling together a number of passages that seemed to add significance to the death of Jesus' false but well-known disciple Judas. The reference to Jeremiah 19 seemed appropriate because it refers to "innocent blood" and because the place where the prophet broke the jar would eventually be used as a burial ground for those who were to die in the siege of Jerusalem. The reference to Zechariah and his role as a shepherd of the people adds the ideas of the rejection of Jesus as the true shepherd of the flock, his being valued at the price of a mere slave, and the betrayal money being cast into the temple.

If this is the right way to approach this problem, we should probably think that Matthew dealt with Old Testament patterns rather than with specific verbal prophecies. D. A. Carson probably summarizes it best when he writes, "Matthew sees in Jeremiah 19 and Zechariah 11 not merely a number of verbal and thematic parallels to Jesus' betrayal but a pattern of apostasy and rejection that must find its ultimate fulfillment in the rejection of Jesus, who was cheaply valued, rejected by the Jews, and whose betrayal money was put to a purpose that pointed to the destruction of the nation."[3] In any case,

Judas's role in the betrayal was not unknown to or unplanned by God, since it had been prophesied that one who was close to Jesus would lift up his heel against him (Ps. 41:9; John 13:18; Acts 1:16) and because Judas was appointed to this end from the beginning (John 17:12).

No Help from the Wicked

What lessons can we learn from Judas's actions? First, partners in evil are not friends. It is common to speak of honor among thieves or imagine sentimental bonds among those who do evil, but nothing could be farther from the truth. Those who share in evil actions are not friends. They do not live for one another or to help one another. Evil persons live for themselves, and when a comrade gets in trouble, they are the first to abandon him to save their own skin. This was the case with the priests and elders who responded to Judas's confession, "What is that to us? That's your responsibility" (v. 4). That is how evil friends will treat you if you link up with them.

What Judas did should have meant something to them. If Judas had sinned against innocent blood, as he claimed, so had they. They had condemned to death one whom Judas was now declaring to be innocent. They were even guiltier than he was. Besides, according to Jewish law, the person arranging for the arrest of an offender had to be the one to make the formal legal accusation. Judas should have been the one to do that. He had not, of course. The Sanhedrin lost many hours trying to find a sustainable accusation. Judas had not made an accusation, and he was now doing the precise opposite, declaring that the one whose arrest he had brought about was not guilty. "What is that to us?" they replied. It should have meant everything to them. Their eternal destiny hung on their rejection of Jesus Christ. They needed to repent of their sin and turn to him for forgiveness and salvation. But they did not. They did not repent, and in their sin they had no use for their accomplice. They were too hardened to despair, as he did, but they perished anyway, as will all who reject Jesus Christ.

A Downward Course

One of the bad things about sin is that its course is always downhill. Judas had a bad end, but we should remember that it did not come about at once. He was an evil man, just like the rulers of the day, but Judas did not start out that way. At one time he must have been an innocent-looking baby smiling in his mother's arms. We all begin like that. But somewhere Judas's life took an evil turn, and his eventual suicide was the result. What was Judas's life story like? We do not have many details, but what we do know about him goes something like this.

1. *He was greedy.* Judas was the one who kept the disciples' money, complained when Mary broke her ointment on Jesus' head, saying that it was a waste of a year's wages, and stole from the money bag when he was able to

(John 12:6). If getting wealth was his aim, he must have been profoundly disappointed and angry when it finally dawned on him that Jesus was not going to set up an earthly kingdom and appoint disciples like himself to positions of honor and economic privilege. I suggested in an earlier chapter that his anger over how the three years of ministry were turning out was probably the root cause of his betrayal, but even that was done for money! Thirty pieces of silver was not much money, the price of a mere slave, but Judas decided to cut his losses and get out, grabbing what he could.

2. *He betrayed Jesus.* Not every disappointment leads to betrayal, least of all a betrayal of someone as holy and unsurpassable as Jesus, but this was no ordinary disappointment. It was a fierce resentment of one who had not conformed to Judas's plans. He didn't care about Jesus; he only cared about himself. So he betrayed his Lord and took the cash.

3. *He despaired and died.* When Judas was approaching the religious leaders to arrange for his betrayal of Jesus, he must have been telling himself that he was right to do it because Jesus had betrayed him. Jesus was not going to become an earthly king, and Judas had wasted three years of his life on this pathetic loser. Jesus deserved what he would get. But reality has a way of creeping up even on the most hardened sinners, and in this case, reality shouted that Jesus was an innocent man. Reality, however, did not lead Judas to repentance. It led him only to remorse and ultimately to suicide. Judas died without hope, as will all who harden their hearts and repudiate the Savior.

True Confession, True Faith

Let me end on a better note. I have shown how Judas confessed his sin without repentance. "I have sinned," he said. The words did not save him, because they were uttered from an unrepentant heart. But this is not the only place those words are spoken in the Bible. According to my count, seven individuals uttered these exact words: Pharaoh, Balaam, Achan, Saul, Shimei, David, and Judas, plus the prodigal son in Jesus' parable. In most of those cases the words do not denote a true repentance. But David repented; he confessed his sin openly, sought cleansing by the blood of the sacrifice, and pled for a restoration of God's favor. So did the prodigal son. He "came to his senses" and set out for home, crying, "Father, I have sinned against heaven and against you. I am no longer worthy to be called your son" (Luke 15:17, 21). Let those two examples be your pattern. Turn to the Savior, and do not turn away in despair as Judas did.

68

The Roman Trial

Matthew 27:11-31

Meanwhile Jesus stood before the governor, and the governor asked him, "Are you the king of the Jews?"

"Yes, it is as you say," Jesus replied.

When he was accused by the chief priests and the elders, he gave no answer. Then Pilate asked him, "Don't you hear the testimony they are bringing against you?" But Jesus made no reply, not even to a single charge—to the great amazement of the governor.

Now it was the governor's custom at the Feast to release a prisoner chosen by the crowd. At that time they had a notorious prisoner, called Barabbas. So when the crowd had gathered, Pilate asked them, "Which one do you want me to release to you: Barabbas, or Jesus who is called Christ?" For he knew it was out of envy that they had handed Jesus over to him.

While Pilate was sitting on the judge's seat, his wife sent him this message: "Don't have anything to do with that innocent man, for I have suffered a great deal today in a dream because of him."

But the chief priests and the elders persuaded the crowd to ask for Barabbas and to have Jesus executed.

"Which of the two do you want me to release to you?" asked the governor.

"Barabbas," they answered.

"What shall I do, then, with Jesus who is called Christ?" Pilate asked.

They all answered, "Crucify him!"

"Why? What crime has he committed?" asked Pilate.

But they shouted all the louder, "Crucify him!"

When Pilate saw that he was getting nowhere, but that instead an uproar was starting, he took water and washed his hands in front of the crowd. "I am innocent of this man's blood," he said. "It is your responsibility!"

All the people answered, "Let his blood be on us and on our children!"

Then he released Barabbas to them. But he had Jesus flogged, and handed him over to be crucified.

T̲hree chapters ago when we began
the study of Christ's trials, I pointed out that they present a unique situation.
Jesus was tried, on the one hand, by an ecclesiastical court, seeking to apply
the revealed law of God to Jesus' case, and, on the other hand, by a civil
court, seeking to apply what is generally thought to be the most highly developed law known to man. Jewish law was the most humane of legal systems.
It did everything possible to preserve life and avoid executions. Roman law
was known for its comprehensiveness, systematization of statutes, specifica-
tion of procedures, and affixing penalties. It has been said of the ancient
world that Judea gave religion, Greece gave letters, and Rome gave law.

We might think based on the very nature of Roman law that the Roman
part of Jesus' trial would be easy to understand. But the opposite is the case.
We can understand the Jewish trial. Jesus was condemned because he was
hated by the religious leaders who resented his exposure of their sin. But
Pilate did not hate Jesus. He seems to have respected him; he pronounced
him innocent. Why then, in the end, did he turn Jesus over to be crucified?

Who Was Pilate?

The greatest puzzle of the Roman trial is the contrast between what we
know of Pilate's character from secular sources and his conduct at the trial
of Jesus as reported in the Gospels. Pilate was not a noble person. He had
come from Spain, served under Germanicus in the wars on the Rhine, and
had risen to his relatively minor post as governor of Judea through his marriage to Claudia Proculla, a granddaughter of the emperor Augustus. The
marriage was a smart career move but a moral disgrace. Claudia's mother,
Julia, was notorious for her coarse immorality even in decadent Rome, and
her daughter was like her. Augustus would refer to them saying, "Would I
were wifeless or had childless died."

Pilate revealed his nature by his oversight of Judea. He was the sixth procu-
rator of that region, having assumed his post in A.D. 26. The governors who
had served before him had been sensitive to Jewish sensibilities and had generally avoided acts that could offend or inflame the people. But Pilate showed
no such sensitivity. When he arrived in Judea the first time, he sent his legions
to Jerusalem by night, bearing standards blazoned with the images of Tiberius,
which the Jews considered idolatrous. That he did it by night shows that he
knew what he was doing, but that he did it at all betrays his brutish nature.
On another occasion he appropriated money from the sacred Corban treasury to build a fifty-mile aqueduct to the city, provoking outrage from the citizens. When the people gathered to protest the sacrilege, Pilate sent soldiers
into the crowd disguised as common people who, on a prearranged signal,
pulled out hidden clubs and daggers and attacked the demonstrators. Luke
refers to an apparently similar massacre in which Pilate "mixed" the blood

of certain Galileans "with their sacrifices" (Luke 13:1). Pilate was not an upright nor noble man.

Yet here is the fascinating thing. As far as the trial of Jesus is concerned, at least in its opening stages, no one could have conducted it with greater attention or integrity. Pilate seems to have understood what was going on, recognized that Jesus was innocent, and used every means he could think of to get him acquitted and discharged.

I suggested in an earlier study that Pilate had probably been contacted the previous night by one of the Sanhedrin, probably Caiaphas, to be sure that he would hear the case in the morning. He must have agreed to a quick *pro forma* trial. But when the leaders appeared the next day, they were startled to find that the governor wanted to begin a formal hearing. They seem to have been caught off guard since they did not have their charges against Jesus well thought out. John gives the fullest account of these proceedings, indicating that when Pilate reopened the case, demanding, "What charges are you bringing against this man?" the best they could do was retort, "If he were not a criminal, we would not have handed him over to you" (John 18:29–30). When they were forced to produce a charge, Luke says they dragged up everything they could think of, hoping that one of the accusations might stick: "We have found this man subverting our nation." "He opposes payment of taxes to Caesar and claims to be Christ, a king" (Luke 23:2). The first two of these were lies, but the third was both true and important. Therefore, each of the Gospels records it. It is the charge Matthew presupposes in his shortened account of the trial when he has Pilate demand of Jesus, "Are you the king of the Jews?" (Matt. 27:11).

The leaders must have said, "This man claims to be a king." So Pilate asked if that were true. Jesus admitted that he was indeed a king, but even then Pilate knew this was a religious matter and that Jesus was innocent of treason or rebellion. So he tried to acquit him.

The Warning from Proculla

Why did Pilate try so hard to acquit Jesus, grasping at no less than four stratagems, when he probably did not really care much about such matters and certainly did not have any natural instinct to act justly? One explanation is that he was probably impressed with Jesus. He seems to have marvelled at his calm self-possession and the fact that he did not try to defend himself against his accusers. Matthew reports this reaction saying, "Then Pilate asked him, 'Don't you hear the testimony they are bringing against you?' But Jesus made no reply, not even to a single charge—to the great amazement of the governor" (vv. 13–14).

But there was another reason too, though Matthew is the only one of the four Gospel writers to record it. Pilate's wife sent him a message while he was seated on his judgment seat. "Don't have anything to do with that inno-

cent man, for I have suffered a great deal today in a dream because of him,"
she said (v. 19).

Frank Morison writes more about this incident than others, reminding us
that the Romans were particularly superstitious where dreams were concerned and seldom undertook any great enterprise without inquiring what
the gods or fate deemed favorable. He suggests that Pilate and Proculla were
probably together the night Jesus was arrested, that Proculla would have
known about the Sanhedrin's request for a trial, would have gone to bed
thinking about Jesus and what she had heard about him, and when she awoke
the next morning to find Pilate gone would have known he was beginning
the trial. Her message to him had to be swift and urgent. "Don't have anything to do with that innocent man," she warned him. Her dream would
have been a serious matter for Pilate and may well have been the reason he
sought to release Jesus.

Morison says of Proculla,

> It was she who stiffened the Roman instinct for justice in Pilate, at a moment
> when he was tempted, from personal considerations, to humor the prejudices
> of the Jewish camarilla, and commit Jesus on their recommendation alone. . . .
> While the stimulus lasted his handling of this difficult and perplexing case was
> well-nigh perfect. . . . It was only as the stimulus faded against the grinding and
> growing opposition of the Jewish party that the threat of Caesar's intervention
> became paramount, and he ended as he had intended to begin, by delivering
> the Prisoner into their hands.[1]

Seeking a Way Out

Up to this point Pilate's handling of the trial was fully commendable.
Matthew's account is short, but looking at it carefully and linking it to the
reports of the other Gospel writers, we realize that Pilate followed the four
stages of a proper Roman trial without deviation: (1) the charge, (2) the evidence, (3) the defense, and (4) the verdict. Pilate heard the charge, investigated the evidence, knew that the real reason behind the accusations was
the Jewish leaders' envy of Jesus (Matt. 27:18), and spoke the verdict: "I find
no basis for a charge against him." *Absolvo! Non fecisse videtur!* John says that
Pilate spoke those words three times (John 18:38; 19:4, 6). But instead of
doing what he should have done at that point, releasing Jesus or at least placing him under protective custody as a later Roman commander did with Paul
when his life was threatened by this same judicial body (Acts 21:31–33;
23:12–24), the governor launched a pattern of irregular proceedings that
led eventually to Jesus' execution.

Pilate tried four expedients to avoid pronouncing sentence: (1) sending
Jesus to Herod, when he learned that Jesus was from Galilee, which was under
Herod's jurisdiction (Luke 23:6–12); (2) offering to punish him without an
execution (Luke 23:16, 22); (3) asking the people to choose either Jesus or

Barabbas as the one to be released at the Passover (Matt. 27:20–26; Mark 15:6–15; John 18:38–40); and (4) producing Jesus in a beaten, bloody condition to stir the people's pity (John 19:1–5). All these measures failed.

The only one of the schemes that Matthew includes in his Gospel is the offer to release either Jesus or Barabbas to the crowd, though surprisingly the offer is in each of the Gospels. It is not surprising that we find it in Matthew, however, in light of Matthew's emphasis throughout the Gospel that Jesus was Israel's true King. Barabbas was not just a common murderer. He was an insurrectionist, that is, a revolutionary who wanted to raise an army, drive out the occupying Romans, and establish himself or someone like himself as Israel's king—like Judas Maccabaeus. That is why he was being held for execution. Matthew does not explain who Barabbas was, though John, who was writing for a Gentile audience, explains that he had taken part in a rebellion (John 18:40). Every Jew knew about Barabbas. He must have been something of a celebrity, a hero, what the people wanted. The people wanted a king they could understand, an earthly king offering earthly advantages, rather than a king from heaven who offered truth, righteousness, and eternal salvation.

John makes the nature of the people's choice crystal clear when he records Pilate asking them, "Do you want me to release 'the king of the Jews'?" and they shout back, "No, not him! Give us Barabbas" (John 18:40). It is a powerful lesson. Sinners will always prefer a manageable earthly ruler, however self-serving, violent, or even evil, to Jesus Christ.

Christ's Fate Sealed

Pilate was trapped by his own scheming. He had miscalculated. But his stubborn character still came through. He was caught, but he did not want to be defeated by the Jews' religious rulers whom he obviously despised. "What shall I do, then, with Jesus who is called Christ?" he demanded.

"Crucify him," they answered.

"Why? What crime has he committed?" asked Pilate. He understood very well that Jesus had done nothing at all to merit punishment, certainly not crucifixion.

They had no answer. There was none. All they could do was cry louder, "Crucify him! Crucify him!"

Matthew indicates that the situation was getting out of hand, that "an uproar was starting" (v. 24). The leaders were stirring it up, of course. It was part of their plan. It was the thing Pilate had to avoid at all costs. But the leaders were doing something else too, according to John's version of the story. They were badgering Pilate with the threat of an unfavorable report of his conduct to Caesar. "If you let this man go, you are no friend of Caesar. Anyone who claims to be a king opposes Caesar," they said (John 19:12). That tipped the scales, of course, for although Pilate may actually have feared Jesus a bit—perhaps Jesus was a kind of god (the ancients believed in such things) and might actually do him harm—and although Pilate feared the hatred of the religious leaders and the fickleness of the crowds even more, Pilate feared the emperor most of all and dared not risk his disfavor. So at last he called for water and washed his hands before the crowd. "I am innocent of this man's blood," he said. "It is your responsibility!" (v. 24).

How ironic! Innocent? That is precisely what Pilate was not. All the water in the world could not wash the guilt of Jesus Christ's blood from his hands, as countless generations since have realized. There was another great irony too. When Pilate told the Jews, "It's your responsibility," he was saying precisely what they had said to Judas earlier: "What is that to us? That's your responsibility" (v. 4). They had not escaped their guilt by passing it off on Judas, and neither could Pilate escape his guilt by passing it off on them. They were all guilty. And so are we! Though we cannot wash away the stains of Christ's blood by any acts of our own or by ceremonial washings, by the blood of Christ we can indeed be cleansed. His death takes away our sins. "What can wash away my sin?" It is a searching question to which there is only one answer: "Nothing but the blood of Jesus!"

"Hail, King of the Jews"

The last verses of this section take the kingship theme a bit further, for Matthew reports that even after Jesus had been flogged in preparation for the crucifixion, he was given to the soldiers who mocked him mercilessly, placing a scarlet robe on his shoulders, a crown of thorns on his head, and a staff in his hand. Then they fell before him in mock homage, crying, "Hail, king of the Jews." They spit on him and struck him on the head again and again. This was human nature in its most brutal and inhumane form. Yet even so, theirs was an innocent brutality, if one can use that word, for it was a lesser sin than that of Pilate, who sinned against his knowledge and responsibility, or that of the leaders, who sinned against their law and knowledge of the Bible, or that of Judas, who had betrayed his Lord.

At the moment of this sadistic beating, no one on earth looked less like a king than Jesus. His flesh had been stripped to ribbons by the scourging. Roman scourgings were so severe that many prisoners died from them before they could be crucified. Blood would have been running down Christ's head from the wounds inflicted by the thorns. Spit would have been clinging to his face. Jesus didn't look like a king then. But no ruler seated upon any earthly throne at the pinnacle of worldly power was ever more entitled to be called a king than was Jesus.

Jesus was not only a king, he was "the King of kings," not only a lord, but "Lord of lords" (Rev. 19:16). Today he rules the universe, and one day he will return in judgment, as he told Caiaphas, "In the future you will see the Son of Man sitting at the right hand of the Mighty One and coming on the clouds of heaven" (Matt. 26:64).

The King and His Kingdom

This is of immense importance, for what was true of the King in the days of his humiliation is no less true of his kingdom. Charles H. Spurgeon, a great Baptist preacher, wrote about the similarity between the King and his kingdom more than a century ago. He wrote that today "pure Christianity in its outward appearances is an equally unattractive object and wears upon its surface few royal tokens. It is without form or comeliness, and when men see it there is no beauty that they should desire it." Nominal Christianity is tolerantly approved by most men, but the pure gospel is scorned and rejected. "The real Christ of today, among men, is unknown and unrecognized as much as he was among his own nation eighteen hundred years ago," Spurgeon said.

> Evangelical doctrine is at a discount, holy living is censured, and spiritual-mind-edness is derided. . . .
>
> Few now-a-days will side with the truth their fathers bled for. The day for covenanting to follow Jesus through evil report and shame appears to have gone by. Yet, though men turn round upon us and say, "Do you call your gospel divine? Are you so preposterous as to believe that your religion comes from God and is to subdue the world?"—we boldly answer: "Yes!"

Spurgeon continues:

> Even as beneath the peasant's garb and the wan visage of the Son of Mary we can discern the Wonderful, the Counselor, the Mighty God, the Everlasting Father! so beneath the simple form of a despised gospel we perceive the royal lineaments of truth divine. We care nothing about the outward apparel or the external housing of truth; we love it for its own sake. To us, the marble halls and the alabaster columns are nothing, we see more in the manger and the cross. We are satisfied that Christ is the king still where he was wont to be king, and that is not among the great ones of the earth, not among the mighty and the learned, but amongst the base things of the world and the things which are not, which shall bring to nought the things that are, for these hath God from the beginning chosen to be his own.[2]

Is Jesus King?

No one can be neutral concerning Jesus Christ, for Jesus claims to be the only ultimate King whether we acknowledge or refuse to acknowledge him. Which brings us back to Pilate. Pilate was not a follower of Jesus. He only wanted to be neutral, to be innocent of his death, but he failed miserably. He was not able to be neutral, and in the end he took his stand against Jesus. So will you unless you decide for Jesus now.

When Pilate awoke that morning, he did not expect to be confronted by the greatest crisis of his career. All he expected to do was go through a *pro forma* trial for which he cared nothing. He would humor the Jewish leaders. Yet suddenly Jesus stood before him, and Jesus was either the King he claimed to be, or he was not. He was either innocent or guilty. What would Pilate do? We know what he did. He failed in his great crisis and condemned to death the very Son of God despite his knowledge of the case, his better judgment, and even the warnings of his wife.

Don't let that happen to you. Jesus is before you every bit as much as he was before Pilate in a physical form that day. "Are you the King?" you ask. "Yes," Jesus answers. Is he right? You have to face that claim. If he is the King, say, "Yes, Jesus, I acknowledge who you are, and I want to become your subject today." Bow before him. If you do not, you will bow before him in terror at the judgment.

69

The King on a Cross

Matthew 27:32–44

As they were going out, they met a man from Cyrene, named Simon, and they forced him to carry the cross. They came to a place called Golgotha (which means The Place of the Skull). There they offered Jesus wine to drink, mixed with gall; but after tasting it, he refused to drink it. When they had crucified him, they divided up his clothes by casting lots. And sitting down, they kept watch over him there. Above his head they placed the written charge against him: THIS IS JESUS, THE KING OF THE JEWS. Two robbers were crucified with him, one on his right and one on his left. Those who passed by hurled insults at him, shaking their heads and saying, "You who are going to destroy the temple and build it in three days, save yourself! Come down from the cross, if you are the Son of God!"

In the same way the chief priests, the teachers of the law and the elders mocked him. "He saved others," they said, "but he can't save himself! He's the King of Israel! Let him come down now from the cross, and we will believe in him. He trusts in God. Let God rescue him now if he wants him, for he said, 'I am the Son of God.'" In the same way the robbers who were crucified with him also heaped insults on him.

Where do you go to find kings today? It is difficult to find kings anywhere, because we live in a democratic age and most kings have been replaced by presidents and other elected officials. Some have been supplanted by dictators. Still, a few kings are left, and if you find them anywhere, you will find them in a king's house, in a palace. You do not find them in apartments or common digs or hovels or merely walking down the street. The last place you would ever expect to find a king is on a cross. Yet here in Matthew 27, we find the King of Kings, the ruler of the universe, occupying the lowest possible place that men in their baseness have devised. He is hanging on a cross of rough wood, beaten, bleeding, mocked, and left to die.

The Offense of the Cross

The cross was so offensive to the Romans that they refused to allow their own citizens to be crucified, no matter what they had done. Cicero (106–43 B.C.) called crucifixion "a most cruel and disgusting punishment."[1] He said, "It is a crime to put a Roman citizen in chains, it is an enormity to flog one, sheer murder to slay one; what, then, shall I say of crucifixion? It is impossible to find the word for such an abomination."[2] Indeed, writes Pastor Philip Ryken, "There was no word for it. No polite word, at any rate, for the word for 'cross' was taboo in Roman society."[3] That is why Cicero also said, "Let the very mention of the cross be far removed not only from a Roman citizen's body, but from his mind, his eyes, his ears."[4]

If mention of the cross was offensive to the Romans, it was even more abhorrent to the Jews, for they saw it in the light of Deuteronomy 21:22–23, which reads, "If a man guilty of a capital offense is put to death and his body is hung on a tree, you must not leave his body on the tree overnight. Be sure to bury him that same day, because anyone who is hung on a tree is under God's curse." They understood this to mean that a crucified person was abandoned by God. This explains why Jesus was crucified outside Jerusalem. The act was so offensive to the Jews that they would not allow it to take place within the sacred precincts of their city.

The early Christians knew all this. They often spoke of Jesus having been hanged on a tree, in specific reference to those critical verses in Deuteronomy (see Acts 5:30; 10:39; 13:29; Gal. 3:13; 1 Peter 2:24). Yet they were not ashamed of Christ's cross. Nor are we! Like the apostle Paul, who wrote about the glory of the cross, we do not hesitate to let everyone know that Jesus died in this way. In fact, we use crosses to mark our graveyards and churches, and many wear crosses on their lapels or on chains around their necks. Why this remarkable transformation? Obviously because Christians know that it was by crucifixion on a cross that Jesus took the curse of God for our sin on himself. Paul made this explicit when he wrote, "Christ redeemed us from the curse of the law by becoming a curse for us, for it is written: 'Cursed is everyone who is hung on a tree'" (Gal. 3:13). The cross is not our shame but our glory, which is why we sing,

> In the cross of Christ I glory,
> Towering o'er the wrecks of time;
> All the light of sacred story
> Gathers round its head sublime.

Simon of Cyrene

None of the Gospels describes the actual crucifixion in detail. The details were well known; there was no point in dwelling on its horrors. But the Gospels do tell in general terms what happened. Matthew begins by telling of a man from the North African town of Cyrene who was drafted by the soldiers to carry Jesus' cross. His name was Simon. A condemned person usually carried his own cross, but Jesus must have been too weakened from his scourging and beatings to do it. Jesus carried his cross from the Praetorium to the gates of the city, but when he staggered, the soldiers seized the first able-bodied man they could find, who just happened to be Simon.

Simon is an interesting person. Mark calls him the father of Alexander and Rufus (Mark 15:21), who may be the persons referred to in Acts 19:33 (Alexander) and Romans 16:13 (Rufus). The sons must have been known by the church to which Mark wrote or he would not have had a reason to mention them. Cyrene is mentioned in Acts 2:10; 6:9; 11:20; and 13:1.

William Barclay considers this one of the great "hidden romances" of the New Testament. Simon was a Jew who, like all Jews, would have hated the Romans. To be pressed into service by a Roman soldier and forced to carry the cross of a condemned man must have been a bitter experience for him. But something important may have happened to Simon that day. Instead of merely flinging down the cross at Golgotha, Simon may have been struck by the person of Jesus, stayed to watch the crucifixion, and either then or shortly afterward been converted. After the Passover he would have returned to Cyrene and may have told his family about Jesus. It is not unlikely that the family became Christians through his testimony.

William Barclay goes further, remembering that it was "men from Cyprus and Cyrene" who came to Antioch and first preached the gospel to the Gentile world (Acts 11:20). Was Simon one of the men from Cyrene? Was Rufus with him? In Ephesus, a riot is instigated by people who served Diana of the Ephesians, and the crowd would have killed Paul if they could have gotten to him. Who stands out to face the mob? A man called Alexander (Acts 19:33). And when Paul sends greetings to the Christians in Rome in the last chapter of Romans, two of the people he addresses are "Rufus . . . and his mother" (Rom 16:13).[5] Are these the same people? We do not know. Simon, Alexander, and Rufus were common names. But stranger histories have unfolded. These events may have happened as a result of an apparently chance encounter between Simon and Jesus on the road to Calvary.

The Crucifixion

If Simon remained by the cross that day, he would have witnessed the aspects of the crucifixion that Matthew reports. There are six of them, and most are fulfillments of specific Old Testament prophecies, mostly from Psalms. Matthew frequently cites Old Testament passages that Jesus fulfilled, but surprisingly, he does not call attention to them specifically.

1. *"Wine . . . mixed with gall" (v. 34).* Each of the Gospels contains a reference to this, but it is likely that two different acts were involved. Matthew and Mark describe an offer that Jewish sources say was customarily made by wealthy women of the city as a compassionate attempt to deaden pain. They

offered the victim wine mixed with gall. This drink was offered at the start of the crucifixion, and Matthew and Mark both say that Jesus refused to drink it, presumably to experience the fullness of his suffering and retain a clear mind to the end. John seems to refer to something the soldiers did later. He reports that when Jesus said, "I am thirsty" (in order to fulfill Ps. 69:21), the soldiers soaked a sponge in cheap wine, put it on a staff, and lifted it to his mouth, and that this time Jesus took what was offered. This happened at the end of his ordeal, for immediately after this, Jesus said, "It is finished," and gave up his spirit (John 19:28–30).

2. *Gambling for Christ's clothes (v. 35)*. Each of the Gospels reports how the soldiers divided Christ's clothing, though John alone explains that the gambling was actually only for Christ's seamless outer robe. John is also the only one who says specifically that this was to fulfill Psalm 22:18, which says, "They divided my garments among them and cast lots for my clothing" (see John 19:24). A few Greek manuscripts of Matthew include this verse, but it seems to be a late addition made to conform Matthew's text to that of John.

3. *The written charge against Jesus (v. 37)*. Each of the Gospels also records this detail, though they vary in the actual wording of the placard. Matthew states, "This is Jesus, the king of the Jews." Mark writes, "The king of the Jews" (15:26). Luke reports the words as: "This is the king of the Jews" (23:38). John, who has the fullest version, writes: "Jesus of Nazareth, the king of the Jews" (19:19).

Bible students have wrestled with these slight variations, trying to reconcile them, but the effort is unnecessary in my judgment. Some suggest that since the words were in "Aramaic, Latin and Greek," according to John 19:20, the Gospels translate different languages. That is unlikely. What we have are probably partial reports. The full text might have read, "This is Jesus of Nazareth, the king of the Jews." The important thing is that Jesus was killed for claiming to be the Messiah, which is exactly what he was. He was rejected as king by both the Jews and Romans, but he lives today as the only true ruler of all people, whether Jew or Gentile, bond or free, male or female. Jesus is indeed the King of kings and Lord of all.

4. *"Two robbers . . . with him" (vv. 38, 44)*. Each of the Gospels also reports that two others were crucified at the same time, though only the first three call them robbers and only Luke reports the conversion of one. *Robber* is the same word that was used to describe Barabbas *(leistes)*, and it probably means more than just "thief." The word refers to what we would call a guerrilla soldier or revolutionary and probably suggests that those who were crucified along with Jesus were Barabbas's companions. This is more than likely because stealing was not a capital offense. Was Barabbas intended for the cross in the center? Probably. If so, Jesus literally took his place, just as in a figurative sense he took the place of all who believe on him and trust him alone for their salvation.

Luke explains that both robbers cursed Jesus along with everyone else, but one eventually settled down and rebuked his friend: "Don't you fear

God, since you are under the same sentence? We are punished justly, for we are getting what our deeds deserve. But this man has done nothing wrong."

Then, turning to the Lord, he pled, "Jesus, remember me when you come into your kingdom."

Jesus replied, "I tell you the truth, today you will be with me in paradise" (Luke 23:39–43). What a wonderful promise! One Bible student said, "One thief was saved so that no one might despair, but only one so that no one might presume." None of the Gospels refers to Isaiah 53:12 at this point, but it is difficult not to think of these strange circumstances as its fulfillment. Isaiah wrote, "He poured out his life unto death, and was numbered with the transgressors."

5. *Insults from those passing by (vv. 39–40).* The insults of those who were passing by seem to have fulfilled Psalm 22:7: "All who see me mock me; they hurl insults, shaking their heads." It is a sorry observation on our corrupt natures that people are seldom more heartless than when they see another person suffering, as Jesus was.

6. *Mocking by the chief priests, teachers of the law, and elders (vv. 41–43).* Reference to these three groups of people indicates that they were members of the Sanhedrin, the very body that had arrested, tried, and then condemned the Lord. They challenged him to have God deliver him, unwittingly fulfilling the taunt of Psalm 22:8: "He trusts in the LORD; let the LORD rescue him. Let him deliver him, since he delights in him."

He Died for You

That is the straightforward account, but this is where we have to stop and go back over it in our mind, remembering what Jesus did for us. Can we imagine it? Perhaps we can think of a lacerated body bleeding from head to foot. His form is so marred that he is hardly recognizable, even to his friends. No representation of Jesus' crucifixion that I have ever seen, even by the greatest of artists, does justice to this horror. They are all too clean, too sterile. The crucifixion was bloody and vulgar, ugly and repulsive. Yet he was the Son of God! Think of that and try to understand something of the horror of your sin and of the grace, love, mercy, and compassion of our God.

Do you understand that it was for you that Jesus endured this? And not just as an example of how to endure great suffering. Jesus endured the agonies of the cross in your place. The cross was God's punishment for your sins, and when Jesus cried out, "My God, my God, why have you forsaken me?" it was for you that his eternally ancient bond with the Father was broken. We find this theme again and again in the Bible. "He himself bore our sins in his body on the tree, so that we might die to sins and live for righteousness; by his wounds you have been healed" (1 Peter 2:24). "Christ died for sins once for all, the righteous for the unrighteous, to bring you to God" (1 Peter 3:18). "God made him who had no sin to be sin for us, so that in him we might become the righteousness of God" (2 Cor. 5:21). "Christ redeemed us from the curse of the law by becoming a curse for us" (Gal. 3:13). "Christ was sacrificed once to take away the sins of many people" (Heb. 9:28). Best of all perhaps, this great text from Isaiah:

> But he was pierced for our transgressions,
>   he was crushed for our iniquities;
> the punishment that brought us peace was upon him,
>   and by his wounds we are healed.
> We all, like sheep, have gone astray,
>   each of us has turned to his own way;
> and the LORD has laid on him
>   the iniquity of us all.
>
>   53:5–6

The great evangelical Anglican bishop John Ryle, who refers to these texts, drives their point home.

> Was he scourged? It was that "through his stripes we might be healed." Was he condemned, though innocent? It was that we might be acquitted, though guilty. Did he wear a crown of thorns? It was that we might wear the crown of glory. Was he stripped of his raiment? It was that we might be clothed in everlasting righteousness. Was he mocked and reviled? It was that we might be honored and blessed. Was he reckoned a malefactor, and numbered among transgressors? It was that we might be reckoned innocent, and justified from all sin. Was he declared unable to save himself? It was that he might be able to save others to the uttermost. Did he die at last, and that the most painful and disgraceful of deaths? It was that we might live for evermore, and be exalted to the highest glory.[6]

Let us remember these things and never forget them. Substitution! A vicarious atonement! These texts and the doctrines they express are the very foundation of the gospel.

The Mocking

All the Gospels tell about Jesus' crucifixion, of course, for it is the chief point of their narratives. But each also contains its own special emphasis, and the mocking of Jesus seems to be the dominant note in Matthew. The paragraphs we are studying contain thirteen verses, but five of them are about the taunts of those passing by and of the leaders. The last verse even adds that the robbers "also heaped insults on him" (v. 44).

The interesting thing about these insults is that they were all highly ironic. The first was about Jesus' claim to destroy the temple and rebuild it in three days. This accusation had been raised at his trial, but the leaders had been unable to prove it by the strict standards of Jewish legal procedure. Yet Jesus had said it, and the accusation seemed to have been floating among the people. "You who are going to destroy the temple and build it in three days, save yourself! Come down from the cross, if you are the Son of God!" (v. 40). They ridiculed him for his words, but it was by his death that he was destroying the temple of his body, and it was by his resurrection that he would raise it again.

The leaders did not address Jesus directly. They spoke to one another, probably to show their scorn for him: "He saved others, but he can't save himself! He's the King of Israel! Let him come down now from the cross, and we will believe in him. He trusts in God. Let God rescue him now if he wants him, for he said, 'I am the Son of God'" (vv. 41–43). Ironically, they used the words that Satan had used in two of his temptations of the Lord, recorded in Matthew 4: "If you are the Son of God, tell these stones to become bread" (v. 3) and, "If you are the Son of God, throw yourself down" (v. 6). They were saying the same thing now: "If you are the Son of God, ask God to save you!"

"They thought they were so clever," writes D. A. Carson,

> but the foolishness of God is wiser than human wisdom. Precisely by voluntarily going to the cross, Jesus *was* destroying "this temple"—the temple of his body—and in three days it *would* be "rebuilt." And precisely because he *was* the Son of God, he would *not* come down from the cross! Similar double irony extended to all the mockery he endured. "He saved others . . . but he can't save himself!" (27:42) they taunted. At one level, they were questioning the legitimacy and reality of his claims. Surely the *real* Messiah would not be forced to bear such shame and suffering. But at a deeper level, the taunt was largely right. If the Lord Jesus was to save others, he *had* to sacrifice himself, and he *could not* save himself.[7]

Surely God's wisdom is beyond our understanding. We would never have thought up a gospel like this, but this is true Christianity. Jesus died for us because without that death we could not be saved. To God be the glory!

70

The Death of Jesus Christ

Matthew 27:45–56

From the sixth hour until the ninth hour darkness came over all the land. About the ninth hour Jesus cried out in a loud voice, "Eloi, Eloi, lama sabachthani?"—which means, "My God, my God, why have you forsaken me?"

When some of those standing there heard this, they said, "He's calling Elijah."

Immediately one of them ran and got a sponge. He filled it with wine vinegar, put it on a stick, and offered it to Jesus to drink. The rest said, "Now leave him alone. Let's see if Elijah comes to save him."

And when Jesus had cried out again in a loud voice, he gave up his spirit.

At that moment the curtain of the temple was torn in two from top to bottom. The earth shook and the rocks split. The tombs broke open and the bodies of many holy people who had died were raised to life. They came out of the tombs, and after Jesus' resurrection they went into the holy city and appeared to many people.

When the centurion and those with him who were guarding Jesus saw the earthquake and all that had happened, they were terrified, and exclaimed, "Surely he was the Son of God!"

Many women were there, watching from a distance. They had followed Jesus from Galilee to care for his needs. Among them were Mary Magdalene, Mary the mother of James and Joses, and the mother of Zebedee's sons.

We are nearing the end of Matthew, which means we are coming face to face with the core doctrines of Christianity. That is particularly the case in this and the next two studies, which cover Matthew 27:45–28:15.

621

In 1 Corinthians 15, where Paul sums up the gospel, which he says had been given to him and which he is passing on to others, the great apostle writes, "For what I received I passed on to you as of first importance: that Christ died for our sins according to the Scriptures, that he was buried, that he was raised on the third day according to the Scriptures, and that he appeared to Peter, and then to the Twelve" (vv. 3–5). Those verses contain three core doctrines: (1) Christ's death, (2) Christ's burial, and (3) Christ's resurrection, attested to by Peter and the others who saw him. We come to these doctrines now and must deal carefully with them in these studies.

The Miracles of Calvary

We begin with Jesus' death. All the Gospels report it, but Matthew, unlike the other writers, surrounds it with reports of the miracles that took place when Jesus died. It is not surprising that miracles accompanied the death of Jesus since they also accompanied his birth, but most of us don't think about them very often. We talk about the birth miracles—the virgin birth itself, the angel visitations, the star that guided the wise men—but we do not pay much attention to the miracles that took place at the crucifixion.

There is probably a good reason for that. Jesus' death was followed by his resurrection, which is the most important miracle of all, and we focus on that event. Nevertheless, it is striking that the first three Gospels record miraculous events that took place at the time Jesus was on the cross and when he died, though Matthew's account is the most complete. Matthew tells of five miracles: (1) the darkening of the sky between noon and three in the afternoon, when Jesus was on the cross; (2) the tearing of the veil of the temple from top to bottom, when Jesus died; (3) the earthquake that opened many of the tombs near the place of the crucifixion; (4) followed by the resurrection to life of many holy people who had died; and (5) the cry of the centurion who said of Jesus when he saw these things, "Surely he was the Son of God."

The last was the greatest miracle of all.

Dark amid the Blaze of Noon

That the sky should grow dark for a time is not in itself miraculous. A severe storm can cause darkness. The sky grew dark over Pompeii in A.D. 79 when Vesuvius erupted. An eclipse can cause darkness. But there are no volcanoes in Israel, it seldom rains, and this was certainly not an eclipse. An eclipse lasts only a few minutes. This darkness lasted for three hours. Besides, the crucifixion took place during Passover week, and Passover was always observed at the time of a full moon. An eclipse cannot take place at the time of the month when the moon is full. This was a special divine intervention in the normal workings of nature by which the sky grew dark in the middle of the day, at the sixth hour, which is twelve o'clock, and continued dark until three in the afternoon, when Jesus cried with a loud voice and gave up his spirit.

This must have been a striking, sober, and well-observed phenomenon. Tertullian, the early Christian apologist, referred to the darkness when he reminded his heathen readers that the "wonder is related in your own annals and is preserved in your archives to this day." But notice how restrained Matthew and the other Gospel writers are as they report it (Matt. 27:45; Mark 15:33; Luke 23:44). They do not embellish their stories or speculate about the nature of the darkness or its source. In a manner that can only enhance their credibility as historians, they report only that "from the sixth hour until the ninth hour darkness came over all the land" (Matt. 27:45).

These are utterly silent hours. They represent a gap in the narrative, a time about which we know absolutely nothing. Much was going on before the darkness descended. Jesus had prayed for the soldiers who were crucifying him. He had words of promise for the believing criminal who was beside him on his cross. He commended his mother to the care of the beloved disciple. The chief priests, the teachers of the law, and the elders taunted him. But with the descent of the darkness all narrative ends, as if a veil had been drawn over the unspeakable suffering of God's Son.

What happened during those hours of darkness? We know the answer. During those hours the Son of God took the burden of our sins on himself, was punished for them in our place, and experienced such terrible alienation from his Father that he cried out at the end of that dark period, *"Eloi, Eloi, lama sabachthani?"* which means, "My God, my God, why have you forsaken me?" (v. 46). The darkness veiled the anguish of the Son of God while he was bearing the punishment for our sins, because it was not right for human eyes to look on him in his suffering. At the same time, the darkness cried out against the blackness of our sin and testified to the tremendous cost to God of our redemption.

The Tearing of the Veil

The second miracle that took place at the time of Jesus' death was the tearing in two of the great veil that separated the Holy Place from the Most Holy Place in the temple. Matthew, Mark, and Luke all report the tearing of the veil, but Matthew and Mark add that it was torn in two "from top to bottom" (Matt. 27:51; Mark 15:38), suggesting that this was something God did and that the event was heavy with spiritual significance.

The temple area was designed as a series of courts in the center of which was the temple building itself, divided into two parts. The first and larger part was the Holy Place. It contained the table where the shewbread was placed and the large seven-branched candlestick. A veil separated this room from the outer courts and another veil separated it from the innermost room called the Most Holy Place. In the early days of Israel's history before the destruction of the temple by the Babylonians, this innermost room contained the ark of the covenant with its mercy seat and cherubim between the wings of which God was understood to dwell in a symbolic sense. The presence of

God above the ark in the Most Holy Place testified to the presence of God among his people. In a contrary way, the veil that divided the Holy Place from the Most Holy Place also pointed to the enormous gulf that existed between the holy God and the people because of their sin. The veil was a way of saying symbolically but also unmistakably, "Thus far you may come, but no farther."

Only one day during the year could the high priest pass the veil, and that was on the Day of Atonement when the high priest took the blood of an animal killed moments before in the courtyard, carried it past the veil, and then sprinkled it on the mercy seat of the ark. The mercy seat was the ark's cover or lid. The figures of two angels faced each other on the lid, and their wings stretched backward and upward, making a space in which God symbolically dwelled. The ark contained the two tablets of the law below the space where God was thought to dwell.

The ark was a picture of judgment, for the righteous, holy God of the universe looked down on the law, knew that it had been broken and that he had to punish the people for their sin. This dramatic illustration stood on the temple mount day after day throughout the year as a constant reminder of God's judgment. When blood was sprinkled on the mercy seat on the Day of Atonement, however, coming between God and the law that had been broken, the act indicated that an atonement for sin had been made, illustrating grace. An innocent victim (the animal) had died in the people's place, and rather than pouring forth wrath, God was now able to show grace and mercy to the people. This pointed forward to the true and final atonement that Jesus Christ would make on the cross. It pointed forward to his death, as did all the other sacrifices of the Old Testament.

Here we see the significance of the tearing of the veil. When Jesus died everything the Old Testament sacrifices pointed to was fulfilled. There was no need for further sacrifices, and the way to God was open for all who would put their trust in Jesus. God showed this in a dramatic way by tearing the veil.

In addition, the veil was torn in two at three o'clock in the afternoon, which was the time of the beginning of the evening sacrifice. The priests would have been in the temple, engaged in their duties, when the veil was torn. They would have seen it, no doubt standing aghast before the now-exposed innermost recess of the temple, and they would have known that the age in which they had served was over and a new age of God's dealings with his people had begun. This may be the explanation of what we read later in Acts: "So the word of God spread. The number of disciples in Jerusalem increased rapidly, and *a large number of priests* became obedient to the faith" (Acts 6:7, emphasis added).

Specifically, the rending of the veil teaches three things.

1. *The old system of offering sacrifices year by year was over.* The priests probably sewed the veil back together and went on with their traditional religious practices, but in the sight of God the old age had ended and a new age had

begun. The new age embraces both Jew and Gentile within Christ's church, which is why Paul was able to write to the Ephesians as he did. "For he himself [Jesus] is our peace, who has made the two one and has destroyed the barrier, the dividing wall of hostility, by abolishing in his flesh the law with its commandments and regulations. His purpose was to create in himself one new man out of the two, thus making peace, and in this one body to reconcile both of them to God through the cross, by which he put to death their hostility" (Eph. 2:14–16).

2. *Jesus' offering of himself was the perfect and final sacrifice; so nothing more needs to be done or can be done to reconcile sinful men and women to God.* Jesus' sacrifice was a real sacrifice for sin, not a symbol that pointed forward to something else, as the Old Testament system did. Previous sacrifices pointed forward to the atonement he would make, but they were not themselves that atonement. Jesus put away our real sin by his real death. To suggest that anything more is necessary for salvation is to deny the doctrine known as *solus Christus* (Christ alone), the slogan by which the Reformers expressed the completeness and total sufficiency of Christ's work. To add anything to Christ's work is to preach "another gospel," which the Bible condemns (Gal. 1:6–9).

The author of the Book of Hebrews is particularly concerned with this theme, developing it in various ways throughout the book. However, in one place he says very clearly:

> [Christ did not] enter heaven to offer himself again and again, the way the high priest enters the Most Holy Place every year with blood that is not his own. Then Christ would have had to suffer many times since the creation of the world. But now he has appeared once for all at the end of the ages to do away with sin by the sacrifice of himself. Just as man is destined to die once, and after that to face judgment, so Christ was sacrificed once to take away the sins of many people; and he will appear a second time, not to bear sin, but to bring salvation to those who are waiting for him.
>
> Hebrews 9:25–28

Likewise, Paul insists that "there is one God and one mediator between God and men, the man Christ Jesus, who gave himself as a ransom for all men—the testimony given in its proper time" (1 Tim. 2:5–6). As a result, today we insist that there is no Savior but Jesus and that we must believe on him and commit ourselves to him if we are to be saved.

3. *Because of Christ's work it is now possible for those who believe on him to approach God directly.* The people of God could not do this before Christ's death. They needed to approach God indirectly, asking a priest to intercede for them. But now the way is open for everyone. The author of Hebrews wrote on this point:

> Therefore, brothers, since we have confidence to enter the Most Holy Place by the blood of Jesus, by a new and living way opened for us through the curtain, that is, his body, and since we have a great priest over the house of God, let us

draw near to God with a sincere heart in full assurance of faith. . . . Let us hold unswervingly to the hope we profess, for he who promised is faithful. And let us consider how we may spur one another on toward love and good deeds.

Hebrews 10:19–24

The Shaking of the Earth

The earthquake that split the rocks and broke open many of the tombs was the third miracle. Earthquakes themselves are not miraculous, but the timing of this one was. It took place at the precise moment when Jesus died. Moreover, it served as the prelude to the resurrection of many holy persons. Matthew does not explain what the earthquake meant, but it probably corresponded to the giving of the law at Sinai, when the earth also trembled. That was a time of fear for those who had been brought out of Egypt, for God is a holy God and the law is a terrible thing for those who have broken it. The revelation of the presence of God on Mount Sinai was so terrifying that even Moses said, "I am trembling with fear" (Heb. 12:21). The earthquake at Calvary parallels the earthquake at Sinai and reminds us that although "the law was given through Moses; grace and truth came through Jesus Christ" (John 1:17).

Foretaste of the Final Resurrection

We do not understand certain aspects of these miracles. The meaning of the torn veil is the easiest to decipher because of the way it is developed in the Book of Hebrews. But the darkness is unexplained. So is the earthquake. And so is the miracle to which we come now: the resurrection of many of the Old Testament saints and their appearance to many in Jerusalem following Jesus' resurrection. We do not know whether these saints had died long ago or only recently. We do not know how long they remained alive. Was this a permanent resurrection? If it was, what happened to them? Were they transported to heaven, like Elijah? Or did they die again? We do not even know whom they went into Jerusalem to see or why they went or what they said to those they saw.

What we do know is that the report must be historical. Otherwise, why would Matthew have recorded such an amazing thing at all? And why so soberly and with no explanation of its meaning? What we can suppose is that the resurrection of these believers was a foretaste and pledge of the final resurrection of all who believe on Jesus. Just as Christ was raised from the dead, so also will God raise from the dead those who die in him. Jesus had taught this clearly. When his friend Lazarus had died and Jesus had returned to Bethany at the request of Lazarus's sisters, Martha went out to meet him, saying, "Lord, if you had been here, my brother would not have died."

Jesus told her, "Your brother will rise again."

That was orthodox teaching among the Jews of that day, no doubt drawn from Old Testament texts. But Martha was thinking of the future, and her reply showed that she did not connect this future resurrection with Jesus in any specific way. "I know he will rise again in the resurrection at the last day," Martha said.

Jesus replied, "I am the resurrection and the life. He who believes in me will live, even though he dies; and whoever lives and believes in me will never die" (John 11:21–26). This was comprehensive teaching, indicating that true life is spiritual life and that those who believe in Jesus have it. His words also taught about a final resurrection. Therefore, it is correct to say of those who believe that they "will never die." All this is because of Christ and is experienced through faith in him. It is why Jesus began his teaching by saying, "I am the resurrection and the life" (v. 25). By raising some to life at the time of Jesus' death, God indicated that this is the destiny of all who believe on Jesus Christ as their Savior.

Later on Jesus told his disciples, "Because I live, you also will live" (John 14:19). And still later, Paul wrote to the Corinthians:

Christ has indeed been raised from the dead, the firstfruits of those who have fallen asleep. For since death came through a man, the resurrection of the dead comes also through a man. For as in Adam all die, so in Christ all will be made alive. But each in his own turn: Christ, the firstfruits; then, when he comes, those who belong to him.

1 Corinthians 15:20–23

This does not mean that the resurrection of those who came out of their tombs at the time of Christ's death was their final resurrection. I imagine that they all died again. But while theirs was not the *final* resurrection, it was *a* resurrection, and it pointed to the day when all who are Christ's will be raised by him.

Paul wrote,

Listen, I tell you a mystery: We will not all sleep, but we will all be changed—in a flash, in the twinkling of an eye, at the last trumpet. For the trumpet will sound, the dead will be raised imperishable, and we will be changed. For the perishable must clothe itself with the imperishable, and the mortal with immortality. When the perishable has been clothed with the imperishable, and the mortal with immortality, then the saying that is written will come true: "Death has been swallowed up in victory."

"Where, O death, is your victory?
Where, O death, is your sting?"

The sting of death is sin, and the power of sin is the law. But thanks be to God! He gives us the victory through our Lord Jesus Christ.

1 Corinthians 15:51–57

The resurrection of many of the saints who had died was a pledge of the final resurrection and an encouragement for those who wait for it.

The Greatest Miracle of All

We have examined four great miracles: the hours of darkness, the tearing of the veil, the earthquake, and the resurrection of many holy persons who had died. The fifth miracle, however, was the greatest one of all.

Standing by the cross was a Roman centurion, the leader of those who had been given the task of crucifying Jesus. We can assume he was a pagan, but when he saw what happened when Jesus died, God quickened him to spiritual life, and he cried out with true faith, "Surely he was the Son of God" (v. 54). It may not have been a full confession. It lacked much that he would undoubtedly come to know later. But it was correct as far as it went, and we cannot doubt that Matthew included it as an example of what is required of all who come face to face with Jesus. Have you made that vital confession, acknowledging that Jesus is both the Son of God and your Savior? It is the only way that anyone can be saved.

71

The Burial of Jesus Christ

Matthew 27:57–66

As evening approached, there came a rich man from Arimathea, named Joseph, who had himself become a disciple of Jesus. Going to Pilate, he asked for Jesus' body, and Pilate ordered that it be given to him. Joseph took the body, wrapped it in a clean linen cloth, and placed it in his own new tomb that he had cut out of the rock. He rolled a big stone in front of the entrance to the tomb and went away. Mary Magdalene and the other Mary were sitting there opposite the tomb.

The next day, the one after Preparation Day, the chief priests and the Pharisees went to Pilate. "Sir," they said, "we remember that while he was still alive that deceiver said, 'After three days I will rise again.' So give the order for the tomb to be made secure until the third day. Otherwise, his disciples may come and steal the body and tell the people that he has been raised from the dead. This last deception will be worse than the first."

"Take a guard," Pilate answered. "Go, make the tomb as secure as you know how." So they went and made the tomb secure by putting a seal on the stone and posting the guard.

The burial of Jesus is the second of the core doctrines of Christianity listed by the apostle Paul in 1 Corinthians 15: "For what I received I passed on to you as of first importance: that Christ died for our sins according to the Scriptures, that he was buried, that he was raised on the third day according to the Scriptures, and that he appeared to Peter, and then to the Twelve" (vv. 3–5). It occupies a significant amount of space in each of the four Gospels: ten verses in Matthew, six verses in Mark, six in Luke, and five in John. But we do not generally give much thought to Jesus' burial. After the death, we move on instinctively to the good news of the resurrection since so much depends on it. It is proof that the God of the Old Testament, the God of Abraham, Isaac, and Jacob, is the true God; that

Jesus is who he claimed to be, the Son of God and the Savior; that Jesus' death was accepted by his Father as an atonement for our sins; that those who believe on Jesus are in a justified state before God; that there is power for victory over sin for all who belong to Jesus; and that those who are united to Jesus by faith will themselves be raised from death to life in heaven. But between the death of Jesus and the resurrection, the writers of the Gospels record the burial. Why is the burial so important?

Why the Burial Is Important

The New Testament stresses the burial of Jesus for several reasons. One is obvious. The second can be found by careful Bible students. The third is not obvious at all.

1. *The burial proves that Jesus was really dead.* If Jesus had not been buried after the centurion had certified to Pilate that Jesus was truly dead (Mark 15:44–45); by Joseph of Arimathea, a member of the Sanhedrin, accompanied by Nicodemus (John 19:39); after a careful preparation of the body; in a new tomb that was then sealed with a large stone (Matt. 27:59–60), it would have been possible for skeptics to argue that Jesus had not really died. Perhaps he only seemed to die. Perhaps he swooned and was somehow able to revive and convince his followers that he had triumphed over death. That is extremely improbable, of course, though some nineteenth-century rationalists were foolish enough to suggest it. A resuscitation such as that would have been impossible in view of the burial and the way it was accomplished. The burial of Jesus assures us that Jesus was really dead and that his resurrection was a true resurrection.

2. *The details of the burial fulfilled Scripture.* The most obvious passage is Isaiah 53:9:

> He was assigned a grave with the wicked,
>   and with the rich in his death,
> though he had done no violence,
>   nor was any deceit in his mouth.

Matthew does not call attention to this verse, though earlier in the Gospel he cites many other texts that Jesus fulfilled. Nor does John mention the verse, though in chapter 19 he refers to four other verses that he says were fulfilled at the time of the crucifixion: Psalm 22:18 in verse 24; Psalm 69:21 in verse 28; Exodus 12:46 (and others texts) in verse 36; and Zechariah 12:10 in verse 37. Nevertheless, Matthew probably has Isaiah 53:9 in mind, since he alone of the Gospel writers says that Joseph of Arimathea was "a rich man," and *rich* is the critical word in Isaiah 53:9.

3. *The burial has theological significance.* This point is not so obvious, but it strikes us when we study what is said about the grave in the Old Testament and about the burial of Jesus in the New Testament. Old Testament texts speak of

the grave with dread. Examples include Genesis 37:35 ("In mourning will I go down to the grave") and 2 Samuel 22:6 ("The cords of the grave coiled around me"). Often the word translated "grave" in our Bibles is *Sheol*, which has overtones of hell, as in Psalm 116:3 ("the anguish of the grave") or Job 10:21, which calls it "the land of gloom and deep shadow." To say that Jesus not only died but was also buried in the grave means that he descended as low as he could go in order to raise us up to heaven. Herman N. Ridderbos wrote, "Jesus endured not only pain and suffering and the curse of death but even the terror of the grave, so that he could save his people from this forever."[1]

Yet there is more. In Romans, Paul speaks of Christians being buried with Jesus in his death, just as they are raised with him in his resurrection. He does this while discussing the Christian life, explaining why believers cannot continue in sin. For example, "We were . . . buried with him through baptism into death in order that, just as Christ was raised from the dead through the glory of the Father, we too may live a new life" (Rom. 6:4).

When theologians work out these parallels, they have little trouble showing how we have been crucified with Jesus, raised with him, or even made to ascend into heaven with him. But they have trouble with the burial. How were we buried with Christ? they ask. What does this add that is not already covered by our death to sin?

I suggest that the reason burial is an important step even beyond death is that burial puts the deceased person out of this world permanently. A corpse is dead to life, but in a sense it is still in life, as long as it is around. When it is buried, when it is placed in the ground and covered with earth, it is removed from the sphere of this life permanently. It is gone. That is why Paul, who wanted to emphasize the finality of being removed from the rule of sin and death, emphasizes it. He is repeating but also intensifying what he said about our death to sin earlier. "You have not only died to it," he says. "You have been buried to it." To go back to sin once you have been joined to Christ is like digging up a dead body.

I do not think the Gospel writers had this in mind when they wrote about Christ's burial, but guided by the Holy Spirit, they were laying down as a detail of history what Paul in particular would later unfold in its full theological significance.

Joseph of Arimathea

As Matthew tells the story, the burial of Jesus was arranged by Joseph of Arimathea, "a rich man" who went to Pilate to ask that the body be given to him. Matthew calls him "a disciple of Jesus" (v. 57). Mark and Luke add that he was "a member of the Council," which means that he was a member of the Sanhedrin. Mark says that he was "waiting for the kingdom of God" (Mark 15:43) and Luke that he was "a good and upright man, who had not consented to their decision and action" (Luke 23:50–51). John alone reports that he was assisted in his work by Nicodemus, who brought the spices. The

Romans did not normally allow crucified persons to be buried, least of all traitors. The fact that Joseph approached Pilate is a testimony to his courage.

It is an interesting fact that this is the first and only time we hear of Joseph. He has not been mentioned before in the Gospels, nor does his name appear again after this event. Yet at the very moment when Christ's other disciples (save John) had forsaken him, he alone came forward boldly to identify with Jesus. He did it at great personal cost too, for if Joseph was a member of the Sanhedrin, as Mark and Luke say he was, his care for Jesus' body must have ended his career with that court. The Sanhedrin would have had no use for him once he had shown an interest in their enemy.

The Guard at the Tomb

When Pilate consented to the crucifixion and washed his hands of it, he must have thought he was finished with the case. But then Joseph of Arimathea arrived, asking for the body. Now others had a continuing interest in Jesus—those irritating Jewish leaders. They were back again, this time asking that a guard be placed at the tomb "until the third day" lest "his disciples . . . come and steal the body and tell the people that he had been raised from the dead" (v. 64). Their fear of what they call "this last deception" as well as their mention of the third day shows that they had understood Jesus' words about destroying the temple and rebuilding it in three days. They knew Jesus had promised to prove he was the Messiah by his resurrection. They did not believe him. They would not believe him even after his resurrection, but they wanted to do everything they could to keep this terrible thing from happening.

Pilate may have been irritated by the intrusion, but I think he must have been amused too. They were asking for Roman soldiers to guard the tomb. I do not think he gave them. "You have a guard," is what he literally said; that is, they had their own temple guard and did not need his troops. But he gave them permission to seal and guard the tomb with their soldiers if they were really worried. "Go, make the tomb as secure as you know how," he told them. I think he said that with amusement and scorn, for what could Pilate possibly have meant? He must have meant one of two things, as Matthew Henry suggests. Either Pilate was laughing at the leaders for their folly—imagine setting a guard to watch a dead man!—or, more likely, he was mocking them for their fears. It was as if he were saying, "Do your worst, try your wit and strength to the uttermost; but if he be of God, he will rise in spite of you and all your guards."[2] That is what Charles H. Spurgeon thought the words meant. He described the priests begging Pilate "to do what he could to prevent the rising of their victim."[3]

Fear of Jesus

When the chief priests and Pharisees came to Pilate, they explained their request by stating that they feared "his disciples may come and steal the body and tell the people that he has been raised from the dead" (v. 64). But that is probably not what they were really afraid of. For one thing, the disciples were not worth fearing. Any doubts the religious leaders may have had on that score had been settled in the garden when Christ's companions forsook him and fled. Only Peter and John seem to have made it to Jerusalem to witness the crucifixion, and neither of them was any help to Jesus. Peter had even denied his Lord. Besides, if the priests had actually feared what the disciples might do, they could easily have arrested them when they arrested Jesus or rounded them up afterward. The fact that they did not shows they had no real concerns on their account.

In my judgment, what they actually feared was the resurrection. These men were not imperceptive. They had been watching Jesus for the better part of three years. They had seen him heal the sick, give sight to the blind, cleanse lepers, and restore strength to the physically impotent. Most amazing of all, just a few days before these events, Jesus had actually raised Lazarus of Bethany from the grave.

There was no denying the miracles. The leaders had tried to deny them at first, but in the end there were too many miracles and too many witnesses. After a while, they simply acknowledged the miracles but attributed them to the devil. This amazing and obviously powerful teacher had claimed that three days after he had been put to death he would be raised from death by God. Was that possible? What if it was? Were they not afraid that the one who had raised Lazarus might actually conquer death and shatter their small religious world forever?

What were they to do? They did what they could. They sealed the stone that had been rolled across the tomb's mouth. Who would dare to break their seal, thereby setting himself against the united spiritual and political powers of their world? They also posted guards drawn from the same company that had arrested Jesus in the garden. These were their men, Jews. If anyone could be trusted, they could.

The guard was set. Everything was in order. The hours and days rolled by. All seemed well. Suddenly, "there was a violent earthquake, for an angel of the Lord came down from heaven and, going to the tomb, rolled back the stone and sat on it. His appearance was like lightning, and his clothes were white as snow. The guards were so afraid of him that they shook and became like dead men" (Matt. 28:2–4). In this manner, the seal was broken and the tomb was shown to be empty. Jesus was no longer there. He was risen as he said. The rule of the priests was broken, and Christianity began its triumphant expansion into the Greek and Roman world.

"Go, make the tomb as secure as you know how." But how? How can anyone secure anything against the shattering power of Jesus' resurrection?

The Conversion of Saul

A few years after Jesus' resurrection, a young rabbi rose to prominence. He had studied under Gamaliel and had achieved some stature among the

Pharisees, the very sect that had been instrumental in securing Jesus' death. Christianity had not died out after Jesus' crucifixion, and this young rabbi— his name was Saul—decided to stamp it out forcefully. He uprooted the Christians in Jerusalem, brought them to trial, and killed at least one (Acts 7). Then, not satisfied with his work in Jerusalem, he went to the high priest and secured letters of introduction to the synagogues in Damascus so that if he found Christians there he might arrest them and bring them to Jerusalem for trial too.

Saul was in the company of those who had tried to secure the tomb of Jesus years before. He was trying to secure two things. First, he was trying to secure Judaism from the vitality of the Nazarene's sect, as some would have called it. He considered Christianity a heresy and Jesus a blasphemer, a child of Satan. By arresting Christians he hoped to destroy it and secure his own religion.

Second, he was trying to secure himself, since later he confessed that he had been trying to "kick against the goads" (Acts 26:14), like an animal fighting one who is prodding it to go in the right direction. Although Saul was fighting Christianity with zeal, he was at the same time fighting an even more intense struggle in his heart. His outward zeal may be explained by his inward struggle. He had given his life to Judaism, but suppose the Christians were actually right? Suppose Jesus really was the Son of God? Suppose he really was the Messiah and that his death really was a vicarious sacrifice for sin? Suppose Jesus really had risen from the dead? Saul couldn't think about that. On with the work! Onward in the war against Christians!

In this turbulent state of mind, Saul made his way northward to Damascus when suddenly a bright light flashed about him and he fell blinded to the ground.

He heard a voice. "Saul, Saul, why do you persecute me?"

"Who are you, Lord?" Saul asked. His answer showed that he sensed what was coming.

"I am Jesus, whom you are persecuting," the voice replied. "Now get up and go into the city, and you will be told what you must do" (Acts 9:1–6). When Saul, hereafter known as Paul, obeyed and went into Damascus, God sent a disciple named Ananias to confirm him in faith and tell him of God's call to world evangelism. The dreaded persecutor of the Christians became the infant church's first great missionary. Saul had tried to make himself secure against Jesus, but suddenly there was the bright light, Jesus spoke to him, and the resurrection became an undeniable reality.

Jesus and You

Have you been confronted by the power of Jesus' resurrection? Or are you still trying to make your life secure against Jesus? Perhaps you have heard of Christ's gospel, but you have been trying to keep Jesus politely in his place. I warn you: Jesus is not that easily contained. You can push him down, but he will crop up again. You can banish him from your thoughts, but he will come back when you least expect him. What are you going to do against the power of the one so many call Lord? How are you going to make yourself secure against Jesus?

Let me suggest what you can do. You can begin with activity. That should not be too difficult in our hectic times. Our world is preoccupied with activity and even rewards those who are busiest. If you are busy enough, you will not have time to think about Jesus. Fill up your time. Schedule your idle hours. Then you will not have to go to a Bible study. When Christians invite you to church, you can say you are too busy. Fill your evenings with television so you will not have time to read your Bible.

Here is something else you can do. You can fill your life with sin and sin's pleasures. Jesus is the sinless Son of God; sin should keep you from him. Fill your life with the evil pleasures of the world. There are many. Make your life as secure as you can against Jesus.

I have one more suggestion: Become religious. If you take this path, however, I suggest that you do not learn too much about Christianity. Instead, sink yourself in ceremony. Do things not because they are meaningful—you might have to think about their meaning—but for tradition's sake or for mere aesthetics. Make your life as secure as you can with religion. Attach your seals! Post your guards! Erect your barricades!

Alas, it will not be enough. Jesus has broken seals before. He has scattered countless guards. What will you do when the light bursts forth from heaven and Jesus confronts you in resurrection splendor? I will tell you what I would do. I would give up fighting altogether. I would lay down my seals and stones and guards and feverish activity. I would abandon my sins, and I would fall before him and confess him as Thomas did. I would say, "My Lord and my God." Then Jesus will make you his, and he will tell you what you are to be and do for his sake.[4]

72

The Resurrection of Jesus Christ

Matthew 28:1-15

After the Sabbath, at dawn on the first day of the week, Mary Magdalene and the other Mary went to look at the tomb.

There was a violent earthquake, for an angel of the Lord came down from heaven and, going to the tomb, rolled back the stone and sat on it. His appearance was like lightning, and his clothes were white as snow. The guards were so afraid of him that they shook and became like dead men.

The angel said to the women, "Do not be afraid, for I know that you are looking for Jesus, who was crucified. He is not here; he has risen, just as he said. Come and see the place where he lay. Then go quickly and tell his disciples: 'He has risen from the dead and is going ahead of you into Galilee. There you will see him.' Now I have told you."

So the women hurried away from the tomb, afraid yet filled with joy, and ran to tell his disciples. Suddenly Jesus met them. "Greetings," he said. They came to him, clasped his feet and worshiped him. Then Jesus said to them, "Do not be afraid. Go and tell my brothers to go to Galilee; there they will see me."

While the women were on their way, some of the guards went into the city and reported to the chief priests everything that had happened. When the chief priests had met with the elders and devised a plan, they gave the soldiers a large sum of money, telling them, "You are to say, 'His disciples came during the night and stole him away while we were asleep.' If this report gets to the governor, we will satisfy him and keep you out of trouble." So the soldiers took the money and did as they were instructed. And this story has been widely circulated among the Jews to this very day.

Have you ever noticed that when Hollywood tries to portray the life of Jesus it inevitably spiritualizes the resurrection? A few years ago I saw one of these films on television. It was well

637

done. The death of Jesus was real enough. When the Roman soldier took a hammer and drove the nail through Jesus' hand, you really could believe you were seeing real metal, flesh, and wood. But when they came to the resurrection, all you could hear was music. You couldn't see Jesus. People rushed about in what was supposedly the joy of the resurrection. But where was the Lord? He wasn't there. At last there was a ghostly view of Jesus in the clouds, but it was no resurrection. If the resurrection had been like that, I am sure that Thomas for one never would have believed in it, and I do not think that Peter or John or any of the others would have either.

The only resurrection that counts for anything is a resurrection of the body. The disciples knew Jesus' resurrection was real when they touched his body, and it was only because of their deeply grounded conviction that he was raised that they were willing to launch out from their obscure corner of the earth to the whole of the Roman world with the gospel.

Paul believed in this kind of resurrection and knew that it was basic to the Christian faith, which is why he expounds it as Christianity's third great doctrinal foundation in 1 Corinthians 15:3–5. Later in that chapter he goes so far as to say that if the resurrection did not occur, then Christianity is an utterly empty hope and that those who believe in it are yet in their sins. Why is this? Because if Jesus did not rise from the dead, Jesus was mistaken in the announcement that he would rise, he was mistaken that he was the divine Son of God, and if he is not God, his death on the cross was not a true atonement for our sins.

The Gospel Records

Each of the writers has his own way of telling about the resurrection, of course, and Matthew is no exception. Matthew alone of the evangelists tells about the soldiers sent to guard the tomb and how they were shaken by the angel. He also tells about a visit Mary Magdalene and "the other Mary" (the mother of James) made to the tomb "at dawn on the first day of the week" and how an angel appeared to them with the first announcement of Christ's victory: "Do not be afraid, for I know that you are looking for Jesus, who was crucified. He is not here; he has risen, just as he said. Come and see the place where he lay. Then go quickly and tell his disciples: 'He has risen from the dead and is going ahead of you into Galilee. There you will see him'" (vv. 5–7).

Over the years critics have complained about what they consider serious discrepancies in these accounts. The number of women, for instance. Matthew mentions two (v. 1). Mark has three (Mark 16:1). Luke refers to three by name and speaks of "others" also (Luke 24:10). John mentions only Mary (John 20:1). Another alleged discrepancy is the time the women set out. Matthew says it was "at dawn" (v. 1). Mark has "very early . . . just after sunrise" (v. 2). Luke says "very early" (v. 1). John writes, "while it was still dark" (v. 1). Again, the number of angels varies: one in Matthew and Mark, two in Luke and John.

These are not discrepancies, of course. They are each only partial tellings of the story. If there were two angels, there was certainly one. As for the time of day, it is easy to imagine that the women set out for the tomb early in the morning, while it was still dark, and arrived as the sun was rising. Variations in the tellings of an obviously identical story actually attest to the reliability of the narratives. They prove that these are independent accounts, not imaginary tales worked out in collusion by the writers, and their essential agreement proves that the four independent records are factual.

Events of Easter Morning

Besides, it is not difficult to put the details of the narratives together. Jesus had been crucified either on Friday (which the church has traditionally believed) or on Thursday (which is less widely held but, in my judgment, seems to fit the evidence better).[1] In any case, Jesus was in the tomb until the resurrection, which certainly took place before dawn on Sunday morning. At this point the women came to the tomb from Jerusalem bearing spices to anoint his body. There were at least five women and probably more. We have already seen that Matthew mentions Mary Magdalene and the other Mary and that Mark adds Salome. Luke writes of the two Marys, Joanna, and others. These women started out while it was still dark and arrived at the tomb in the very early dawn.

On reaching the tomb, they were astonished to find that the stone had been moved from the entrance. We can imagine them standing at a distance, afraid to move closer, wondering what had happened. Who moved the stone? Had the body of Jesus been stolen? Grave robbing was a common crime in the ancient world. Perhaps the robbers were still around. Or had Pilate ordered the body's removal? What should they do? At last they decided the disciples should be told. So Mary Magdalene was sent back to the city to find them. Not one of them imagined that Jesus had been raised from the dead.

After a while it began to grow lighter and the women grew bolder. They decided to look into the tomb. There they saw the angels. The women were afraid, but an angel told them not to be afraid, that Jesus was risen, and that they were to tell his disciples.

Meanwhile, Mary had found the two chief disciples, Peter and John, who alone of the eleven were present in the city that weekend. The two disciples immediately started for the tomb, running and leaving Mary far behind. John was the younger of the two. Consequently, he arrived at the tomb first, stooped to look through the narrow opening, and saw the graveclothes. Then Peter arrived, out of breath and in a hurry as usual. He brushed John aside and went in. When John saw the graveclothes, he saw them in a cursory manner from outside the tomb. The Greek uses the most common word for seeing (*blepo*); it suggests nothing more than sight. But when Peter arrived, he scrutinized the graveclothes closely. The account uses a special word (*theoreo*) for what Peter did. We get our words *theory* and *theorize* from it. He was trying to figure things out.

John, who tells this part of the story because he was there and lived through it, records what Peter saw: "He saw the strips of linen lying there, as well as the burial cloth that had been around Jesus' head. The cloth was folded up by itself, separate from the linen" (John 20:6–7). At last John entered also, saw what Peter had seen—now the verb is *orao* ("to see with understanding")—and believed in Jesus' resurrection. John understood that the only way to explain the unusual arrangement of the graveclothes was that Jesus' resurrection body had passed through them, just as it would later pass through closed doors.

After this the appearances of the Lord began. Jesus appeared first to Mary Magdalene, who arrived back at the tomb after Peter and John had returned to the city. He appeared to the women next, then to Peter alone, then to the Emmaus disciples, finally, later that night to all the disciples as they were gathered in the upper room.

The way these accounts fit together makes the narrative compelling, and it may not be overstating the case to say, as Matthew Arnold once did, that the resurrection of Jesus Christ is "the best attested fact in history." Lawyers in particular have found this to be true, such as Frank Morison, Gilbert West, J. N. D. Anderson, and others. Sir Edward Clark, a well-known English lawyer, wrote, "As a lawyer I have made a prolonged study of the evidences for the first Easter day. To me the evidence is conclusive, and over and over again in the High Court I have secured the verdict on evidence not nearly so compelling. As a lawyer I accept it as the testimony of men to facts that they were able to substantiate."[2]

Four Imperatives

At this point, however, neither Peter nor John had seen the resurrected Lord. He was seen by the women first, those who had been last at the cross and were now first at the tomb. Jesus met them on their way home after they had gone to the tomb, seen the angels, and heard about Jesus' resurrection. The angel's message contains four imperatives that are as important today as they were on that first Easter day for those women (vv. 6–7).

1. *Come.* The first of the angel's imperatives was "come." This was an important statement because much might have hindered the women from coming. The place itself might have hindered them. They were in a graveyard early in the morning. They might have said to each other, "Let's go back; it's not safe here. Let's come back when it is brighter and there are more people around." Fear of Rome might have hindered them. The stone had been sealed, but the seal was broken and the stone removed. Rome had been defied. They might be implicated in the crime. They might have said, "We can't go closer. Rome forbids it." Their sin might have hindered them. Something mysterious, holy had taken place here. They might have rea-

soned, "This is sacred ground. We can't go closer." None of this stopped them, of course. The invitation to come was from God, and they recognized the voice of God in the invitation and obeyed it.

Through the preaching of the gospel, the Lord invites you to come to him. He is speaking to you when he says, "Come to me, all you who are weary and burdened, and I will give you rest. Take my yoke upon you and learn from me, for I am gentle and humble in heart, and you will find rest for your souls" (Matt. 11:28–29). Have you come? Have you obeyed that invitation? There can be no knowledge of God, no salvation, no growth in the Christian life until you do.

2. *See.* The second imperative was "see." The angel said, "Come and *see* the place where he lay" (v. 6). What should we see when we look into the tomb? Years ago Charles H. Spurgeon preached a message on this verse in which he suggested five things.

First, we should see in Christ's grave *the condescension of Jesus Christ.* Jesus was not a man for whom death would be natural. Jesus is God. He was with the Father from all eternity and will be with him forever. We would never expect Jesus to die. But Jesus did in fact die for us. We should marvel at the condescension of such an amazing God, that he should be placed in a tomb to save us.

Second, we should see *the horror of our sin,* for it was our sin that put him there. Death is the punishment for sin. But Jesus had no sin; he was sinless. Why then did Jesus die? The answer is clear: "He was pierced for our transgressions, he was crushed for our iniquities; the punishment that brought us peace was upon him, and by his wounds we are healed" (Isa. 53:5). When we look into the tomb, we begin to see the horror of our sin and develop a proper hatred for it.

Third, we should look into the tomb to be reminded that *we too will die.* Unless the Lord returns for his own before that moment, we will also die and be separated from those we know and love. The tomb speaks of our mortality and warns us that there is a life beyond this life for which we must prepare.

Fourth, and most important, we must look into the tomb to see that *Jesus is not in it.* He is risen as he said. He has conquered death. The empty tomb is one great evidence of the resurrection. Most people who have written seriously about the events of this momentous week have noticed, if they have been honest, that in all the reports we have, whether in the New Testament or in secular sources of the time, there is not one attempt to deny that the grave was empty. There are alternative explanations. One of them is in the verses that follow these in Matthew: The disciples stole the body. But not one writer anywhere denied that the tomb was empty. What can account for it? Not theft by Christ's enemies: If they had stolen the body, they would have produced it later when the resurrection was proclaimed by Jesus' followers. Not the disciples either: If they had stolen the body, they would not have been willing to die, as many of them later did, for what they knew was a fabrication. The only adequate explanation of the empty tomb is that Jesus had been raised from the dead as the Bible teaches.

The fifth reason we should look into the tomb is to learn that *we shall also rise, as Jesus did,* if we are joined to him. Jesus did not come to earth merely to teach, die, and rise again, so that in the end he might lose those for whom he died. He came to save his own "completely" (Heb. 7:25), to take them to heaven to be with him. When we look at the tomb, we are assured that one day we will be with him and will be as he is (1 John 3:2).[3]

3. *Go.* This was the third of the angel's imperatives. It is a strong reminder that however tempting it may be to remain near the tomb to learn its lessons, there is nevertheless work that remains to be done and we must get on with it. This is the way the Gospel ends, of course, for the last words of Jesus to his disciples, reported just three paragraphs after this, are, "Go and make disciples of all nations, baptizing them in the name of the Father and of the Son and of the Holy Spirit, and teaching them to obey everything I have commanded you" (vv. 19–20). This is the greatest work any person can ever have, and it is for all Christians.

4. *Tell.* The last of the angel's imperatives was "tell." It rightly came last, for if we have come to the tomb, have seen that it is empty, know that Jesus was raised, and then obeyed Jesus by going into the world, clearly we must speak of what we know. We must say to people, "He is not here; he has risen, just as he said." This is powerful, even astonishing good news. But good news must be told. If we do not tell it, our actions can only be the result of unbelief or that we do not understand what a great, powerful, and astonishing gospel it is.

Let me give an illustration. I have three children, and over the years I noticed that children never find an egg on Easter without telling you about it. Since there were three children in my home, there were usually three reports of each discovery. The youngest would find an egg and cry, "I found an egg." The oldest one would confirm it. "She's right, Daddy. Jennifer found an egg." The middle one would join in, "Jennifer really found an egg." Three tellings.

Shouldn't you likewise report the good news? The greatest news the world has ever heard is that Jesus Christ has been raised from the dead. It is great because it is true and because of what it proves. It proves that the God of the Old Testament is the true God, that Jesus is God's Son and our Savior, that his death has been accepted by his Father as a true atonement for our sins, that those who believe on Jesus are in a justified state before God, that there is power for victory over sin for all who belong to Jesus, and that those who are joined to Jesus by faith will themselves be raised from death to life in heaven. That is a tremendous message. How can we not tell it boldly to those who are perishing apart from Jesus Christ?

The Beginning of Lies

Yet we must not be naive about the opposition, for the women who went to the tomb were not the only ones who knew about the resurrection, according to Matthew. The soldiers also knew about it. They were present when the angels rolled away the stone and were terrified by it. They went to the religious leaders to report what had happened. "Angels came! They opened the tomb! The body is not there!"

How perverse are the sinful hearts of men. When Jesus was dying on the cross, the leaders taunted him, saying, "Let him come down now from the cross, and we will believe in him" (Matt. 27:42). But now Jesus had done something even greater than that. He had been raised from death. Did they believe on him? Of course not. They could not believe because they would not believe. They hated Jesus, so they drew the soldiers into an evil conspiracy. They gave them money, telling them, "You are to say, 'His disciples came during the night and stole him away while we were asleep.' If this report gets to the governor, we will satisfy him and keep you out of trouble" (vv. 13–14). Matthew concludes, "So the soldiers took the money and did as they were instructed. And this story has been widely circulated among the Jews to this very day" (v. 15).

What "day" was that? Matthew meant up to the day he was writing. But the lie of the leaders did not end then. It has been repeated throughout history even to our own day by those who are the enemies of Jesus and the gospel. A recent example is *The Passover Plot* by Hugh J. Schonfield, a book that attempted to explain the resurrection as an accident resulting from a plot that went wrong. Schonfield argued that Jesus had planned to be crucified but had arranged to be drugged with fortified wine, rescued from the tomb in his drugged state by Joseph of Arimathea, and revived by him. Jesus would then appear to his disciples as if resurrected. What ruined the plot was the soldier's unanticipated spear thrust into Christ's side. Those who had moved the body to revive it and failed then buried the body elsewhere, leaving the puzzle of the now evacuated tomb.[4]

What astonishing nonsense! But the book sold one hundred thousand copies in its first five months and received good reviews! William Barclay, the author of the well-known *Daily Study Bible*, called it "a book of enormous learning and erudition, meticulously documented. . . . It demands to be read."[5] All of this only proves Jesus' teaching in the parable of the rich man and Lazarus: "If they do not listen to Moses and the Prophets, they will not be convinced even if someone rises from the dead" (Luke 16:31). True. But those who have been given to Jesus by the Father do believe, since it is God himself who draws them to faith in Jesus Christ. Many do not yet believe. It is our solemn task to take the good news to them.

73

The Great Commission

Matthew 28:16–20

Then the eleven disciples went to Galilee, to the mountain where Jesus had told them to go. When they saw him, they worshiped him; but some doubted. Then Jesus came to them and said, "All authority in heaven and on earth has been given to me. Therefore go and make disciples of all nations, baptizing them in the name of the Father and of the Son and of the Holy Spirit, and teaching them to obey everything I have commanded you. And surely I am with you always, to the very end of the age."

I am sure you have noticed in your study of the New Testament that nearly all the resurrection appearances of Jesus end with Jesus telling those present to announce the good news. This was the case with Mary Magdalene: "Go . . . to my brothers and tell them, 'I am returning to my Father and your Father, to my God and your God'" (John 20:17). This was the case with the women who were returning from the tomb. The angel had told them: "He is not here; he has risen, just as he said. Come and see the place where he lay. Then go quickly and tell his disciples: 'He has risen from the dead'" (Matt. 28:6–7). When Jesus appeared to the women shortly after that he said, "Do not be afraid. Go and tell my brothers to go to Galilee; there they will see me" (v. 10).

The New Testament indicates that there were at least ten appearances of the risen Lord, plus another some years later to the apostle Paul. In eight of these appearance accounts, Christ gives an explicit commission, and in five he commands his followers to go into all the world and preach the gospel.

Matthew does not end his Gospel with the resurrection itself. Even more striking, he does not include an account of Christ's ascension. Instead, he ends the Gospel with the Lord's Great Commission. Apparently it was evident to him, as it also should be to us, that the life and death of Christ should affect our speech and conduct. He reports:

> Then the eleven disciples went to Galilee, to the mountain where Jesus had told them to go. When they saw him, they worshiped him; but some doubted. Then Jesus came to them and said, "All authority in heaven and on earth has been given to me. Therefore go and make disciples of all nations, baptizing them in the name of the Father and of the Son and of the Holy Spirit, and teaching them to obey everything I have commanded you. And surely I am with you always, to the very end of the age."
>
> Matthew 28:16–20

These words are for all Jesus' disciples, of course, not only for the apostles. They are for you if you have turned from your sin to trust Jesus Christ alone for your salvation and have become his disciple. If you have, then you are to work with other Christians to lead people to faith through the preaching and teaching of the gospel, bring them into the fellowship of the church through the sacrament of baptism, and, within that fellowship, continue to teach them all that Jesus has commanded. What is wonderful about all this is that Jesus promised he will be with us as we do it. We witness in a hostile environment, but as we do, we know that Jesus will be with us to bless our efforts.

When we study the Great Commission, we notice that the word *all* occurs four times, though this is obscured in some versions: (1) Jesus possesses *all* authority, (2) he sends us to *all* nations, (3) we are to teach people *all* he has commanded, and (4) as we do, we are to know that Jesus will be with us *all* the days, or always.

All Authority

Jesus begins with his authority: "All authority in heaven and on earth has been given to me" (v. 18). This is no weak authority, because the one who spoke it is no weak master. He is the risen Lord, and "*all* authority in heaven and on earth" has been given to him.

The fact that all authority in heaven has been given to Jesus could mean merely that the authority he exercised on earth would be recognized in heaven. If that is the case, it would be an affirmation of Jesus' divinity. Authority such as that would be nothing other than Jehovah's authority. Yet there is probably more to Christ's statement than this. For one thing, when the Bible speaks about heavenly "powers" or "authorities," it usually means spiritual or demonic powers. When it speaks of Christ's victory through his death and resurrection, it usually also has those powers in mind.

We think of Ephesians 6:12, which says of the Christian's warfare, "For our struggle is not against flesh and blood, but against the rulers, against the authorities, against the powers of this dark world and against the spiritual forces of evil in the heavenly realms." Or Ephesians 1:20–21, which tells us that God "raised [Jesus] from the dead and seated him at his right hand in the heavenly realms, far above all rule and authority, power and dominion, and every title that can be given, not only in the present age but also in the one to come."

When we put Christ's announcement in that context, we sense that he is not merely talking about an acknowledgment of his earthly authority in heaven. Rather, his authority is superior to and over all other authorities whether spiritual, demonic, or otherwise. His resurrection proves his authority over any power that can possibly be imagined. Consequently, we do not fear Satan or anyone else while we are engaged in Jesus' service.

Second, Jesus announces that he has authority over everything on earth. He has authority over us, his people. How can it be otherwise? If we are truly his people, we have confessed to him that we are sinners, that he is the divine Savior, and that we have accepted his sacrifice on our behalf and have pledged ourselves to follow him as Lord. Such a confession is hypocrisy if it does not contain a recognition of his authority over us in every area. Jesus told his disciples, "You are my friends if you do what I command" (John 15:14). If we do not obey Jesus, we are not his friends. Worse than that, we are not even Christians. Clearly, Jesus' authority extends to the work we are called to do, including what is demanded by the Great Commission. Because we are under Jesus' authority we are to take his gospel to the world and "make disciples" of the nations (v. 19).

Again, the declaration of Christ's authority on earth means that he has authority over those who are not yet believers. That is, his authority extends to the people to whom he sends us with the gospel. It follows, on the one hand, that Christianity is to be a world religion. No one is outside the sphere of his authority or is exempt from his call. On the other hand, this is also a statement of Jesus' ability to bring fruit from our efforts, for it is through the exercise of his authority that men and women actually come to believe and follow him.

John Stott summarizes this well:

> The fundamental basis of all Christian missionary enterprise is the universal authority of Jesus Christ, "in heaven and on earth." If the authority of Jesus were circumscribed on earth, if he were but one of many religious teachers, one of many Jewish prophets, one of many divine incarnations, we would have no mandate to present him to the nations as the Lord and Savior of the world. If the authority of Jesus were limited in heaven, if he had not decisively overthrown the principalities and powers, we might still proclaim him to the nations, but we would never be able to "turn them from darkness to light, and from the power of Satan to God" (Acts 26:18). Only because all authority on earth belongs to Christ dare we go to all nations. And only because all authority in heaven as well is his have we any hope of success.[1]

All Nations

The second great universal of this text is "*all* nations." It refers, as I have just anticipated, to the universal authority of Jesus over all people and thus also to the worldwide character of Christianity.

It is a bit surprising that Matthew should end on this note. Each of the Gospels has its unique character, as commentators have frequently noted. John's is the most universal; it presents Jesus as "the Savior of the world" (John 4:42). Luke's is a Gentile or Greek book; it is usual to think of Luke presenting Jesus as the ideal man (as well as God incarnate). Mark seems to have written for a largely Roman audience; he stresses Jesus as a miracle worker, giving less attention to his discourses than the others. By general consent, Matthew is the preeminently Jewish Gospel. It is written to show Jesus as the son of David and the fulfillment of the Old Testament prophecies of the Messiah. No other Gospel is so limited to the immediate historical and ethnic climate into which Jesus was born and in which he ministered. Yet it is this Gospel that ends on the most universal note. In this commission we learn that the Jewish disciples who had followed Jesus through the days of his ministry and who were being commissioned formally to his service were not to limit their operations to Judaism, as we might expect, but were to go to all the people of the world with this gospel.

Whenever the church has done this it has prospered. When it has failed to do this it has stagnated and dried up. Why? Because discipleship demands evangelism; it is an aspect of our obedience as Christ's followers, and Jesus blesses obedience. If we are following Jesus, we will go to others for whom he died. A disobedient church is one that does not evangelize, begins to dry up, or even dies.

What does it mean to evangelize? Jesus tells us how to do it. First, he tells us to "make disciples." In the King James Version this is rendered "teach all nations," but the word translated "teach" is not the same word as the "teach" that comes later. The later word *(didasko)* actually does mean "teach." It is the word from which we get our word *didactic.* However, the first word is *matheteuo,* which literally means "to make one a disciple." This is the way the New International Version renders the phrase: "make disciples of all nations," that is, "make them disciples of Christ." Preach the gospel to them so that through the power of the Scriptures and the work of the Holy Spirit they are converted from sin to Christ and thereafter follow him as their true Lord. In this commission, evangelism is the primary task.

On the other hand, without what follows, evangelism is at best one-sided and perhaps even unreal, for Jesus goes on to show that those who are his must lead converts to the point of baptism "in the name of the Father and of the Son and of the Holy Spirit." This does not mean that empty rites or ceremonies are to take the place of a vital relationship with Christ. Rather, first, at some point one's commitment to Jesus as Savior and Lord must become public, for baptism is a public act (it is a declaration before the world that a person intends to follow Jesus); and, second, the person is uniting with the church, which is Christ's visible body. This is both natural and necessary. If a person is truly converted, he or she will want to join with other similarly converted people.

All I Have Commanded

The third universal of the Great Commission is the command to teach those we have evangelized. Christ commanded us to teach them "to obey everything" (or *all* things), which means that for all Christians a lifetime of learning must follow conversion and membership in Christ's church. This command is particularly important in our extremely superficial age.

What we observe seems to be the opposite. Instead of striving to teach *all* Christ commanded, many are trying to eliminate as much of his teaching as possible, concentrating instead on things that are easily comprehended and unobjectionable. But a core such as this is distorted. It is usually grace without judgment, love without justice, salvation without obedience, and triumph without suffering. The motivation of some of these reductionists may be good: They want to win as many people to Christ as possible. But the method is the world's, and the results will be the world's results. Robust disciples are not made by watered-down teaching.

Today's church needs to recapture the entire counsel of God. To many this seems the most foolish of pursuits. If we were to ask many so-called Christians what should be done in our day to win the world for Christ, it is likely they would talk about literature campaigns, the use of radio and television, the founding of seeker-sensitive churches, recruitment of workers, and how to raise funds. In other words, most of the discussion would center on methods rather than on content. By contrast, Jesus spoke about teaching his commandments. What should our teaching include? Clearly any short list of doctrines is inadequate. We must teach the entire Bible. Nevertheless, faithfulness to the Great Commission must involve at least the following:

1. *A high view of Scripture.* In our day, liberal teachers are trying to undercut the church's traditionally high view of the Bible, saying that it is only a human book, that it contains errors, that it is therefore at best only relatively trustworthy or authoritative, or that, while it may be true, it is not sufficient for dealing with today's challenges. Such attitudes have produced a weak church. It is significant that with only a few exceptions even these liberal detractors of Scripture acknowledge that Jesus regarded the Bible (in his case, the Old Testament) as authoritative. Kirsopp Lake was no friend of historic Bible-believing Christianity, but he wrote, "The fundamentalist may be wrong; I think that he is. But it is we who have departed from the tradition, not he; and I am sorry for the fate of anyone who tries to argue with a fundamentalist on the basis of authority. The Bible and the *corpus theologicum* of the church are on the fundamentalist side."[2]

If we are to be faithful to *all* Christ's teachings, we must teach his high view of the Bible as a fundamental part of our theology.

2. *The sovereignty of God, especially in salvation.* The English Bible translator J. B. Phillips wrote a book entitled *Your God Is Too Small.* That title, which is also a statement, might well be spoken of many of today's professing Christians who, in their ignorance of Scripture, inevitably scale God down to their own limited and fallible perspectives. We need to capture a new, elevated sense of who God is, particularly in regard to his grace in saving sinners. Sovereignty refers to rightful rule. To say that God is sovereign, therefore, as the Bible does, is to say that God rules in all matters and all places. Nothing is an accident. No one catches God off guard. Moreover, he does what seems best to him. Paul wrote, "God has mercy on whom he wants to have mercy, and he hardens whom he wants to harden" (Rom. 9:18).

3. *The depravity of man.* Church people are willing to speak of sin in the sense that we are "less perfect than God" and need help to live a godly life. That is not offensive to anyone. But it is not the Bible's teaching. The Bible teaches that men and women are in rebellion against God (Ps. 2:1–3). It says not that they are marred by sin but that they are dead in it (Eph. 2:1–3). It says they have been so debased by sin that even their thoughts are corrupted and that in all ways "the LORD saw how great man's wickedness on the earth had become, and that every inclination of the thoughts of his heart was only evil all the time" (Gen. 6:5). So great is this depravity that a person cannot even come to Christ unless God first renews his soul and so draws him. If we are going to be saved, it must be by the grace of God and by the grace of God alone.

4. *Salvation by grace alone.* While it is true that by ourselves we cannot come to Christ and so live under God's judgment, God has nevertheless acted in grace to save some who were perishing. Salvation is by grace alone, through faith alone, because of Christ alone. That is the full meaning of justification, the doctrine by which the church stands or falls, according to Martin Luther. Any teaching about salvation that is less than that teaching is not authentic Christianity.

5. *Work to do.* Although God does the work of saving individuals, drawing them to Christ, he does not abandon them at that point. Rather, he directs and empowers them to do meaningful work for him. Most of Christ's teachings about discipleship fall into this area, as does Ephesians 2:10, which says, "For we are God's workmanship, created in Christ Jesus to do good works, which God prepared in advance for us to do." It is necessary that we do these good works (as Christians in all ages have), for unless we do we have no assurance that we are really Christ's followers. Like Jesus himself, Christians are to stand for justice and do all in their power to comfort the sick, rescue the outcast, defend the oppressed, and save the innocent. We are also to oppose those who perpetrate or condone injustice.

6. *The security of the believer in Christ.* Jesus was strong in cautioning against presumption. He let no one think that he or she could presume to be a

Christian while at the same time disobeying God's commandments. He said, "My sheep listen to my voice . . . and . . . follow me" (John 10:27). If we are not listening to Christ and following him in faithful obedience, we are not his disciples. However, although he warned against presumption, Jesus also spoke the greatest words of assurance and confidence for those who do indeed follow him. He said that they will never be lost. Indeed, how could they be lost if he is responsible for their salvation? Jesus said, "I give them eternal life, and they shall never perish; no one can snatch them out of my hand" (John 10:28). No one? No one! And no thing either! For nothing either in heaven or on earth "will be able to separate us from the love of God that is in Christ Jesus our Lord" (Rom. 8:39).

This does not mean that Christians will not encounter dangers. In fact, the verse implies them, for if Jesus promises that no one will be able to snatch us from his hands, he must have said so because he knows some will try. Christians will always face dangers—dangers from without, from enemies, and dangers from within. Paul lists some of them in Romans 8. Still, the promise is that those who have believed in Jesus will not be lost. The Christian may be deprived of mere things. He may lose his job, his friends, even his good reputation, but he will not be lost.

Today's Christians need to articulate these great biblical doctrines afresh rather than just adopt the theology of our culture. We need to speak of the depravity of man, so much so that there is no hope for him apart from God's grace. We need to speak of God's electing love, showing that God enters the life of an individual by his Holy Spirit to quicken understanding and draw the rebellious will to himself. We must show that God is able to keep and does keep those whom he so draws. These truths and the supporting doctrines that go with them need to be proclaimed forthrightly. We need to say, "This is where we stand. We do not adopt the world's theology. We do not accept the theology of the worldly church." Unless we do this we cannot consider ourselves to be obedient disciples of Jesus Christ—or even his disciples at all. Without this commitment our churches will not prosper and our work will not be blessed.

"I Will Be with You Always"

The final universal of Matthew 28:18–20 is "al[l]-ways" or, as the Greek text literally says, "all the days, even to the consummation of the age." This is a great, empowering promise, and it is wonderfully true.

In the first chapter of Matthew, Jesus was introduced as "Immanuel"—which, we are told, means "God with us" (Matt. 1:23). Here, in the last verse, that very same promise is repeated. John Stott adds:

> This was not the first time Christ had promised them his risen presence. Earlier in this Gospel . . . he had undertaken to be in their midst when only two or three disciples were gathered in his name. Now, as he repeats the promise of

his presence, he attached it rather to their witness than to their worship. It is not only when we *meet* in his name, but when we *go* in his name, that he promises to be with us. The emphatic "I," who pledges his presence, is the one who has universal authority and who sends forth his people.[3]

So ends the first and longest of the Gospels: Jesus will be with us as we go. We have been given a very great task, but we do not need to attempt it in our own strength. We have the Lord's power at work within us as well as his promise to be with us to the very end as we obey the Great Commission.[4]

Notes

Chapter 40

1. John R. W. Stott, *The Message of Acts: To the Ends of the Earth* (Leicester, England: Inter-Varsity Press, 1960), 41.

2. D. A. Carson, *God with Us: Themes from Matthew* (Ventura, Calif.: Regal Books, 1985), 112.

3. John Charles Ryle, *Expository Thoughts on the Gospels: St. Matthew* (Cambridge: James Clarke, 1974), 220.

4. William Hendriksen, *New Testament Commentary: Exposition of the Gospel according to Matthew* (Grand Rapids: Baker, 1985), 690.

Chapter 41

1. Howard Vos, *Matthew* (Grand Rapids: Zondervan, 1979), 129.

2. John A. Broadus, *Commentary on Matthew* (Grand Rapids: Kregel, 1990), 384.

3. Careful readers will note that in most translations verse 11 ("For the Son of Man has come to save that which was lost") is omitted. Some ancient manuscripts have this verse, which is why it appears in some translations, but the majority do not. The verse was probably added to Matthew mistakenly from the parallel passage in Luke 19:10.

Chapter 42

1. The first is in Matthew 16:18.

2. In Matthew 16:19.

3. The Tractate *Joma* quotes Rabbi Jose ben Judah (c. A.D. 180) as saying, "If a brother sins against you once, forgive him; a second time, forgive him; a third time, forgive him; but a fourth time, do not forgive him." There are other examples as well.

4. Jesus' reply is probably an allusion to Genesis 4:24, where Lamech boasts of having revenged himself by that number of times. It has the effect of turning Lamech's declaration of revenge into a principle of forgiveness.

5. The section of this chapter dealing with the parable of the unmerciful servant is adapted from James Montgomery Boice, *The Parables of Jesus* (Chicago: Moody Press, 1983), 179–87.

Chapter 43

1. Women had no rights of divorce; that was not even a question.

2. The Mishna has an entire tractate on divorce *(Gittin)*, the last paragraph of which reads: "The school of Shammai says, no one shall put away a wife unless there has been found in her something disgraceful, as written, 'because he hath found something unseemly in her'; the school of Hillel says, even if she has burnt his food, as written, 'because he has found something unseemly in her'; Rabbi Akiba says, even if he find another more beautiful than she is, as written, 'if she find no favor in his eyes'" (cited by John A. Broadus, *Commentary on Matthew* [Grand Rapids: Kregel, 1990], 396).

3. The interpretation of verse 9 and its "exception clause" is discussed at length in some of the major commentaries. An example is D. A. Carson, "Matthew," in *The Expositor's Bible Commentary*, vol. 8, *Matthew, Mark, Luke* (Grand Rapids: Zondervan, 1984), 412–18. But fuller treatments can be found in books dealing with divorce and remarriage issues specifically, for example, J. Carl Laney, *The Divorce Myth* (Minneapolis: Bethany House, 1981).

4. C. S. Lewis, *Mere Christianity* (New York: Macmillan, 1958), 87.

5. This last section is borrowed with changes from an earlier book of mine that has been out of print for years: *The Sermon on the Mount* (Grand Rapids: Zondervan, 1972), 139–41.

Chapter 44

1. Walter J. Chantry, *Today's Gospel: Authentic or Synthetic?* (London and Carlisle, Pa.: The Banner of Truth Trust, 1972), 55.

2. John A. Broadus, *Commentary on Matthew* (Grand Rapids: Kregel, 1990), 407.

Chapter 45

1. It is developed theologically and at length in the middle section of Paul's great letter to the Romans (chaps. 9–11).

2. R. A. Torrey, *The Power of Prayer and the Prayer of Power* (Grand Rapids: Zondervan, 1955), 138–39.

3. Portions of this chapter have been adapted from a study of this same parable appearing in James Montgomery Boice, *The Parables of Jesus* (Chicago: Moody Press, 1983), 57–64.

Chapter 46

1. The other predictions are in Matthew 16:21 and 17:22–23.

2. A number of problems concerning this incident are discussed by the major commentators. The first is that Mark and Luke mention only one blind

man; Mark names him: Bartimaeus (Mark 10:46). That is not much of a problem, however. There may well have been two men with only one being singled out, perhaps because he came to some prominence later. It may be why his name was remembered. A second, more serious problem is that Matthew and Mark say Jesus met the blind man as he was leaving Jericho on his way to Jerusalem, while Luke says it was as he approached the city (Luke 18:35). The answer may be that the blind men followed Jesus for some time as he approached and then passed through the city, or even that two locations were involved. There seems to have been an ancient Jericho, which went back to the time of the Jewish conquest, and a newer city that had developed since. The healing could have taken place between the two places.

Chapter 47

1. See Mark 11:1–10; Luke 19:28–40; and John 12:12–19.

2. I discuss my reasons for placing the triumphal entry on the tenth of Nisan, when the lambs were purchased for the Passover, in my study of John 12:12–19. See James Montgomery Boice, *John*, vol. 3, *Those Who Received Him: John 9:1–12:50* (Grand Rapids: Baker, 1999), 927–32.

3. John R. W. Stott, *Basic Christianity* (Grand Rapids: Eerdmans, 1958), 21.

4. C. S. Lewis, *Mere Christianity* (New York: Macmillan, 1958), 41.

5. The last section of this chapter is adapted from James Montgomery Boice, *Foundations of the Christian Faith* (Downers Grove, Ill.: InterVarsity Press, 1986), 275–77.

Chapter 48

1. Matthew describes the cleansing of the temple immediately after his account of the triumphal entry. But Mark points out that the cleansing of the temple actually took place the next day, that is, on Monday of passion week (Mark 11:12). Mark places the cursing of the fig tree at the start of this second day, as does Matthew, but he locates the account of the temple cleansing after it.

2. Much has been written about these cleansings, the prevailing view being that only one event took place and that John placed it at the start of Jesus' ministry and the Synoptics placed it at the end. It is true that the Gospel writers often arranged their material topically rather than chronologically. We have seen several examples of this in Matthew. But there are significant differences in the two cleansing accounts, and it is not unreasonable to conclude that there were in fact two cleansings. D. A. Carson discusses some of the reasons for this in "Matthew," *The Expositor's Bible Commentary*, vol. 8, *Matthew, Mark, Luke* (Grand Rapids: Zondervan, 1984), 441.

3. A helpful discussion of these abuses is found in William Barclay, *The Gospel of Matthew*, vol. 2, *Chapters 11–28* (Philadelphia: Westminster Press, 1958), 269–71.

4. John White, *The Golden Cow: Materialism in the Twentieth-Century Church* (Downers Grove, Ill.: InterVarsity Press, 1979), 38.

5. Ibid., 98.

6. Ibid., 134.

7. Ibid., 170.

8. See D. A. Carson, "Matthew," in *The Expositor's Bible Commentary,* vol. 8, *Matthew, Mark, Luke* (Grand Rapids: Zondervan, 1984), 443.

Chapter 49

1. John A. Broadus, *Commentary on Matthew* (Grand Rapids: Kregel, 1990), 435. In Mark, the only other Gospel to record this incident, the story is split into two parts with the cleansing of the temple in between (Mark 11:12–14, 20–26).

2. John Charles Ryle, *Expository Thoughts on the Gospels: St. Matthew* (Cambridge: James Clarke, 1974), 270.

3. John Charles Ryle, *Expository Thoughts on the Gospels: St. Luke,* vol. 1 (Cambridge: James Clarke, 1976), 195.

4. Howard F. Vos, *Matthew* (Grand Rapids: Zondervan, 1979), 148.

Chapter 50

1. Jonathan Edwards, "Men Naturally Are God's Enemies," in *The Works of Jonathan Edwards* (Edinburgh and Carlisle, Pa.: The Banner of Truth Trust, 1974), vol. 2, 131.

2. Ibid.

3. Ibid.

4. Sections of this chapter are adapted from James Montgomery Boice, *The Parables of Jesus* (Chicago: Moody Press, 1983), 131–38, 189–97.

Chapter 51

1. Charles Haddon Spurgeon, "The Wedding Was Furnished with Guests," in *Metropolitan Tabernacle Pulpit* (London: The Banner of Truth Trust, 1970), vol. 34, 254–55.

2. Charles Haddon Spurgeon, "Making Light of Christ," in *The New Park Street Pulpit* (Pasadena, Tex.: Pilgrim Publications, 1975), vol. 2, 358.

3. Spurgeon, "The Wedding," 261–63.

4. Sections of this chapter are adapted from James Montgomery Boice, *The Parables of Jesus* (Chicago: Moody Press, 1983), 65–73.

Chapter 52

1. John Calvin, *Institutes of the Christian Religion,* 2 vols., ed. John T. McNeill, trans. Ford Lewis Battles (Philadelphia: Westminster Press, 1960), 1512.

2. John H. Gerstner, "The Atonement and the Purpose of God," in *Our Savior God: Man, Christ and the Atonement,* ed. James Montgomery Boice (Grand Rapids: Baker, 1980), 107.

Chapter 53

1. Cited at length by Charles Haddon Spurgeon, *The Treasury of David*, vol. 2b, *Psalms 88–110* (Grand Rapids: Zondervan, 1966), 464–65.

2. Ibid., 460.

3. This is not the case in Matthew 22:44, where Jesus cites Psalm 110:1, because the New Testament is written in Greek and the word in Matthew's text is *kyrios*, which means "lord" only.

4. For example, Leslie C. Allen largely ignores its claims to have been written by David, even though much is at stake (see *Word Biblical Commentary*, vol. 21, *Psalms 101–150* [Waco: Word, 1983], 83–87).

5. See John A. Broadus, *Commentary on Matthew* (Grand Rapids: Kregel, 1990), 459–60, for a good discussion of these arguments.

6. See D. A. Carson, "Matthew," in *The Expositor's Bible Commentary*, vol. 8, *Matthew, Mark, Luke* (Grand Rapids: Zondervan, 1984), 467–68.

7. Derek Kidner, *Psalms 73–150: A Commentary on Books III–V of the Psalms* (Leicester, England, and Downers Grove, Ill.: InterVarsity Press, 1975), 391–92.

8. Walter J. Chantry, *Praises for the King of Kings* (Edinburgh and Carlisle, Pa.: The Banner of Truth Trust, 1991), 59.

9. Quoted by Walter R. Martin, *Essential Christianity: A Handbook of Basic Christian Doctrines* (Grand Rapids: Zondervan, 1962), 23.

Chapter 54

1. Edward Gibbon, *The History of the Decline and Fall of the Roman Empire* (Norwalk, Conn.: Easton Press, 1974), vol. 1, 22.

2. Matthew Henry's *Commentary on the Whole Bible*, vol. 5, *Matthew to John* (New York: Revell, n.d.), 329.

3. The woe that appears as verse 14 in some Bibles does not appear in the oldest manuscripts and seems to be a later insertion drawn from Mark 12:40 or Luke 20:47. This seems the more certain in that the point of insertion is different in some of these Greek texts.

4. William Barclay, *The Gospel of Matthew*, vol. 2, *Chapters 11–28* (Philadelphia: Westminster Press, 1958), 326–27.

5. Verse 35 presents a well-known problem for which no final solution has been found. The verse must be referring to the Zechariah whose death is described in 2 Chronicles 24:21–22, because he is said to have been killed "in the courtyard of the LORD's temple" and because, in the Hebrew Bible, 2 Chronicles comes at the end of the Old Testament and Jesus seems to be speaking of the martyrs from Abel at the beginning of the Bible to Zechariah at the end. But Zechariah's father was Jehoiada. Berekiah was the father of the better known Zechariah, who was the eleventh of the twelve minor prophets. Many commentators simply call this a mistake on Matthew's part, but this is a serious charge to make of an inspired biblical writer. H. N. Ridderbos suggests that although this is a wrong identification, it was prob-

ably made by a scribe who was copying the text (*Matthew* [Grand Rapids: Zondervan, 1987], 433). John A. Broadus suggests that Jehoiada may have had Berekiah as a surname; Berekiah was a common name possessed by six or seven other persons in the Bible. Or Jehoiada, who had just died a short time before at the age of 130 (24:15), may have been the grandfather of Zechariah, and Berekiah was his father (*Commentary on Matthew* [Grand Rapids: Kregel, 1990], 477). D. A. Carson discusses these and other possibilities in "Matthew," in *The Expositor's Bible Commentary*, vol. 8, *Matthew, Mark, Luke* (Grand Rapids: Zondervan, 1984), 485–86.

Chapter 55

1. See my study of these events in James Montgomery Boice, *Daniel: An Expositional Commentary* (Grand Rapids: Zondervan, 1989), 99, 121–22.

2. The story is retold from Barnhouse's original studies of the "Epistle to the Romans," part 55 (Philadelphia: The Bible Study Hour, 1955), 4–12. It does not appear in the later, bound edition of the Romans series. I have told it in a slightly longer version than here in James Montgomery Boice, *The Last and Future World* (Grand Rapids: Zondervan, 1974), 132–39.

Chapter 56

1. Bertrand Russell, *Why I Am Not a Christian: And Other Essays on Religion and Related Subjects*, ed. Paul Edwards (New York: Simon & Schuster, 1957), 16–17.

2. R. C. Sproul, *The Last Days according to Jesus* (Grand Rapids: Baker, 1998).

3. J. Stuart Russell, *The Parousia: A Study of the New Testament Doctrine of Our Lord's Second Coming* (Grand Rapids: Baker, 1983).

4. D. A. Carson, "Matthew," in *The Expositor's Bible Commentary*, vol. 8, *Matthew, Mark, Luke* (Grand Rapids: Zondervan, 1984), 493.

5. There are three ways to understand "this generation." It can be the generation then living, which is what I maintain. It might refer to the Jews or to "this kind of people," the view of most dispensationalists. Or it can refer to the generation living at the end of history. John Broadus, like most modern commentators, argues that it must refer to the people living in Jesus' day, though he still regards verses 29–31 as referring to the final, second coming of Christ. "All the things predicted in vv. 4–31 would occur before or in immediate connection with the destruction of Jerusalem. But like events might again occur in connection with another and greater coming of the Lord, and such seems evidently to be his meaning" (John A. Broadus, *Commentary on Matthew* [Grand Rapids: Kregel, 1990], 492). William Hendriksen regards "this generation" as the Jews, and one reason he gives is that "things that will take place" are things spread out over the centuries, such as the preaching of the gospel throughout the whole world. The following section, which clearly describes the final return of Jesus, picks up on the coming in verses 29–31; hence, Jesus must be talking about a generation living at least at that

time (William Hendriksen, *New Testament Commentary: Exposition of the Gospel according to Matthew* [Grand Rapids: Baker, 1985], 868–69).

Chapter 57

1. D. A. Carson, *God with Us: Themes from Matthew* (Ventura, Calif.: Regal Books, 1985), 146.

2. John Charles Ryle, *Expository Thoughts on the Gospels: St. Matthew* (Cambridge: James Clarke, 1974), 326–27.

3. John A. Broadus, *Commentary on Matthew* (Grand Rapids: Kregel, 1990), 495. As far as this context is concerned, "It is neither clear nor particularly important whether 'taken' means 'taken in judgment' . . . or 'taken to be gathered with the elect,'" says D. A. Carson ("Matthew," in *The Expositor's Bible Commentary*, vol. 8, *Matthew, Mark, Luke* [Grand Rapids: Zondervan, 1984], 509).

4. Carson, "Matthew," 510.

5. I have borrowed these three points from William Hendriksen, *New Testament Commentary: Exposition of the Gospel according to Matthew* (Grand Rapids: Baker, 1985), 873.

6. The story is in William Barclay, *The Gospel of Matthew*, vol. 2, *Chapters 11–28* (Philadelphia: Westminster Press, 1958), 350–51.

Chapter 58

1. Charles Haddon Spurgeon, "Entrance and Exclusion," in *Metropolitan Tabernacle Pulpit* (Pasadena, Tex.: Pilgrim Publications, 1976), vol. 43, 30.

2. William M. Taylor, *The Parables of Our Saviour Expounded and Illustrated* (New York: A. C. Armstrong and Son, 1900), 170–71.

Chapter 59

1. A similar story occurs in Luke 19:11–27, but it has a different setting and varies in important details. There is no reason to suppose that Matthew derived his story from Luke or vice versa. Jesus must have told similar stories on many occasions.

2. John Charles Ryle, *Expository Thoughts on the Gospels: St. Matthew* (Cambridge: James Clarke, 1974), 336–37.

3. William Hendriksen, *New Testament Commentary: Exposition of the Gospel according to Matthew* (Grand Rapids: Baker, 1985), 881.

4. D. A. Carson, *God with Us: Themes from Matthew* (Ventura, Calif.: Regal Books, 1985), 149. The Alford quotation is from Henry Alford, *The Greek New Testament*, vol. 1 (Chicago: Moody Press, 1958).

Chapter 60

1. G. Barrois, "On Medieval Charities," in *Service in Christ*, ed. James I. McCord and T. H. L. Parker (London: Epworth Press, 1966), 72.

2. William Barclay, *The Gospel of Matthew*, vol. 2, *Chapters 11–28* (Philadelphia: Westminster Press, 1958), 360.

3. Ibid., 359.

4. David Hill, *The Gospel of Matthew*, in *The New Century Bible Commentary* (Grand Rapids: Eerdmans; London: Marshall, Morgan & Scott, 1981), 331.

5. Harry A. Ironside, *Expository Notes on the Gospel of Matthew* (Neptune, N.J.: Loizeaux Brothers, 1948), 339–40.

6. John A. Broadus, *Commentary on Matthew* (Grand Rapids: Kregel, 1990), 510.

7. D. A. Carson, *God with Us: Themes from Matthew* (Ventura, Calif.: Regal Books, 1985), 150.

8. William Hendriksen, *New Testament Commentary: Exposition of the Gospel according to Matthew* (Grand Rapids: Baker, 1985), 886.

9. R. V. G. Tasker, *The Gospel according to St. Matthew* (Grand Rapids: Eerdmans, 1961), 239.

10. Charles Haddon Spurgeon, *The Gospel of the Kingdom: A Popular Exposition of the Gospel according to St. Matthew* (Pasadena, Tex.: Pilgrim Publications, 1974), 228.

11. John Charles Ryle, *Expository Thoughts on the Gospels: St. Matthew* (Cambridge: James Clarke, 1974), 344–45.

Chapter 61

1. This is also the beginning of the last of the ten sections of Matthew as I have outlined them for this volume: (1) "The Coming of the King" (chaps. 1–4); (2) "The Sermon on the Mount" (chaps. 5–7); (3) "The Power of the Kingdom" (chaps. 8–10); (4) "Is Jesus Really God's King?" (chaps. 11–12); (5) "The Parables of the Kingdom" (chap. 13); (6) "The Withdrawal of the King" (chaps. 14–17); (7) "The Citizens of the Kingdom" (chaps. 18–20); (8) "The King's Final Break with Judaism" (chaps. 21–23); (9) "The Sermon on the Mount of Olives" (chaps. 24–25); and (10) "The King's Death and Resurrection" (chaps. 26–28).

2. The story is told in the booklet "How to Study Your Bible," prepared by Ralph L. Keiper from material supplied by Barnhouse (Philadelphia: The Bible Study Hour, 1961), 9–10.

3. Parts of the material about Mary have been borrowed with changes from James Montgomery Boice, *John: An Expositional Commentary*, vol. 3 (1977; reprint, Grand Rapids: Baker, 1999), 915–20.

Chapter 62

1. See D. A. Carson, *The Expositor's Bible Commentary*, vol. 8, *Matthew, Mark, Luke* (Grand Rapids: Zondervan, 1984), 528–32; and John A. Broadus, *Commentary on Matthew* (Grand Rapids: Kregel, 1990), 524–25.

2. R. T. France, *The Gospel according to Matthew: An Introduction and Commentary* (Grand Rapids: Eerdmans, 1985), 365.

3. The Greek text of Matthew 28:1 is literally "after the sabbaths" (plural), though this is usually translated as a singular in English Bibles.

4. John Charles Ryle, *Expository Thoughts on the Gospels: St. Matthew* (Cambridge: James Clarke, 1974), 351.

5. Ibid., 353.

6. These four arguments are presented well in ibid., 355–57, but they occur in various forms in most commentaries.

7. The only other place "blood" and "covenant" are found together is in Zechariah 9:11.

8. The word is in a few of the manuscripts, but they are a minority. It seems to have been added by copyists to conform Matthew and Mark's account to Luke's and to Paul's words in 1 Corinthians 11:25.

Chapter 63

1. Charles Haddon Spurgeon, *The Gospel of the Kingdom: A Popular Exposition of the Gospel according to Matthew* (Pasadena, Tex.: Pilgrim Publications, 1974), 237.

2. William Barclay, *The Gospel of Matthew,* vol. 2, *Chapters 11–28* (Philadelphia: Westminster Press, 1958), 384.

3. D. A. Carson, *The Expositor's Bible Commentary,* vol. 8, *Matthew, Mark, Luke* (Grand Rapids: Zondervan, 1984), 543.

4. Quoted by William Hendriksen, *New Testament Commentary: Exposition of the Gospel according to Matthew* (Grand Rapids: Baker, 1985), 917.

5. John Charles Ryle, *Expository Thoughts on the Gospels: St. Matthew* (Cambridge: James Clarke, 1974), 363.

6. Reuben A. Torrey, *The Power of Prayer and the Prayer of Power* (Grand Rapids: Eerdmans, 1955), 76.

Chapter 64

1. Frank Morison, *Who Moved the Stone?* (1930; reprint, Grand Rapids: Zondervan, 1977).

2. William Barclay suggests that "when Judas stepped up to kiss Jesus, he kissed him as a disciple kissed a master, and that he meant it; that he stood back with expectant pride waiting on Jesus to blast these people and at last to act" (*The Gospel of Matthew,* vol. 2, *Chapters 17–22* [Philadelphia: Westminster Press, 1958], 370–71). Comments such as this say more about how we view ourselves than about these past events.

3. John Charles Ryle, *Expository Thoughts on the Gospels: St. Matthew* (Cambridge: James Clarke, 1974), 351.

4. Ibid., 368.

5. Martin Luther, "Admonition to Peace" (April 1525). Cited by Will Durant, *The Story of Civilization,* vol. 6, *The Reformation: A History of European Civilization from Wycliffe to Calvin: 1300–1564* (Norwalk, Conn.: Easton Press, 1992), 386.

Chapter 65

1. Walter M. Chandler, *The Trial of Jesus from a Lawyer's Standpoint* (Atlanta: The Harrison Company, 1956), xvi. Much of the following is taken from a more extensive handling of the Jewish trial in James Montgomery Boice, *John: An Expositional Commentary*, vol. 5 (Grand Rapids: Baker, 1999), 1383–1410.

2. Frank Morison, *Who Moved the Stone?* (1930; reprint, Grand Rapids: Zondervan, 1977), 24.

Chapter 66

1. Herman N. Ridderbos, *Matthew*, trans. Ray Togtman (Grand Rapids: Zondervan, 1987), 506.

2. Harold Lindsell, *The Battle for the Bible* (Grand Rapids: Zondervan, 1976), 174–76.

3. Clarence Edward Macartney, *Peter and His Lord: Sermons on the Life of Peter* (Nashville: Cokesbury Press, 1937), 102.

Chapter 67

1. But see Peter's reference to Judas's fate in Acts 1:18.

2. Robert Herrick, "To His Savior," in *The Poems of Robert Herrick*, ed. L. C. Martin (London: Oxford University Press, 1965), 357.

3. D. A. Carson, "Matthew," in *The Expositor's Bible Commentary*, vol. 8, *Matthew, Mark, Luke* (Grand Rapids: Zondervan, 1984), 566. For a fuller discussion of this problem, see pages 562–66.

Chapter 68

1. Frank Morison, *Who Moved the Stone?* (1930; reprint, Grand Rapids: Zondervan, 1977), 59.

2. Charles Haddon Spurgeon, "Jesus, the King of Truth," *Metropolitan Tabernacle Pulpit* (Pasadena, Tex.: Pilgrim Publications, 1971), vol. 18, 699.

Chapter 69

1. Marcus Tullius Cicero, *In Verrem*, II, 5, 165; in John R. W. Stott, *The Cross of Christ* (Downers Grove, Ill.: InterVarsity Press, 1986), 24.

2. Cicero, *In Verrem*, II, 5, 170; in Stott, *The Cross of Christ*, 24.

3. Philip Graham Ryken, "The Offense of the Cross," in *The Heart of the Cross*, ed. James Montgomery Boice and Philip Graham Ryken (Wheaton: Crossway Books, 1999), 138.

4. Cicero, *Pro Rabirio*, 5; in F. F. Bruce, *The Epistle to the Hebrews* (Grand Rapids: Eerdmans, 1990), 338.

5. William Barclay, *The Letter to the Romans* (Philadelphia: Saint Andrews Press, 1969), 236–37.

6. John Charles Ryle, *Expository Thoughts on the Gospels: St. Matthew* (Cambridge: James Clarke, 1974), 392.

7. D. A. Carson, *God with Us: Themes from Matthew* (Ventura, Calif.: Regal Books, 1985), 161.

Chapter 71

1. Herman N. Ridderbos, *Matthew,* trans. Ray Togtman (Grand Rapids: Zondervan, 1987), 541.

2. Matthew Henry, *Matthew Henry's Commentary on the Whole Bible,* vol. 5, *Matthew to John* (New York, London, and Edinburgh: Revell, n.d.), 436.

3. Charles Haddon Spurgeon, *The Gospel of the Kingdom: A Popular Exposition of the Gospel according to Matthew* (Pasadena, Tex.: Pilgrim Publications, 1974), 253.

4. The last section of this chapter is borrowed with changes from James Montgomery Boice, *The Christ of the Empty Tomb* (Chicago: Moody Press, 1985), 35–41.

Chapter 72

1. See my discussion in *Matthew,* vol. 1, chap. 26. One bit of evidence for placing the crucifixion on Thursday is Matthew's use of the plural word *sabbaths* in verse 1, though this is usually translated singular ("after the Sabbath") in most English Bibles. I believe that there were two Sabbaths in this particular week, the special Passover Sabbath, which fell on Friday in the year A.D. 30, and the normal Saturday Sabbath the next day. This explains Matthew's plural and provides for the "three days and three nights" that Jesus said he would remain in the grave (Matt. 12:40).

2. The quotations come from John R. W. Stott, *Basic Christianity* (Downers Grove, Ill.: InterVarsity Press, 1981), 47. I have borrowed portions of the preceding material with changes from James Montgomery Boice, *The Gospel of John,* vol. 5 (Grand Rapids: Baker, 1999), 1564–65, 1583.

3. See Charles Haddon Spurgeon, "A Visit to the Tomb," in *Metropolitan Tabernacle Pulpit* (Pasadena, Tex.: Pilgrim Publications, 1971), vol. 18, 637–48.

4. Hugh J. Schonfield, *The Passover Plot: New Light on the History of Jesus* (New York: Bantam Books, 1967).

5. From the cover of *The Passover Plot.*

Chapter 73

1. John R. W. Stott, "The Great Commission," in *One Race, One Gospel, One Task: World Congress on Evangelism, Berlin 1966, Official Reference Volumes,* ed. Carl F. H. Henry and W. Stanley Mooneyham (Minneapolis: World Wide Publications, 1966), vol. 1, 46.

2. Kirsopp Lake, *The Religion of Yesterday and Tomorrow* (Boston: Houghton Press, 1926), 61.

3. Stott, "The Great Commission," 49.

4. This chapter is adapted from James Montgomery Boice, *The Christ of the Empty Tomb* (Chicago: Moody Press, 1985), 119–25.

Subject Index

Scripture Index